A Study of Non Impacting Employees Performace

By,
Kumawat, Kunal Shriram

ACKNOWLEDGEMENT

It gives me a great esteem and pleasure to submit my thesis titled as **"A study of Non-Monetary factors impacting employee's performance in selected automobile manufacturing industry"**, to the Savitribai Phule Pune University.

I my honored to have valuable guidance of **Dr. Kuldip S. Charak** (Director - Navsahyadri Group of Institutes, Faculty of Management, Pune) for this research work. His constant encouragement, coaching, step by step guidance has made this thesis to see the light of the day. He, besides a source of inspiration, was always helpful in exploring the various dimensions of the research subject and enriched my learning curve. I am extremely thankful for the blissful insights I gained through the focused discussion and deliberations I had with him on the research subject. His personal touch & professional competence made my research journey memorable.

I am highly grateful to **Dr. E. B. Khedkar** (Ex-Dean, Faculty of Management, SSPU and Director, School of Management, Ajinkya DY Patil Insitute of Management, Charoli, Pune),

Dr. O. P. Haldar (Coordinator-PhD Research Center), **Dr. Ashutosh Misal** (Director, DYPIMS).

I am also obliged to all my colleagues and friends, more so Dr. Kavita Joshi, for their instantaneous help, support and inspiration throughout my research work.

Last but not the least, I have no words to express my deepest feelings for the support and encouragement from my Parents, Father – Shriram Z Kumawat, Mother – Seema S Kumawat, wife – Pallavi Kunal Kumawat and my Son Vihaan Kunal Kumawat for supporting me as I was using their time for the research. I am thankful to my beloved Sister Dr. Priya and my lovely Brother-in-law Dr. Ritesh for their constant support and encouragement.

Without their treasured love and support, the completion of this work would not have been possible at all.

Date: January 2022   **Mr. Kunal Shriram Kumawat**

Place: Pune   (Research Student)

TABLE OF CONTENTS

Sr. No.	Particular	Page No.
1	Title Page	i
2	Certificate of the Guide	ii
3	Declaration by the Candidate	iii
4	Acknowledgement	iv
5	Table of Contents	vi
6	Chapter Scheme	vi
6	Index of Study	vii
7	List of Tables	ix
8	List of Figures	x
9	List of Graphs	x
10	Abbreviations	xii
11	Abstract	xiii

CHAPTER SCHEME

Chapter. No.	Name of the Chapter	Page No.
1	Introduction	1
2	Literature Review	66
3	Research Methodology	130
4	Data Analysis	149
5	Findings and Discussion	225
6	Conclusion	236
7	Scope for Further Study	242
8	Bibliography	243
9	Annexures-1	257

INDEX OF STUDY

Ch. No	Name of Chapter	Page No.
1	Introduction	1
	1.1 About Automotive Industry	1
	1.2 History of Automotive Industry	1
	1.3 Employee Performance	27
	1.4 Tools to Evaluate employee performance	33
	1.5 Factors Impacting Employees Performance	41
2	Literature Review	66
	2.1 Research Gap	95
3	Research Methodology	130
	3.1.1 Introduction	130
	3.1.2 What is Research	130
	3.1.3 What are types of Research	131
	3.1.4 Different Tools used in Research	138
	3.2 Defining Research	142
	3.3. Research Process	143
	3.4 Need of the Study	144
	3.5 Statement of Research Problem	144
	3.6 Objectives of Study	144
	3.7 Research Hypothesis	145
	3.8 Research Methodology – Sample Size Calculation	145
	3.9 Scope of Study	148
	3.10 Limitation of Study	148
4	Data Analysis	149
	4.1 Factorization	149
	4.2 Normality of data	153
	4.3 Reliability of Questionnaire	161
	4.4 Objective 2 Analysis	167
	4.5 Objective 3 Analysis	171
	4.6 Objective 4 Analysis	175
	4.7 Hypothesis 1	201
	4.8 Hypothesis 2	205
	4.9 Hypothesis 3	208
	4.10 Hypothesis 4	210
	4.11 Hypothesis 5	213
	4.12 Hypothesis 6	216
	4.13 Hypothesis 7	219
5	Findings	225
	5.1 Leadership/Managerial Findings	225
	5.2 Institutional Factors Findings	226
	5.3 Job Related Factors Findings	227
	5.4 Organizational Culture Findings	227
	5.5 Opportunity Factors	228
	5.6 Motivational Factors	229
	5.7 Performance Factors	229

	5.8 Summary of Regression Model	230
	5.9 Conceptual Model	232
	5.10 Top 10 Factors Impacting Employees Performance	233
6	Conclusion	236
7	Further Research Suggestion	242
8	Bibliography	243
9	Annexure	257

LIST OF TABLES

Table 1: Sample Size Calculation – determination of Population size ... 146
Table 2: Factors and sub factors considered for study ... 149
Table 3: Skewness and Kurtosis of Data ... 153
Table 4: Reliability Statistics table ... 161
Table 5: Cronbach alpha questions wise ... 162
Table 6: Descriptive Statistics with Dependent Variable as Performance of Employee (Y). 167
Table 7: Table showing summary of model ... 169
Table 8: Table showing results of ANOVA ... 169
Table 9: Table showing the regression coefficients & T stat ... 170
Table 10: Calculation Table ... 171
Table 11: Anova Table ... 172
Table 12: Post Hoc Tests ... 172
Table 13: The ranking & frequencies of respondents with respect to Section A responses are as given below. ... 176
Table 14: The ranking & frequencies of respondents with respect to Section B responses are as given below. ... 178
Table 15: The ranking & frequencies of respondents with respect to Section C responses are as given below ... 179
Table 16: The ranking & frequencies of respondents with respect to Section D responses are as given below. ... 181
Table 17: The ranking & frequencies of respondents with respect to Section E responses are as given below. ... 183
Table 18: The ranking & frequencies of respondents with respect to Section F responses are as given below. ... 184
Table 19: The ranking & frequencies of respondents with respect to Section G responses are as given below. ... 185
Table 20: Leadership / Managerial Factors ... 187
Table 21: Institutional factors ... 189
Table 22: Job Related Factors ... 192
Table 23: Organisational Cultural Factors ... 193
Table 24: Opportunity Factors ... 196
Table 25: Motivational Factors ... 198
Table 26: Performance of Employee ... 199
Table 27: Calculation table ... 202
Table 28: The Pearson's correlation coefficient between Leadership/Managerial factors & performance of employee is given as below. ... 205
Table 29: Descriptive for Hypothesis2 ... 206
Table 30: Model Summary for Hypothesis2 ... 206
Table 31: ANOVA for Hypothesis2 ... 206
Table 32: Regression coefficients & T stat for Hypothesis2 ... 207
Table 33: Descriptive for Hypothesis 3 ... 209
Table 34: Model Summary for Hypothesis 3 ... 209

Table 35: ANOVA for Hypothesis 3 209
Table 36 : Regression coefficients & T stat for Hypothesis 3 210
Table 37: The Pearson's correlation coefficient between Job Related factors & performance of employee is given as below. 211
Table 38: Descriptive for Hypothesis 4 211
Table 39 : Model Summary for Hypothesis 4 212
Table 40: ANOVA for Hypothesis 4 212
Table 41 :Regression coefficients & T stat for Hypothesis 4 212
Table 42: The Pearson's correlation coefficient between Organisational Cultural factors & performance of employee is given as below 214
Table 43 : Descriptive for Hypothesis 5 214
Table 44: Model Summary for Hypothesis 5 215
Table 45 : ANOVA for Hypothesis 5 215
Table 46: Regression coefficients & T stat for Hypothesis 5 215
Table 47: The Pearson's correlation coefficient between Opportunity factors & performance of employee is given as below. 217
Table 48 : Descriptive for Hypothesis 6 217
Table 49: Model Summary for Hypothesis 6 217
Table 50: ANOVA for Hypothesis 6 218
Table 51: Regression coefficients & T stat for Hypothesis 6 218
Table 52: The Pearson's correlation coefficient between Motivational factors & performance of employee is given as below. 219
Table 53: Descriptive for Hypothesis 7 220
Table 54: Model Summary for Hypothesis 7 220
Table 55: ANOVA for Hypothesis 7 221
Table 56: Regression coefficients & T stat for Hypothesis 7 221
Table 57: Summary of Regression Model for all the factors. 230
Table 58: – Top 10 Factors Impacting Employee's Performance 233
Table 59: Regression Summary 238
Table 60:Regression Summary 239

LIST OF FIGURES

Figure 1: Maslow's theory of needs 51
Figure 2: Factors and subfactors considered for study impacting employee's performance. 149
Figure 3: Conceptual Model 232
Figure 4: Factors and subfactors Identified for study impacting employee's performance...237
Figure 5: Creation of Model/structure to enhance performance of employees. 240

LIST OF GRAPHS

Graph No 1 : The Histogram of Leadership Factors to check outliers 154
Graph No 2: The Histogram of Institutional Factors to check outliers 155
Graph No 3: Histogram of Job-Related Factors to check outliers. 155
Graph No 4: The Histogram of Organizational Cultural Factors to check outliers 156

Graph No 5: The Histogram of Opportunity Factor to check outliers 156
Graph No 6: The Histogram of Motivational Factors to check outliers 157
Graph No 7: The Histogram of Performance measures to check outliers 157
Graph No 8: Showing P-P plot deviation and normality of data for Leadership 158
Graph No 9: Showing P-P plot deviation and normality of data for Institutional 158
Graph No 10: Showing P-P plot deviation and normality of data for Job Related 159
Graph No 11: Showing P-P plot deviation and normality of data for Organisational Cultural
.... 159
Graph No 12: Showing P-P plot deviation and normality of data for Opportunity 160
Graph No 13: Showing P-P plot deviation and normality of data for Motivational 160
Graph No 14: Showing P-P plot deviation and normality of data for Performance 161
Graph No 15: The means plot showing means of all non-monetary factors is as given below.
.... 175
Graph No 16: Plot of ranking & frequencies for Institutional Factors 179
Graph No 17 :Plot of ranking & frequencies for Job Related Factors 180
Graph No 18: Plot of ranking & frequencies for Organisational Cultural Factors 182
Graph No 19: Plot of ranking & frequencies for Opportunity Factors 183
Graph No 20: Plot of ranking & frequencies for Motivational Factors 185
Graph No 21: Plot of ranking & frequencies for Performance of Employee 186
Graph No 22: Plot of Frequency Distributions of Leadership / Managerial Factors 191
Graph No 23: Plot of Frequency Distributions of Institutional Factors 191
Graph No 24: Plot of Frequency Distributions of Job Related Factors 193
Graph No 25: Plot of Frequency Distributions of Organisational Cultural Factors 196
Graph No 26: Plot of Frequency Distributions of Opportunity Factors 197
Graph No 27: Plot of Frequency Distributions of Motivational Factors 199
Graph No 28: Plot of Frequency Distributions of Performance of Employee 201

ABBREVATIONS

HR – Human Resource

HRM – Human Resource Management

OEM – Original Equipment Manufacturer

HRD - Human Resource Management

L&D – Learning and Development

T&D – Training and Development

RM – Research Methodology

Auto – Automobile

KRA – Key Result Areas

KPI – Key Performance Indicator

PMS – Performance Management System

MBO – Management by Objective

ABSTRACT

Scheme of study: After understanding, analyzing, and evaluating various aspects of research titled "A study of Non-Monetary factors impacting employee's performance in selected automobile manufacturing industry". The researcher has presented the research in the following chapter scheme.

Chapter 1: Introduction

This chapter focuses on various aspects about India & Global Automotive industry, Employee performance, managing employee performance, Purpose of effective performance management process, Significant factors impacting employee performance and Non-Monetary Factors impacting employee performance.

Chapter 2: Review of literature

This chapter consists of review of literature. The researcher has reviewed the literature in regard to factors impacting employee performance, Which factors impact employee's performance – monetary and non-monetary, different articles on, Research papers, Books and School of thoughts which and how non-monetary factors impact employee performance at work.

Chapter 3: Research Methodology

This chapter presents the research methodology implemented to carry out the research work. It consists of statement of research problem, objectives of the research, type of research, research design for collection of data.

Chapter 4: Data Analysis

This chapter extensively focuses on analysis of collected data, and interpretation. This chapter explores the results, outcomes and interpretations of analysis of data.

Chapter 5: Finding of data

This unit focuses on the findings from the analysis, results, literature, and evaluation of the studies.

Chapter 6: Suggestions and conclusion

This chapter consists of conclusions to this research work. This section concludes with contribution by researcher, limitations of the study, future scope and finally recommendations and suggestions to various stakeholders based on the research.

Chapter 7: Bibliography and Annexures

This includes the books, sources, references and website references followed by annexures consisting of the questionnaire used in the study.

Introduction

About Automotive industry[1]

Automotive industry, all those companies and activities involved in the manufacture of motor vehicles, including most components, such as engines and bodies, but excluding tires, batteries, and fuel. The industry's principal products are passenger automobiles and light trucks, including pickups, vans, and sport utility vehicles. Commercial vehicles (i.e., delivery trucks and large transport trucks, often called semis), though important to the industry, are secondary. The design of modern automotive vehicles is discussed in the article's automobile, truck, bus, and motorcycle; automotive engines are described in gasoline engine and diesel engine. The development of the automobile is covered in transportation, history of: The rise of the automobile.

The history of the automobile industry, though brief compared with that of many other industries, has exceptional interest because of its effects on history from the 20th century. Although the automobile originated in Europe in the late 19th century, the United States completely dominated the world industry for the first half of the 20th century through the invention of mass production techniques. In the second half of the century the situation altered sharply as western European countries and Japan became major producers and exporters.

Definition of Employee Performance[2]

Employee performance refers to your employees' behaviour in the workplace and their ability to accomplish the job obligations you've assigned to them. Typically, your firm establishes performance goals for individual employees and the organisation as a whole in order to ensure that your business provides value to consumers, minimizes waste, and functions efficiently.

Performance can refer to the efficacy, quality, and efficiency of an individual employee's work at the task level. For example, your salesperson may be expected to make a particular number of calls to potential leads every hour, with a certain percentage of those calls resulting in closed sales. On the other side, a production worker may be required to meet performance standards for product quality and hourly production.

Individual performance has an effect on the performance of your team and company. If you have staff that are unable to keep up or who perform mediocre work, this may need other employees to pick up the slack or require work to be redone. When employees perform poorly, they may be unable to satisfy clients, resulting in negative effects on profits, corporate reputation, and sales.

Employee Performance Metrics That Are Frequently Used
The measures used to evaluate employee performance will ultimately depend on the sort of work performed by your organisation. However, there are some measurements that are universally applicable.

Businesses should check work quality, individual employee objectives, training efficacy, and staff efficiency. Evaluating work quality and efficiency helps you avoid costly mistakes, increases the likelihood that your employees will meet deadlines, and minimises wasted time, materials, and effort. Evaluating the success of training and individual employee work goals will assist you in determining if employees are adequately prepared to do their duties and in providing necessary guidance.

Depending on the nature of your firm, you may wish to employ additional particular performance measures such as the following:

- **Achievement of Goals / KRA**
- **Production Efficiency - Number of units produced per day or per months based on efficiency of setup/plant.**
- **The quantity of defective products**
- **The total number of errors**
- **The quantity of sales**
- **The quantity of units manufactured**
- **The duration of the call**
- **Initial contact resolution**
- **Rate of absenteeism**

Performance Evaluation of Employees

Your firm has numerous ways for evaluating employee performance, and you may find it beneficial to combine them to obtain a fuller picture of individual, team, and organizational performance. Among these are the following:

Management according to objectives: This approach of reviewing employee performance relies on goal setting between managers and employees. It has the advantage of setting clear expectations for how people should execute their jobs and tracking progress toward these goals through the use of deadlines.

360-degree feedback: This strategy entails soliciting feedback on an employee's performance from a variety of individuals with whom the employee interacts. Along with having a direct supervisor assess work-performance measures such as effectiveness and efficiency, coworkers, other managers, and anybody else to whom the employee reports can offer insight about the person's abilities and character.

Scale and rating methods: There are numerous employee performance assessment choices that assess an employee using lists or scales of desired attributes. Employees may be ranked according to their performance from best to worst in order to quickly discover individuals who may be desirable for higher-level positions as well as those who require additional training.

Self-evaluation of employees: Often used in conjunction with another review approach, self-evaluation allows employees to reflect on their own work performance and identify their strengths and faults. However, this strategy has the disadvantage of making it difficult for employees to be subjective about themselves.

Increasing Employee Productivity

Along with conducting frequent performance evaluations, you'll need an employee performance improvement strategy to address your results. It's beneficial to begin by determining why your staff fall short of performance objectives. Perhaps they lack enough training, motivation, morale, or a grasp of performance objectives.

Once the root reason has been identified, it is time to take action by providing more training, developing an effective reward system, changing the work atmosphere, empowering your employees, and integrating relevant technologies.

Taking Charge of Employee Performance (Managing Employee Performance)[3]

Managing employee performance is a critical component of organisational success in the current environment of organisations attempting to embrace a resource-centered organisational vision. As previously demonstrated, integrating human resource management methods with organisational goals and strategy boosts a firm's competitive edge. Similarly, firms that value people as a vital asset must manage employee performance within the context of organisational goals. As previously stated, organisations in the service sector that place a high premium on people must guarantee that employee performance is handled holistically.

A Two-Way Road

When we discuss employee performance, we must keep in mind that it is a two-way street that connects the manager and the employee, with the HR manager acting as a mediator. For example, any discussion of employee performance must include both the management and the employee, or the manager and those who are managed. As a result, it is critical that both parties to this transaction understand their respective obligations and collaborate to ensure that the process runs well. The next sections describe the manager's and employee's roles, as well as how an organisational focus on controlling employee performance can play a role.

The Manager's Function

The manager owes it to his or her staff to ensure that their management is devoid of biases and prejudices. It has been documented across industries and verticals that employees feel discriminated against, resulting in turnover, decreased employee morale, and, in extreme circumstances, lawsuits against the organisation. As a result, the manager must "walk the walk" and not simply pay lip service to the company's performance policies. While operating as a team, there are certain to be occasions of friction between the management and the team, as well as within the team. The manager's responsibility is to ensure that this does not deteriorate into a corrosive effect that threatens the team's very existence.

The Employee's Role

The preceding section discussed the manager's role. The manager has a responsibility to manage the team effectively, and each employee also has comparable responsibilities. Absenteeism, Disappeared Work, Negative attitudes and a casual attitude toward work are two characteristics that the employee must avoid. It is beneficial for the employee to understand that once classified as having an attitude problem, it will be tough to overcome the perception and function well. This is not to say that the employee must accept whatever is thrown his or her way. The notion is that the employee must pursue remedy through accessible avenues rather than sulking at work if he or she has issues against the manager.

Organizational Objectives

Though the HR manager's and organization's roles appear to be little, it is a reality that organisational goals and culture play a critical role in ensuring that employee performance is managed to the organization's benefit. The majority of us have read or heard about the perks of working for multinational corporations (MNCs) in India. The reason they are so well-known is that potential and aspiring employees have a positive image of how these organisations handle their staff. Though the purpose of this section is not to disparage Indian businesses, it does emphasize the ways in which organisations can influence how people are treated in theory and reality.

1. As a result, human resource management has a considerable impact on performance. [4]

The performance of an organisation may be traced back to the actions of its employees on the shop floor. Employees work in a given way or act in a certain way in order to contribute to the organization's (objective). [5]

Employee behaviour can present itself in three distinct ways in relation to organisational performance.[6]

Execution of tasks

Behaviour centered on completing the task. Task performance is frequently seen as the most critical part of job behaviour and is frequently used interchangeably with overall job performance.

Behaviour of Organizational Citizenship

This is sometimes referred to as 'soft performance'. In a nutshell, this occurs when individuals perform duties that are not directly related to their immediate area of responsibility or job description, thereby contributing to the organization's objectives.

Deviant Behaviour in the Workplace

This is behaviour in which an employee breaches an organization's standards, thereby endangering the organisation or his coworkers. Spreading false rumors, insulting coworkers, stealing, and sabotage are just a few examples. Employees that are actively disengaged exhibit this behaviour. Employees must receive feedback on their behaviour and performance. If such is not the case, they will use their prior performance as a benchmark to determine:

Which activities they will perform[7]
how much work they will exert[8]
how motivated they are[9]
to what extent they will recognize and rectify errors

The critical nature of performance

If your organisation or organisational unit does not add value, it has no reason to exist. This may include value for customers, society, and shareholders, as well as value for employees within the organisation. Each person offers a unique contribution to the organisational unit's performance, and consequently to the overall success of your organisation. If an organisational unit or individual employee's performance lags over an extended period of time, reorganization or redundancy are likely. The necessity of ongoing performance is growing, even more so in a context where competition is fiercer than ever.

What Is the Purpose of an Effective Performance Management Process (PMP)?[10]

A dependable and stable Employee Performance Management Process, along with all of its associated strategies, tools, and ratings, contribute significantly to improving the performance of employees and supervisors throughout the firm. An efficient employee performance management programme contributes to the following benefits for the organisation:
- Produces efficacy, adaptability, and equality

- The objectives established are precise, reasonable, and quantifiable.
- Enhances employee productivity, engagement, and development
- Encourages both proactive and ongoing succession planning
- Consistency throughout the organization's departments to foster development and talent usage
- Develops a more capable staff
- Develops, moulds, and engages employees in all circumstances
- Prior performance is taken into account when setting new targets.
- Additionally, a future viewpoint is examined to aid in the creation of development chances.
- Enhances communication by ensuring that everyone respects the rules
- Reduced stress among coworkers as a result of communication
- Employee education and development

The entire performance management process revolves around four pillars: developing, recognizing, planning, and assessing. All of this is accomplished with the assistance of supervisors. The primary tools used throughout the procedure are as follows:

Individual Development Plan (IDP): This is a tool that assists managers and employees in developing annual personal development plans. IDP and the department share a common aim of success.

Dialogue in Performance (PD): The team develops the PD in order to evaluate their current and previous updates.

How Should Employee Performance Be Measured?

Any business owner is always reliant on his staff efficiency. To motivate their personnel to achieve at their peak levels, they must work diligently. They will constantly require someone who can strive to elevate their firm and also track the performance of their personnel. Certain tools aid in the evaluation of employee performance.

The following tools are used to evaluate employee performance:

Productivity Evaluations

Productivity measurement demonstrates how well your employees are meeting expectations. These tests are fairly prevalent in factories where output is quantified.

Management by Objectives

The assessment process evaluates employees' performance in technical, skilled, communicative, and motivational domains. Certain employees' performance is evaluated based on their annual percentage of goal achievement.

Performance Evaluations

This is one of the most critical, comprehensive, and successful methods of evaluating your employees' business performance. Annual evaluations ensure that the results are correct.

360° Feedback

This input enables the organization's management sector to be quantified. It benefits supervisors, trainers, and human resource management leaders, among others.

As a result of all of this, we may infer that performance management is important in order to establish a more efficient organization.

Literature review

1. **Anna Mokhniuk and Larysa Yushchyshyna (2018)** in their research paper titled **"The Impact of Monetary and Non-Monetary Factors of Motivation on Employee Productivity"** concluded as . Our research, as described in this paper, sought to ascertain the elements that inspire various personnel groups and to investigate their effect on Labour productivity. The findings indicate that a successful motivation system should incorporate a variety of rewards for various staff groups. The findings corroborate Maslow's (1954) theory of motivation by indicating that the top two elements employees value most are their base income and bonuses.

Thus, the base income plays a critical role in enhancing employee motivation. To begin, it satisfies fundamental human wants. Second, it serves as a barometer of one's profession's status and one's standing inside a corporation. Thirdly, it provides a backdrop for further motivational techniques. It is obvious that all nonmonetary motivational approaches appear to lose effectiveness unless they are complemented by enough cash remuneration. In other words, when employees are content with their compensation, they are far more sensitive to additional forms of stimulation such as recognition, flexible work hours, and autonomy. Regrettably, in Ukraine's current unfavorable business environment, numerous intangible motivating tactics are adopted in place of monetary incentives, primarily due to a scarcity of cash resources. Bonuses and profit-sharing arrangements are examples of secondary motivation approaches. They recognize and reward the efforts and accomplishments of individual employees.

There is a high chance that monetary incentives improve employee motivation and motivate employees to follow their superiors' orders. We believe that employees regard base pay and bonuses as a form of compensation and that they must compensate for this by enhancing their performance.

However, compensation and bonus considerations alone cannot achieve the long-term goals of promoting creativity and invention, or of developing foresight and the ability to make successful judgments in tough situations.

It is critical to note the major disparities in how different groups of employees perceived motivational elements. These variables have been ranked according to their significance to the influence, beginning with the most significant.

The following factors are advocated for top-level managers: involvement in decision-making, recognition, public appreciation, base pay, bonuses, competitive spirit, autonomy, flexible hours, profit sharing opportunities, public criticism, and on/off the job training.

Bonuses, recognition, profit sharing, autonomy, competitive spirit, basic salary, demanding work, flexible hours, participation in decision-making, job happiness, and the availability of free cell phones are all recommended motivator incentives for middle-level managers.

Low-level managers will benefit the most from bonuses, recognition, job satisfaction, autonomy, competitive spirit, flexible hours, on-the-job training, profit sharing, gym membership, demanding work, and a life insurance plan.

2. Pradorn Sureephong, Winai Dahlan, Suepphong Chernbumroong, and Yootthapong Tongpaeng in their research paper titled "The Effect of Non-Monetary Rewards on Employee Performance in Massive Open Online Courses" concluded as This study described and illustrated the effect of several non-monetary rewards on employee performance (tangible, social, and job-related). This study enrolled ninety volunteer employees from a food manufacturing company in Chiang Mai, Thailand. Two field studies were done to assess staff motivation and performance. In field study 1, a questionnaire evaluating Valence, Instrumentality, and Expectancy was used to assess employee motivation for three distinct non-monetary reward categories. The results suggested that the group of non-monetary physical rewards had the greatest valence score.

Employees tended to value physical things more highly than social and job-related benefits. As a result, experts believe that individuals who receive physical non-monetary benefits are more motivated to participate in the online training programme. In field research 2, the same set of participants as in field study 1 was divided into three non-monetary reward groups and assigned to enrol in an online curriculum called "HSC MOOC." Only those participants who met the prerequisites for MOOCs got incentives, which varied by group. The results suggested that about 63% of participants in the group receiving tangible non-monetary rewards completed the MOOC curriculum.

According to the researchers, physical rewards have a beneficial effect on participants' learning performance.

3. Ruth Kanini Bosire and Dr. James Muya(2019) in their research paper titled "NON-MONETARY COMPENSATION PRACTICES AND EMPLOYEE OUTPUT: A CRITICAL REVIEW OF LITERATURE" focused on This research tried to establish some critical non-monetary remuneration practices and their impact on employee output. The research established through a review of the theoretical and empirical literature that non-monetary remuneration systems have a direct effect on motivation levels and, eventually, on productivity. Various organisations have implemented a variety of non-monetary remuneration techniques, including medical plans, work-hour flexibility, staff training, and employee recognition and development opportunities. The study argues that in order for a business to excel in terms of quality and quantity of production, as well as retention of competent individuals, it is critical that they implement non-monetary pay strategies to boost employee morale and demonstrate appreciation. Finally, the report advises that governments, labour unions, and regulatory agencies responsible for salaries and remunerations enact rules that encourage firms to use non-monetary pay to drive employees to perform better.

4. Tavonga Gilson Gudo in his paper titled "An analysis on the impact of non monetary incentives on employee performance" concluded as Due to the diversity of inferences that may be drawn from the findings of this study, the conclusion of the research study on the impact of non-monetary incentives on employee performance at TelOne can be summarized as follows:

i. TelOne, the postal and telecommunications firm, operates a functional nonmonetary incentive structure. The findings indicate that the Institution has a functional non-monetary incentive structure that is well understood by its personnel. According to research findings, the existence of a functional non-monetary incentive system contributes significantly to improving employee performance, as evidenced by TelOne's sustained profitability growth over the years, which the researcher attributes to the non-monetary incentive strategy among a variety of other strategies.

2. Employees assert that non-monetary incentives have had a significant impact on their performance at work, both positively and negatively, depending on the incentive's use. Non-monetary incentives like as career progression opportunities, on-the-job training, promotion, paid time off, vacation, job stability, good communication, work rotation, health care, and goal setting and rewards have all had a favorable effect on employee performance. According to the data, this has resulted in personnel exhibiting increased performance in order to accomplish their assigned tasks. However, it is the unethical and unfair employment practices based on nepotism that have had a detrimental effect on employee performance. The awarding of these non-monetary incentives based on management's personal preferences has hindered efforts to reform the system, as employees are demotivated to perform better as a result of the injustice.

TelOne standards for providing non-monetary rewards should be predicated on transparency, fairness and merit, nepotism and favoritism should not play a crucial part in this regard. Thus, their use must be continuously managed to ensure that they have a beneficial effect on staff performance.

3. TelOne has used non-monetary incentives such as career growth opportunities, on-the-job training, promotion, paid time off, vacation, job stability, effective communication, work rotation, health care, and goal setting and rewards. These non-monetary incentives have been well received by employees and, according to research findings, have contributed to increased employee performance. The most popular initiatives identified in the report were the payment of dependents' school tuition, health

care, and subsidising telephone expenses. These initiatives have increased employee loyalty, which has a positive effect on their performance.

4. That there is a positive linear link between employee performance and non-monetary incentives that must be maintained. There is a significant linear association between employee performance and non-monetary relationships. To be effective, managers must have a working knowledge of the linear relationship between employee performance and non-monetary incentives, as well as motivation and the various motivational theories that attempt to explain motivation. According to the study's findings, when employees are assured non-monetary rewards, they work at their maximum ability.

5. The existing economic environment precludes the use of non-monetary incentives, as institutions struggle to allocate money for motivation in such an economy. According to the study's findings, some institutions have eliminated non-monetary incentives from their strategies in response to the present economic climate, which has seen the majority of businesses running on shoestring budgets and earning the barest of profits. Due to the existing state of the economy, it is impossible to apply nonmonetary incentives. While non-monetary incentives may have a beneficial effect on employee performance, the current economic climate makes their employment nearly impossible.

In light of the foregoing conclusions drawn from the investigation, one can confidently conclude that the research issues addressed by the study were adequately addressed. The conclusions achieved do, in fact, fully address the research issues.

5. ErajesvariePillay and Dr.Shamila Singh in their research paper "The Impact of employee engagement on organisational performance – a case of an Insurance Brokerage company in Gauteng" concluded as The purpose of this study was to determine the effect of employee engagement on the performance of a short-term insurance brokerage. Employee engagement does have an effect on organisational performance, as evidenced by both the literature and the study conducted. Second, communications, work design, incentives and rewards, leadership, employee involvement, culture, and career development have all been highlighted as critical elements in employee engagement. The study's shortcomings include the fact that it was done in a single organisation and was not equally representative of both genders due to the organization's two male employees. Second, while purposive sampling is meant to identify participants with extensive knowledge and expertise in the topic area, the researcher was unable to determine which employees were more informed about employee engagement due to the sample size being insufficient. In light of this study, additional research in the short-term industry is needed to acquire a better knowledge of the impact of employee engagement on organisational success.

6. Zafar, Marium and Karim, Emadul and Abbas, Omair(April 2017) in their paper "Factors of Workplace Environment that Affects Employee Performance in an Organization": A study on Greenwich University of Karachi concluded as For enterprises, employee performance is a critical aspect in their success, as it enables them to stay ahead of the competition, accomplish their objectives, and make profits. The goal of this study was to examine the many elements that influence employee performance at Greenwich University in Karachi. Multiple Linear Regression was used to test the hypothesis, which was done using the SPSS software. Leadership, training and development, and stress had the most impact on the performance of Greenwich University staff, indicating that these independent variables had the greatest effect on the dependent variable.

7. Saharuddin1 , Sulaiman (Oct 2016) The Effect Of Promotion And Compensation Toward Working Productivity Through Job Satisfaction And Working Motivation Of Employees, In The Department Of Water And Mineral Resources Energy North Aceh District concluded as The findings of this study can be interpreted in practice as indicating that variable compensation, promotion, and job satisfaction all have an effect on employee productivity, either directly or indirectly. This demonstrates the critical role of promotion and remuneration as fringe benefits in an organization's continual improvement of productivity, as well as the need of providing capacity building and growth to employees. Career stagnation (no promotion) results in sloth and unhappiness; also, the salary earned by employees does not match their performance, posing a danger of employee dissatisfaction, which results in decreasing work productivity. On the other hand, promotion and compensation serve as a magnet for capable and qualified employees within the organisation, encouraging employees to remain motivated and qualified to remain loyal, ensure fairness, control costs, adhere to the rule of law, improve efficiency and effectiveness, and maintain and/or increase employee productivity.

8. Daniel Njoya Ndungu(2017) The Effects of Rewards and Recognition on Employee Performance in Public Educational Institutions: A Case of Kenyatta University, Kenya focused on The findings of this study reveal that employees at Kenyatta University are less motivated by money and recognition rewards, and that variables only contribute slightly to job performance improvement. This indicates that if Kenyatta University's management places a greater emphasis on reward and recognition, it may have a favourable effect on university workers, resulting in increased job performance.

The findings, however, may be unique to Kenyatta University and may not be generalizable to other universities in Kenya.

Nonetheless, Kenyatta University's administration may use the research findings to evaluate its current incentive and recognition programmes. This will be especially effective if the focus is on the requirements of all employees, regardless of their working status: whether casual, permanent, contract, or any other. According to the research, cash and recognition awards had the lowest mean values. This demonstrates that employees are less motivated by money benefits and frequently overlook aspects of acknowledgment. On the other hand, when the work atmosphere is conducive, employees are nice, they are compensated fairly for their efforts, their jobs are secure, and they have opportunities to advance within Kenyatta University, their motivation remains high.

Employees at Kenya University regard prizes and recognition for their efforts as a means of motivating them to continue working for the institution. This demonstrates that employees desire recognition for their efforts in order to be motivated to repeat the behaviour that results in increased performance levels. The study's findings indicated that few personnel had worked for the institution for an extended period of time, implying that Kenyatta University has a high rate of staff attrition. The majority of staff had spent less than five years at the organisation. According to respondents, awards and recognition should be based on objective performance criteria that are seen to be fair. Low-level employees, the majority of whom were casual workers, saw disparities in wage, benefits, and other characteristics as demotivating. Lack of communication was also identified as a significant impediment to respondents' motivation, which impacted performance. It is therefore essential to communicate incentives and recognition in a timely manner and with appropriate ceremony to ensure that staff are prepared and motivated.

9. Iqbal N , Anwar S and Haider N ( ), Effect of Leadership Style on Employee Performance explored on According to Myron Rush and Cole, participatory leadership has a more beneficial effect on employee performance when employees feel empowered and confident in their ability to execute their jobs and make alternative judgments. And in an autocratic approach, leaders have the right to make decisions that make employees feel inferior in their ability to do tasks and make decisions. Employees in a democratic style have some discretionary authority over their work, which results in higher performance than in an autocratic style.

- The authoritative tone is suitable.
- When new employees are unfamiliar with their duties and lack appropriate knowledge about them
- If an employee abuses their authority on a consistent basis
- When employees breach business policies
- When a single individual is accountable for decision-making and implementation
- Appropriate consultative style
- When a business need innovative issue solving
- When an organisation has planning meetings to improve a department's operations
- When a company prepares individuals for leadership responsibilities
- When you want competent and effective completion of routine organisational chores
- It is appropriate to use a participative style.
- When an organization's team members are skilled and talented
- When a corporation or department has meetings to discuss ways to improve
- When a business has evaluation sessions
- When encouraging an organization's top performers
- When you require inventive and imaginative work.

10. ASAMU Festus Femi(Aug. 2014), "The Impact of Communication on Workers' Performance in Selected Organisations in Lagos State" concluded as According to the study's findings, good communication fosters mutual understanding between management and employees, resulting in the development of true relationships between both sides within businesses. Additionally, this study demonstrates that poor communication might have a negative effect on worker performance. As a result, firms should communicate their policies, aims, and objectives to their employees on a frequent basis in order to boost job performance. That is, communication is the process through which the task and resources required to complete an assignment, the roles and responsibilities, and the expected results are communicated to subordinates, making work easier and resulting in improved performance. Additionally, managers must contact with employees on a frequent basis to solicit feedback and make suggestions for future task assignments; this will help enhance employee performance and organisational productivity. Additionally, top managers should interact directly with their direct reports on critical concerns. Organizations should remove communication barriers and establish efficient, participatory, and transparent communication channels to increase employee commitment.

Research Methodology
Research Process

The process of research includes a series of steps carried out by a research to reach the ultimate conclusion. The general steps to be followed by a researcher in any research work areas follow

1. Defining the research problem
2. Reviewing literature
3. Formulation of hypothesis
4. Development & implementation of a research plan
5. Data Collection
6. Analyzing data & testing of Hypothesis
7. Interpretation of data & reaching conclusions
8. Preparation of report & reporting the findings
9. The researcher in order to carry out this study had followed the systematic research process plan.

Need for the Study

Monetary & Non-Monetary factors both impacting performance of employees in an organization, but over a period as the employees matures, there is shift in impact of both the factors on performance of employee. Generally, it is evident that, for first 4-5 years, monetary factors play important role, but post a certain amount of experience to credit the Non-Monetary factors impact most to performance of an employee. Also, in constantly evolving and disruptive world, where organizations are under tremendous pressures to cut costs and have highly engaged and productive employees, it's very much imperative for them to find ways and means to derive high performance from employees using Non-Monetary Factors. The findings from this study will help organization with deeper insights on relationship between Non-Monetary factors and performance. Further engagement surveys conducted by different renowned consulting firms like Gallup, Mercer and Aon-Hewitt have stress upon evident importance of Non-Monetary factors affecting employee's performance.

Statement of the Research Problem
A study of Non-Monetary factors impacting employee's performance in selected automobile manufacturing industry"- Specifically to 4-wheeler manufacturing - Original Equipment manufacturers spreaded across the country predominantly in with the intent to understand impact of each Non-Monetary factor on employee's performance.

Objective of the Study
The objectives of the proposed study are:
1. Identify of Non- Monetary of Factors which impact performance in Automobile manufacturing industries.
2. To establish relationship between Non-Monetary factors and performance of employee.
3. To establish or rank non-monetary factors based on their positive impact on employee's performance.
4. Based on the finding of study, Creation of Model/structure to enhance performance of employees.

Research Hypothesis
Hypothesis will be drawn in the course of study - Multiple Hypothesis will be tested to establish correlation between various Non-Monetary factors and employee's performance in automobile industry.

H1 : There is impact of non-monetary factors on performance of employee.

H2 :There is positive impact of Leadership/Managerial factors on performance of employee.

H3 :There is positive impact of Institutional factors on performance of employee.

H4: There is positive impact of Job Related factors on performance of employee.

H5: There is positive impact of Organisational Cultural factors on performance of employee.

H6: There is positive impact of Opportunity factors on performance of employee.

H7 : There is positive impact of Motivational factors on performance of employee.

Research Methodology

A) Sampling Design:

The sample universe for this research will be Auto Manufacturing plant in like FIAT CHRYSLER, TATA Motors, Jeep, Mahindra & Mahindra, Skoda and VW. The sample will be collected using random sampling method. We will target samples (employees) with experience range from 5 years to 15 years, the reason being, in early stage of the careers mostly young professionals are behind monetary factors.

B) Sources and Methods of Collection of Data:

The applied methodology of the study is the use of the questionnaires. The participants are the employees that are employed by auto manufacturing OEMs. We will use online software's like survey monkey to collect the data. The participants are allowed to answer on the basis of their work nature. Participants will be classified on the basis of Experience, Gender, and Levels in Organization, Education and Location.

The researcher seeks to collect the data through primary as well as secondary sources.

i) Primary Data:

- Questionnaire: Online Format.

It will be collected through structured Questionnaire from 600 employees working with different auto manufacturing organizations.

ii) Secondary Data:

It will be gathered through the following sources:-

- Use of library-

Relevant data will be collected through books, journals etc.

- Use of Internet-

Internet will be extensively used to seek data from the websites like SHRM, Gallup, and Employee engagement agency sites.

- Published/ Unpublished data-

Journals regarding Employee performance and Organizational Development and HRM.

- Published and unpublished PhD thesis regarding Factors affecting Employee performance and Organizational Development.

C) Methods of Analysis and Statistical Tools:

Both Qualitative and Quantitative methods of analysis will be used by the researcher. Sophisticated statistical tools like SPSS and AMOS will be used for the analysis purpose.

Firstly, a pilot study will be conducted and then the questionnaire will be finalized.

Sample Size Calculation:

I have worked as HR in auto industry for more than 10 Years and during my association I have collected the data related to headcount in different auto OEM'S. the below table summarizes the staff working in different auto OEM's across india. This data has been collected by speaking to different employee working in the auto OEM's and is also validated by checking in against SIAM reference reports.

Table: Sample Size Calculation

Company	Estimated White Collars
FIAT	450
TATA Motors	1400
Honda Cars	550
Mahindra & Mahindra	1400
Skoda	200
VW	500
Force Motors	300
Toyota	500
Mercedes Benz	400
Nissan/Renault	700
Hyundai / Kia	800
Maruti Suzuki	1400
Kohler Engineers	100

Hero Motors	600
Ford Sanand & Chennai	600
Total	**9900**

Population size is approx. 9900 employees working in different auto OEM's.

As per Morgan and Krejcie table the minimum acceptable sample size should be 370 sample

Using the calculations provided by Krejcie & Morgan in their "Determining Sample Size for Research Activities" the sample size for the population mentioned above shall be 384 at a Confidence interval 4.9, Confidence Level of 95% with Margin of Error 5%.

Sample duration: 6 months

Sampling procedure: Random Sample

Sample size determination :

S S using mean

$$\text{Sample size, } n = N * \frac{\frac{z^2 * p * (1-p)}{e^2}}{[N - 1 + \frac{z^2 * p * (1-p)}{e^2}]}$$

N = population size

- e = Margin of error (percentage in decimal form)
- z = z-score (from the table it is 1.96)

N= 342

E=0.05

Z=1.96

P=0.5

And considering confidence interval is 4.9

Sample size :

SS = (9900*(1.96^2)*0.5*(1-0.5)/(0.05^2)/(9900-1+((1.96^2)*0.5*(1-0.5)/(0.05^2))))

Sample is : 384

Scope of study
1. The research is restricted to selected Auto OEMs.
2. The research would comprise of inputs from employees above 5 years of experience to 15 years of experience.
3. Employees from Different levels of Management pyramid would be considered for this research.

Limitation of study
1. Performance is function of both the factors Monetary as well as Non-Monetary, this study is limited to Non-Monetary factors only.
2. Researcher will not consider fresher's or employees with experience less than 4 to 5 years, as for most them primary factors that affect performance are monetary.
3. Study findings may be limited to the data collection period.
4. During this study, data will be collected from respondents, which may be representation of particular time response at that point in time and may be the response from respondent may vary at other point in time.

Data Analysis

Researcher has considered 6 factors to understand their impact on employee's performance. Below is the list of Factors and their subfactors considered for the study.
Table :Factors and subfactors considered for study

F1-Leadership / Managerial	F2 - Institutional	F3 - Job Related
Vision & Mission of Leader	Brand Image	Job Fit
Leadership Style	Reponsiblity	Clear Goals and Expectations
Coaching by Lead	Technology	Tools and Equipment / Resources
Camaradarie with Colleagues	Infrastructure	Work Life Balance
Relationship with Manager	Production Systems	Usage of Technology
Performance Pressure	Structure	Risk associated with Job
Empowement	Indian / MNC	Location of work
	Organisational Stability	Reputation/Status of the Job
	Market Position	Diversity in Job

F4 - Organisational Culture	F5-Opportunity	H-6 Motivation
Culture	Development Opportunities	Motivation
Communication	Career Path	Recognition
social learning	Growth Options	Job Enrichment
Ethics	Job Security	Job Satisfaction
Innovation	Diversity	Passion towards car
Discipline		Ability
Standardisation		Performance Appraisal Process
Reputation in eyes of Customer		

Figure :Factors and subfactors considered for study impacting employee's performance.

Normality of the data
Skewness & Kurtosis

Table : Skewness and Kurtosis of Data

Descriptive Statistics					
	N	Skewness		Kurtosis	
	Statistic	Statistic	Std. Error	Statistic	Std. Error
Leadership / Managerial Factor	416	-.222	.120	-.196	.239
Institutional Factor	416	-.643	.120	.383	.239
Job Related Factor	416	-.366	.120	-.019	.239

Organizational Cultural Factor	416	-.782	.120	.899	.239
Opportunity Factor	416	-.704	.120	.757	.239
Motivational Factor	416	-.738	.120	.537	.239
Performance of Employee	416	-.272	.120	.015	.239
Valid N (listwise)	416				

We can assume normality if skewness is in the range of -0.8 to 0.8 and kurtosis is in the range of -3.0 to 3.0

Histogram, skewness & kurtosis values & P-P plots indicates that the data for factors - Leadership / Managerial Factor, Institutional Factor, Job Related Factor, Organizational Cultural Factor, Opportunity Factor, Motivational Factor and Performance of Employee can be considered as normally distributed.

Reliability of the questionnaire:

The questionnaire includes 5 demographic question & 72 questions related to study. The reliability of the questionnaire is calculated as follows.

Table : Reliability Statistics table

Reliability Statistics	
Cronbach's Alpha	N of Items
.941	72

The reliability of the questionnaire i.e. the Cronbach alpha = 0.941

Hence the Cronbach alpha; reliability of the questionnaire is excellent.

If the reliability alpha (if the question deleted) is less than 0.941, then the corresponding question is important (must be kept in questionnaire). If the reliability alpha (if the question deleted) is greater than 0.941, then the corresponding question is unnecessary (must be removed from questionnaire).

Since there is no high variation of the reliability alpha (if the question deleted) from the Cronbach alpha, which is 0.941; all the questions are equally important. Hence the same questionnaire is applied for main study.

Hypothesis Testing

Hypothesis 1: There is impact of non-monetary factors on performance of employee.

To test the hypotheses,

The null hypothesis, H_0:

There is no impact of non-monetary factors on performance of employee.

Vs.

The alternative hypothesis, Ha:

There is impact of non-monetary factors on performance of employee.

The test used is z test for proportions.

Test statistics:

$$Z = \frac{\hat{p} - p_0}{\sqrt{\frac{p_0(1-p_0)}{n}}}$$

Here $\hat{p}$ = sample proportion, p_0 = hypothetical value = 75% = 0.75, n = sample size

Table: Calculation table:

Sr. No.	Question	Frequency (Often + Always)	Proportion	Z Statistics	P value	Significance
1	Leadership Style of my manager affects me drastically	329	0.79	1.92	0.0271	Significant
2	My leader knows my strengths and Weakness and he guides me accordingly	340	0.82	3.17	0.0008	Significant

3	My Manager is supportive & I like interacting with him	354	0.85	4.76	0.0000	Significant
4	It is my experience that Production systems plays a important role in increasing Productivity	378	0.91	7.47	0.0000	Significant
5	Reporting / Org Structure affects my performance drastically	289	0.69	-2.60	0.9954	Not Significant
6	I like my job if my skills my matching with offered role	391	0.94	8.94	0.0000	Significant
7	Clear Goals & Expectations helps me in achieving my Targets	400	0.96	9.96	0.0000	Significant
8	I feel Training provided helps me grow in the organisation	357	0.86	5.10	0.0000	Significant
9	My Organisation is Agile and Flexible to meet customer & market demand	373	0.90	6.91	0.0000	Significant

10	I feel motivated when I am included/involved in the communication	396	0.95	9.51	0.0000	Significant
11	My Organisation has required level of standardization	354	0.85	4.76	0.0000	Significant
12	I feel passionate to perform when I see development opportunities in my organisation	404	0.97	10.42	0.0000	Significant
13	I feel motivated when in grow in the organisation	383	0.92	8.04	0.0000	Significant
14	I feel good when my efforts are recognized	406	0.98	10.64	0.0000	Significant
15	I feel motivated when additional responsibilities are entrusted upon me.	372	0.89	6.79	0.0000	Significant
16	I give my best when I am satisfied with my Job	412	0.99	11.32	0.0000	Significant
17	I am able to complete my targets	398	0.96	9.74	0.0000	Significant

18	My Organisations management is happy with my work	388	0.93	8.61	0.0000	Significant
19	I am getting recognition I deserve	320	0.77	0.91	0.1825	Not Significant
20	I got the growth that I deserve in the organisation	337	0.81	2.83	0.0023	Significant

If p value < 0.05, the level of significance; the null hypothesis is rejected.
Since p value is less than 0.05 for 18 factors out of 20 factors; the null hypothesis can be rejected for 18 factors out of 20 factors.
Conclusion:
For the majority of parameters the null hypothesis is being rejected.
Hence there is impact of non-monetary factors on performance of employee. Hypothesis 1 is accepted.

Hypothesis 2: There is positive impact of Leadership/Managerial factors on performance of employee.
This hypothesis is assessed by two distinct tools of statistics; first is Pearson's correlation coefficient & second is Regression model.
To test the hypotheses,
The Null Hypothesis, H_0: There is no impact of Leadership/Managerial factors on performance of employee.
Vs.
The Alternative Hypothesis, H_a: There is positive impact of Leadership/Managerial factors on performance of employee.

Part 1] Pearson's Correlation coefficient

Table : The Pearson's correlation coefficient between Leadership/Managerial factors & performance of employee is given as below.

		Correlations	
		Performance of Employee	Leadership / Managerial Factor
Pearson Correlation	Performance of Employee	1.000	.590
	Leadership / Managerial Factor	.590	1.000
P Value	Performance of Employee	-	.000
	Leadership / Managerial Factor	.000	-
N	Performance of Employee	416	416
	Leadership / Managerial Factor	416	416

Since P value is less than 0.05, level of significance; the correlation is significant.

Conclusion:

The correlation between Leadership/Managerial factors & Performance of employee is significant. The positive value of correlation coefficient suggests that one variable increases with the other.

Part 2] Regression Model

The regression model for Performance of employee (Y) on Leadership/Managerial factors (X) is as given below.

Table: Descriptive for Hypothesis 2

Descriptive Statistics			
	Mean	Std. Deviation	N
Performance of Employee	39.24	3.443	416
Leadership / Managerial Factor	74.07	6.659	416

Table : Model Summary for Hypothesis 2

Model Summary				
Model	R	R Square	Adjusted R Square	Std. Error of the Estimate
1	.590a	.348	.347	2.783
a. Predictors: (Constant), Leadership / Managerial Factor				

Since coefficient of determination i.e. R square = 0.348, 34.8% of the total variation in the dependent variable is explained by independent variables in model 1.

Table : ANOVA for Hypothesis 2

ANOVAa						
Model		Sum of Squares	df	Mean Square	F	Sig.
1	Regression	1714.031	1	1714.031	221.379	.000b
	Residual	3205.409	414	7.743		
	Total	4919.440	415			
a. Dependent Variable: Performance of Employee						
b. Predictors: (Constant), Leadership / Managerial Factor						

Since F = 221.379 & p value = 0.00 < 0.05, there is strong evidence to conclude that the regression model is significant.

Table :Regression coefficients & T stat for Hypothesis 2

Coefficientsa						
Model		Unstandardized Coefficients		Standardized Coefficients	t	Sig.
		B	Std. Error	Beta		
1	(Constant)	16.630	1.526		10.901	.000
	Leadership / Managerial Factor	.305	.021	.590	14.879	.000
a. Dependent Variable: Performance of Employee						

The regression model for Performance of Employee (Y) on Leadership / Managerial Factor (X) is given as

$Y = 16.630 + 0.305*X$

Here the intercept is 16.630 implies that the initial Performance of Employee would be 16.630 when the independent variable value is zero.

The slope of variable Leadership / Managerial Factor (X) is 0.305 implies that the Performance of Employee would be increased by 0.305 per unit increase in variable Leadership / Managerial Factor (X).

The positive correlation coefficient (R = 0.590) & positive slope (0.305) indicate that there is positive impact of Leadership/Managerial factors on performance of employee.

Hypothesis 2 is accepted.

Hypothesis 3: There is positive impact of Institutional factors on performance of employee.

This hypothesis is assessed by two distinct tools of statistics; first is Pearson's correlation coefficient & second is Regression model.

To test the hypotheses,

The Null Hypothesis, H_0: There is no impact of Institutional factors on performance of employee.

Vs.

The Alternative Hypothesis, H_a: There is positive impact of Institutional factors on performance of employee.

Part 1] Pearson's Correlation coefficient

Table: The Pearson's correlation coefficient between Institutional factors & performance of employee is given as below.

Correlations			
		Performance of Employee	Institutional Factor
Pearson Correlation	Performance of Employee	1.000	.587
	Institutional Factor	.587	1.000

P value	Performance of Employee	-	.000
	Institutional Factor	.000	-
N	Performance of Employee	416	416
	Institutional Factor	416	416

Since P value is less than 0.05, level of significance; the correlation is significant.
Conclusion:
The correlation between Institutional factors & Performance of employee is significant. The positive value of correlation coefficient suggests that one variable increases with the other.

Part 2] Regression Model

The regression model for Performance of employee (Y) on Institutional factors (X) is as given below.

Table :Descriptive for Hypothesis 3

Descriptive Statistics			
	Mean	Std. Deviation	N
Performance of Employee	39.24	3.443	416
Institutional Factor	39.59	3.176	416

Table: Model summary for Hypothesis 3

Model Summary				
Model	R	R Square	Adjusted R Square	Std. Error of the Estimate
1	.587a	.344	.343	2.791
a. Predictors: (Constant), Institutional Factor				

Since coefficient of determination i.e. R square = 0.344, 34.4% of the total variation in the dependent variable is explained by independent variables in model 1.

Table - Table3. ANOVA

Table :ANOVA for Hypothesis 3

Model		Sum of Squares	df	Mean Square	F	Sig.
1	Regression	1694.255	1	1694.255	217.483	.000[b]
	Residual	3225.185	414	7.790		
	Total	4919.440	415			
a. Dependent Variable: Performance of Employee						
b. Predictors: (Constant), Institutional Factor						

ANOVA[a]

Since F = 217.483 & p value = 0.00 < 0.05, there is strong evidence to conclude that the regression model is significant.

Table: Regression coefficients & T stat for Hypothesis 3

Coefficients[a]

Model		Unstandardized Coefficients		Standardized Coefficients	t	Sig.
		B	Std. Error	Beta		
1	(Constant)	14.050	1.713		8.200	.000
	Institutional Factor	.636	.043	.587	14.747	.000
a. Dependent Variable: Performance of Employee						

The regression model for Performance of Employee (Y) on Institutional factors (X) is given as

Y = 14.050 + 0.636*X

Here the intercept is 14.050 implies that the initial Performance of Employee would be 14.050 when the independent variable value is zero.

The slope of variable Institutional factors (X) is 0.636 implies that the Performance of Employee would be increased by 0.636 per unit increase in variable Institutional factors (X).

The positive correlation coefficient (R = 0.587) & positive slope (0.636) indicate that there is positive impact of Institutional factors on performance of employee.

Hypothesis 3 is accepted.

Hypothesis 4: There is positive impact of Job Related factors on performance of employee.

This hypothesis is assessed by two distinct tools of statistics; first is Pearson's correlation coefficient & second is Regression model.

To test the hypotheses,

The Null Hypothesis, H_0: There is no impact of Job Related factors on performance of employee.

Vs.

The Alternative Hypothesis, H_a: There is positive impact of Job Related factors on performance of employee.

Part 1] Pearson's Correlation coefficient

Table: The Pearson's correlation coefficient between Job Related factors & performance of employee is given as below.

Correlations			
		Performance of Employee	Job Related Factor
Pearson Correlation	Performance of Employee	1.000	.513
	Job Related Factor	.513	1.000
P value	Performance of Employee	-	.000
	Job Related Factor	.000	-
N	Performance of Employee	416	416
	Job Related Factor	416	416

Since P value is less than 0.05, level of significance; the correlation is significant.

Conclusion:

The correlation between Job Related factors & Performance of employee is significant. The positive value of correlation coefficient suggests that one variable increases with the other.

Part 2] Regression Model

The regression model for Performance of employee (Y) on Job Related factors (X) is as given below.

Table: Descriptive for Hypothesis 4

Descriptive Statistics			
	Mean	Std. Deviation	N
Performance of Employee	39.24	3.443	416
Job Related Factor	43.53	3.454	416

Table: Model Summary for Hypothesis 4

Model Summary				
Model	R	R Square	Adjusted R Square	Std. Error of the Estimate
1	.513^a	.264	.262	2.958
a. Predictors: (Constant), Job Related Factor				

Since coefficient of determination i.e. R square = 0.264, 26.4.0% of the total variation in the dependent variable is explained by independent variables in model 1.

Table: ANOVA for Hypothesis 4

ANOVA^a						
Model		Sum of Squares	df	Mean Square	F	Sig.
1	Regression	1296.406	1	1296.406	148.139	.000^b
	Residual	3623.034	414	8.751		
	Total	4919.440	415			
a. Dependent Variable: Performance of Employee						
b. Predictors: (Constant), Job Related Factor						

Since F = 148.139 & p value = 0.00 < 0.05, there is strong evidence to conclude that the regression model is significant.

Table: Regression coefficients & T stat for Hypothesis 4

Model		Unstandardized Coefficients		Standardized Coefficients	t	Sig.
		B	Std. Error	Beta		
1	(Constant)	16.965	1.836		9.242	.000
	Job Related Factor	.512	.042	.513	12.171	.000
a. Dependent Variable: Performance of Employee						

The regression model for Performance of Employee (Y) on Job Related factors (X) is given as

Y = 16.965 + 0.512*X

Here the intercept is 16.965 implies that the initial Performance of Employee would be 16.965 when the independent variable value is zero.

The slope of variable Job Related factors (X) is 0.512 implies that the Performance of Employee would be increased by 0.512 per unit increase in variable Job Related factors (X).

The positive correlation coefficient (R = 0.513) & positive slope (0.512) indicate that there is positive impact of Job Related factors on performance of employee.

Hypothesis 4 is accepted.

Hypothesis 5: There is positive impact of Organisational Cultural factors on performance of employee.

This hypothesis is assessed by two distinct tools of statistics; first is Pearson's correlation coefficient & second is Regression model.

To test the hypotheses,

The Null Hypothesis, H_0: There is no impact of Organisational Cultural factors on performance of employee.

Vs.

The Alternative Hypothesis, H_a: There is positive impact of Organisational Cultural factors on performance of employee.

Part 1] Pearson's Correlation coefficient

Table: The Pearson's correlation coefficient between Organizational Cultural factors & performance of employee is given as below.

		Performance of Employee	Organisational Cultural Factor
Pearson Correlation	Performance of Employee	1.000	.666
	Organisational Cultural Factor	.666	1.000
P Value	Performance of Employee	-	.000
	Organisational Cultural Factor	.000	-
N	Performance of Employee	416	416
	Organisational Cultural Factor	416	416

Since P value is less than 0.05, level of significance; the correlation is significant.

Conclusion:

The correlation between Organisational Cultural factors & Performance of employee is significant. The positive value of correlation coefficient suggests that one variable increases with the other.

Part 2] Regression Model

The regression model for Performance of employee (Y) on Organisational Cultural factors (X) is as given below.

Table : Descriptive for Hypothesis 5

Descriptive Statistics			
	Mean	Std. Deviation	N
Performance of Employee	39.24	3.443	416
Organisational Cultural Factor	62.28	4.572	416

Table: Model Summary for Hypothesis 5

Model Summary				
Model	R	R Square	Adjusted R Square	Std. Error of the Estimate
1	.666a	.444	.442	2.571
a. Predictors: (Constant), Organisational Cultural Factor				

Since coefficient of determination i.e. R square = 0.444, 44.4% of the total variation in the dependent variable is explained by independent variables in model 1.

Table :ANOVA for Hypothesis 5

ANOVAa						
	Model	Sum of Squares	df	Mean Square	F	Sig.
1	Regression	2182.656	1	2182.656	330.176	.000b
	Residual	2736.784	414	6.611		
	Total	4919.440	415			
a. Dependent Variable: Performance of Employee						
b. Predictors: (Constant), Organisational Cultural Factor						

Since F = 330.176 & p value = 0.00 < 0.05, there is strong evidence to conclude that the regression model is significant.

Table: Regression coefficients & T stat for Hypothesis 5

Model		Unstandardized Coefficients		Standardized Coefficients	t	Sig.
		B	Std. Error	Beta		
1	(Constant)	7.996	1.724		4.638	.000
	Organisational Cultural Factor	.502	.028	.666	18.171	.000
a. Dependent Variable: Performance of Employee						

The regression model for Performance of Employee (Y) on Organisational Cultural factors (X) is given as

$Y = 7.996 + 0.502*X$

Here the intercept is 7.996 implies that the initial Performance of Employee would be 7.996 when the independent variable value is zero.

The slope of variable Organisational Cultural factors (X) is 0.502 implies that the Performance of Employee would be increased by 0.502 per unit increase in variable Organisational Cultural factors (X).

The positive correlation coefficient (R = 0.666) & positive slope (0.502) indicate that there is positive impact of Organisational Cultural factors on performance of employee.

Hypothesis 5 is accepted.

Hypothesis 6 : There is positive impact of Opportunity factors on performance of employee.

This hypothesis is assessed by two distinct tools of statistics; first is Pearson's correlation coefficient & second is Regression model.

To test the hypotheses,

The Null Hypothesis, H_0: There is no impact of Opportunity factors on performance of employee.

Vs.

The Alternative Hypothesis, H_a: There is positive impact of Opportunity factors on performance of employee.

Part 1] Pearson's Correlation coefficient

Table: The Pearson's correlation coefficient between Opportunity factors & performance of employee is given as below.

Correlations				
		Performance of Employee	Opportunity Factors
Pearson Correlation	Performance of Employee	1.000	.472
	Opportunity Factors	.472	1.000
P value	Performance of Employee	-	.000
	Opportunity Factors	.000	-
N	Performance of Employee	416	416
	Opportunity Factors	416	416

Since P value is less than 0.05, level of significance; the correlation is significant.

Conclusion:

The correlation between Opportunity factors & Performance of employee is significant. The positive value of correlation coefficient suggests that one variable increases with the other.

Part 2] Regression Model

The regression model for Performance of employee (Y) on Opportunity factors (X) is as given below.

Table: Descriptive for Hypothesis 6

Descriptive Statistics			
	Mean	Std. Deviation	N
Performance of Employee	39.24	3.443	416
Opportunity Factors	22.24	1.937	416

Table: Model Summary for Hypothesis 6

Model Summary				
Model	R	R Square	Adjusted R Square	Std. Error of the Estimate
1	.472[a]	.223	.221	3.039
a. Predictors: (Constant), Opportunity Factors				

Since coefficient of determination i.e. R square = 0.223, 22.3% of the total variation in the dependent variable is explained by independent variables in model 1.

Table: ANOVA for Hypothesis 6

ANOVA[a]						
Model		Sum of Squares	df	Mean Square	F	Sig.
1	Regression	1095.770	1	1095.770	118.642	.000[b]
	Residual	3823.670	414	9.236		
	Total	4919.440	415			
a. Dependent Variable: Performance of Employee						
b. Predictors: (Constant), Opportunity Factors						

Since F = 118.642 & p value = 0.00 < 0.05, there is strong evidence to conclude that the regression model is significant.

Table: Regression coefficients & T stat for Hypothesis 6

Coefficients[a]						
Model		Unstandardized Coefficients		Standardized Coefficients	t	Sig.
		B	Std. Error	Beta		
1	(Constant)	20.575	1.720		11.963	.000
	Opportunity Factors	.839	.077	.472	10.892	.000
a. Dependent Variable: Performance of Employee						

The regression model for Performance of Employee (Y) on Opportunity factors (X) is given as

$Y = 20.575 + 0.839*X$

Here the intercept is 20.575 implies that the initial Performance of Employee would be 20.575 when the independent variable value is zero.

The slope of variable Opportunity factors (X) is 0.839 implies that the Performance of Employee would be increased by 0.839 per unit increase in variable Opportunity factors (X).

The positive correlation coefficient (R = 0.472) & positive slope (0.839) indicate that there is positive impact of Opportunity factors on performance of employee.

Hypothesis 6 is accepted.

Hypothesis 7: There is positive impact of Motivational factors on performance of employee.

This hypothesis is assessed by two distinct tools of statistics; first is Pearson's correlation coefficient & second is Regression model.

To test the hypotheses,

The Null Hypothesis, H_0: There is no impact of Motivational factors on performance of employee.

Vs.

The Alternative Hypothesis, H_a: There is positive impact of Motivational factors on performance of employee.

Part 1] Pearson's Correlation coefficient

Table: The Pearson's correlation coefficient between Motivational factors & performance of employee is given as below.

Correlations		Performance of Employee	Motivational Factor
Pearson Correlation	Performance of Employee	1.000	.651
	Motivational Factor	.651	1.000
P value	Performance of Employee	-	.000
	Motivational Factor	.000	-

N	Performance of Employee	416	416
	Motivational Factor	416	416

Since P value is less than 0.05, level of significance; the correlation is significant.

Conclusion:

The correlation between Motivational factors & Performance of employee is significant. The positive value of correlation coefficient suggests that one variable increases with the other.

Part 2] Regression Model

Table - The regression model for Performance of employee (Y) on Motivational factors (X) is as given below.

Table: Descriptive for Hypothesis 6

Descriptive Statistics			
	Mean	Std. Deviation	N
Performance of Employee	39.24	3.443	416
Motivational Factor	31.81	2.537	416

Table: Model Summary for Hypothesis 6

Model Summary				
Model	R	R Square	Adjusted R Square	Std. Error of the Estimate
1	.651[a]	.424	.422	2.617
a. Predictors: (Constant), Motivational Factor				

Since coefficient of determination i.e. R square = 0.424, 42.4% of the total variation in the dependent variable is explained by independent variables in model 1.

Table: ANOVA for Hypothesis 6

ANOVA[a]					
Model	Sum of Squares	df	Mean Square	F	Sig.

1	Regression	2083.813	1	2083.813	304.236	.000[b]
	Residual	2835.627	414	6.849		
	Total	4919.440	415			
a. Dependent Variable: Performance of Employee						
b. Predictors: (Constant), Motivational Factor						

Since F = 304.236 & p value = 0.00 < 0.05, there is strong evidence to conclude that the regression model is significant.

Table: Regression coefficients & T stat for Hypothesis 6

Coefficients[a]						
Model		Unstandardized Coefficients		Standardized Coefficients	t	Sig.
		B	Std. Error	Beta		
1	(Constant)	11.141	1.616		6.895	.000
	Motivational Factor	.883	.051	.651	17.442	.000
a. Dependent Variable: Performance of Employee						

The regression model for Performance of Employee (Y) on Motivational factors (X) is given as

Y = 11.141 + 0.883*X

Here the intercept is 11.141 implies that the initial Performance of Employee would be 11.141 when the independent variable value is zero.

The slope of variable Motivational factors (X) is 0.883 implies that the Performance of Employee would be increased by 0.883 per unit increase in variable Motivational factors (X).

The positive correlation coefficient (R = 0.651) & positive slope (0.883) indicate that there is positive impact of Motivational factors on performance of employee.

Hypothesis 7 is accepted.

Findings & Suggestions

Table : Summary of Regression Model for all the factors.

Factors	R-Square	Anova	Regression	Correlation Coefficient (R) and +slope
1. Leadership/Managerial factors	R square = 0.348, 34.8% Variations Explained	$F = 221.379$ & p value = $0.00 < 0.05$	$Y = 16.630 + 0.305*X$	+ correlation coefficient ($R = 0.590$) & + slope (0.305)
2. Institutional factors	R square = 0.344, 34.4% variation explained	$F = 217.483$ & p value = $0.00 < 0.05$	$Y = 14.050 + 0.636*X$	+ correlation coefficient ($R = 0.587$) & + slope (0.636)
3. Job Related factors	R square = 0.264, 26.4.0% variation Explained	$F = 148.139$ & p value = $0.00 < 0.05$	$Y = 16.965 + 0.512*X$	+ correlation coefficient ($R = 0.513$) & + slope (0.512)
4. Organizational Cultural factors.	R square = 0.444, 44.4% of variation explained	$F = 330.176$ & p value = $0.00 < 0.05$	$Y = 7.996 + 0.502*X$	+correlation coefficient ($R = 0.666$) & + slope (0.502)
5. Opportunity factors	R square = 0.223, 22.3% Variation Explained	$F = 118.642$ & p value = $0.00 < 0.05$	$Y = 20.575 + 0.839*X$	+ correlation coefficient ($R = 0.472$) & + slope (0.839)
6. Motivational factors	R square = 0.424, 42.4% Explained	$F = 304.236$ & p value = $0.00 < 0.05$	$Y = 11.141 + 0.883*X$	positive correlation coefficient ($R = 0.651$) & positive slope (0.883)

With reference to above table researcher has observed following findings.

1. Motivation Factors are having highest impact on employee's performance considering the slope of variable Motivational factors (X) is 0.883 implies that the Performance of Employee would be increased by 0.883 per unit increase in variable Motivational factors (X).

2. Opportunity Factors are having second highest impact on employee's performance considering the slope of variable Opportunity factors (X) is 0. 839 implies that the Performance of Employee would be increased by 0. 839 per unit increase in variable Opportunity factors (X).

3. Institutional factors are having Third highest impact on employee's performance considering the slope of variable Institutional factors (X) is 0.636 implies that the Performance of Employee would be increased by 0.636 per unit increase in variable Institutional factors (X

4. Job Related Factors are having fourth highest impact on employee's performance considering slope of variable Job-Related factors (X) is 0.512 implies that the Performance of Employee would be increased by 0.512 per unit increase in variable Job-Related factors (X).

5. Organisational Cultural Factors are having fifth highest impact on employee's performance considering slope of variable Organisational Cultural factors (X) is 0.502 implies that the Performance of Employee would be increased by 0.502 per unit increase in variable Organisational Cultural factors (X).

6. Leadership/Managerial Factors are having fifth highest impact on employee's performance considering slope of variable Leadership / Managerial Factor (X) is 0.305 implies that the Performance of Employee would be increased by 0.305 per unit increase in variable Leadership / Managerial Factor (X).

Based on the above study researcher is proposing below model to ensure highest performance of employees in Auto industry.

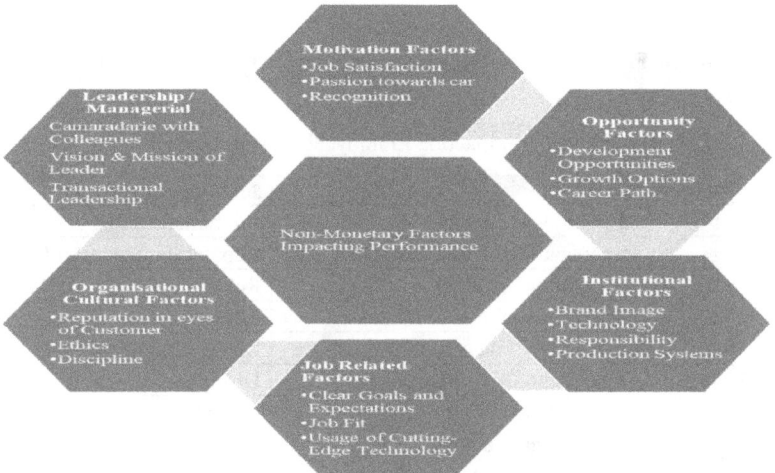

Figure 1: Conceptual Model

Elaboration on Conceptual Model Based on the analysis and findings of study

1. Motivation factor has highest impact on the performance of employee, in which motivation Job satisfaction, Passion towards car and Recognition plays a crucial role in improving the performance of employee.

2. Opportunity Factor has second highest impact on the performance of employee, in which Development opportunities, Growth Options and Clarity of Career path excites employee to deliver high performance

3. Institutional Factors has third highest impact on the performance of employee, in which subfactors like Brand Image, Technology used, Responsibility and Production system used play significant role in supporting employee performance.

4. Job Related Factors has fourth highest impact on the performance of employee, Clear goal setting, Correct Job Fit and Usage of cutting age technology highly positively impacts employee performance.

5. Organisational culture factors has fifth highest impact on performance of employee, sub-factors like Reputation in eyes of Customer, Organisational Ethics and Discipline are important.

6. Leadership / Managerial factor has lowest impact in all the factors, but Camaraderie with Colleagues, Vision & Mission of Leader and Transactional Leadership Subfactors impact most on the employee performance.

Top 10 Factors impacting employee's performance in Auto Industry in Rank Order.

Table: Top 10 Factors Impacting Employee's Performance

Sr No	Factor	Sub-Factor
1	Motivational Factors	Job Satisfaction
2	Organizational Cultural Factors	Reputation in eyes of Customer
3	Motivational Factors	Recognition
4	Organizational Cultural Factors	Ethics
5	Opportunity Factors	Development Opportunities
6	Organizational Cultural Factors	Discipline
7	Job Related Factors	Clear Goals and Expectations
8	Motivational Factors	Passion towards car
9	Organizational Cultural Factors	Communication to Involve
10	Job Related Factors	Job Fit

Conclusion

The study examined the effect of monetary and non-monetary reward factors on employee performance. The organizational challenge is to determine the optimal balance between monetary and non-monetary factors that will improve employee performance supporting in achieving the organization's objectives. Both monetary and Non-Monetary play a crucial role in supporting employee performance.

The study's first purpose was to catalogue the non-monetary factors employed by the automobile industry. According to the study, non-monetary factors considerations such as motivation, recognition, communication, leadership, vision & mission are frequently used the automobile industry. In the automobile industry, non-monetary benefits broadly are categories int 6 categories Motivational, Cultural, Opportunity, Job Related, Institutional and Leadership/Managerial.

A questionnaire containing questions was developed and distributed to the Auto OEM company employees based on the non-monetary aspects in place.The questionnaire included 72 questions on five-point Likert scale about non-monetary factors, in order to explore the research objectives.

Objective 1 - Identify of Non- Monetary of Factors which impact performance in Automobile manufacturing industries.

The study's first purpose was to catalogue the non-monetary factors employed by the automobile industry. According to the study, non-monetary factors considerations such as motivation, recognition, communication, leadership, vision & mission are frequently used the automobile industry. In the automobile industry, non-monetary benefits broadly are categories int 6 categories Motivational, Cultural, Opportunity, Job Related, Institutional and Leadership/Managerial. After exhaustive Literature Review overall we identified 45 factors which were later combined in 6 umbrella factors to carry out the study.

F1-Leadership / Managerial	F2 - Institutional	F3 - Job Related
Vision & Mission of Leader	Brand Image	Job Fit
Leadership Style	Reponsiblity	Clear Goals and Expectations
Coaching by Lead	Technology	Tools and Equipment / Resources
Camaradarie with Colleagues	Infrastructure	Work Life Balance
Relationship with Manager	Production Systems	Usage of Technology
Performance Pressure	Structure	Risk associated with Job
Empowement	Indian / MNC	Location of work
	Organisational Stability	Reputation/Status of the Job
	Market Position	Diversity in Job

F4 - Organisational Culture	F5-Opportunity	H-6 Motivation
Culture	Development Opportunities	Motivation
Communication	Career Path	Recognition
social learning	Growth Options	Job Enrichment
Ethics	Job Security	Job Satisfaction
Innovation	Diversity	Passion towards car
Discipline		Ability
Standardisation		Performance Appraisal Process
Reputation in eyes of Customer		

Figure No. 3 - Factors and subfactors Identified for study impacting employee's performance.

Further for the studies we also considered various dements of Sub-Factors like Communication types, Leadership Styles, Pressure/Stress etc. The identification of these monetary factors impacting performance have given all together a new perspective to factors impacting performance.

Objective 2 - To establish relationship between Non-Monetary factors and performance of employee.

The second purpose of this study was to ascertain the relative importance of monetary and nonmonetary rewards in the case study. As a result, the study establishes a favorable correlation between monetary factors and employee performance. Job Satisfaction and Recognition are the most influential variables. so, the business should develop policies that effectively handle these two factors, which will result in increased motivation and retention rates in the long run. Additionally, automobile industry includes non-monetary incentives, which will result in increased employee motivation in turn resulting into employee performance. Thus, the author can assert that non-monetary benefits have an effect on the organization's employees' performance.

Table: Summary of Regression Model.

Factors	R-Square	Anova	Regression	Correlation Coefficient (R) and +slope
1. Leadership/Managerial factors	R square = 0.348, 34.8% Variations Explained	F = 221.379 & p value = 0.00 < 0.05	Y = 16.630 + 0.305*X	+ correlation coefficient (R = 0.590) & + slope (0.305)
2. Institutional factors	R square = 0.344, 34.4% variation explained	F = 217.483 & p value = 0.00 < 0.05	Y = 14.050 + 0.636*X	+ correlation coefficient (R = 0.587) & + slope (0.636)
3. Job Related factors	R square = 0.264, 26.4.0% variation Explained	F = 148.139 & p value = 0.00 < 0.05	Y = 16.965 + 0.512*X	+ correlation coefficient (R = 0.513) & + slope (0.512)
4. Organizational Cultural factors.	R square = 0.444, 44.4% of variation explained	F = 330.176 & p value = 0.00 < 0.05	Y = 7.996 + 0.502*X	+correlation coefficient (R = 0.666) & + slope (0.502)
5. Opportunity factors	R square = 0.223, 22.3% Variation Explained	F = 118.642 & p value = 0.00 < 0.05	Y = 20.575 + 0.839*X	+ correlation coefficient (R = 0.472) & + slope (0.839)
6. Motivational factors	R square = 0.424, 42.4% Explained	F = 304.236 & p value = 0.00 < 0.05	Y = 11.141 + 0.883*X	positive correlation coefficient (R = 0.651) & positive slope (0.883)

With the help of statistical tools like Annova and Regression we have established relationship between different factors like Motivational, Cultural, Opportunity, Job Related, Institutional and Leadership/Managerial whose summary is mentioned in above table.

Further it can be concluded that there is positive correlation / impact of all the six factors identified on the impact of employee's performance. This was also tested with **Hypothesis 1** of the study.

It's evident from the study that the employers have put calibrated & balanced efforts to ensure these factors in a right mix to have optimum levels of performance from employees.

Objective 3 - To establish or rank non-monetary factors based on their positive impact on employee's performance.
Table No. -

The third purpose of this study was to establish or rank non-monetary factors based on their positive impact on employee's performance. According to respondents, all the 6 factors positively impact employees' performance. Employees are more likely to stay with a company if they are Satisfied, Recognized, Values and Coached. Employees wish to enhance their professional qualifications through exposure to cutting-edge technology and exposure to latest Auto Production systems.

Table: Summary of Regression Model.

Factors	R-Square	Anova	Regression	Correlation Coefficient (R) and +slope
1. Leadership/Managerial factors	R square = 0.348, 34.8% Variations Explained	$F = 221.379$ & p value = $0.00 < 0.05$	$Y = 16.630 + 0.305*X$	+ correlation coefficient (R = 0.590) & + slope (0.305)
2. Institutional factors	R square = 0.344, 34.4% variation explained	$F = 217.483$ & p value = $0.00 < 0.05$	$Y = 14.050 + 0.636*X$	+ correlation coefficient (R = 0.587) & + slope (0.636)
3. Job Related factors	R square = 0.264, 26.4.0% variation Explained	$F = 148.139$ & p value = $0.00 < 0.05$	$Y = 16.965 + 0.512*X$	+ correlation coefficient (R = 0.513) & + slope (0.512)
4. Organizational Cultural factors.	R square = 0.444, 44.4% of variation explained	$F = 330.176$ & p value = $0.00 < 0.05$	$Y = 7.996 + 0.502*X$	+correlation coefficient (R = 0.666) & + slope (0.502)
5. Opportunity factors	R square = 0.223, 22.3% Variation Explained	$F = 118.642$ & p value = $0.00 < 0.05$	$Y = 20.575 + 0.839*X$	+ correlation coefficient (R = 0.472) & + slope (0.839)
6. Motivational factors	R square = 0.424, 42.4% Explained	$F = 304.236$ & p value = $0.00 < 0.05$	$Y = 11.141 + 0.883*X$	positive correlation coefficient (R = 0.651) & positive slope (0.883)

Study concluded that the all the non-monetary factors are positively impacting employee's performance. Further based on the data following is the rank of factors impacting employee's performance.

Rank 1 - Motivational Factors
Rank 2 - Opportunity Factors
Rank 3 - Institutional Factors
Rank 4 - Job Related Factors
Rank 5 - Organisational Culture Factors
Rank 6 – Leadership/Managerial

Based on the above ranking employers can calibrate the Employee life cycle management process, focus of factors and make sure that we have optimum level of performance.

Objective 4 - Based on the finding of study, Creation of Model/structure to enhance performance of employees.

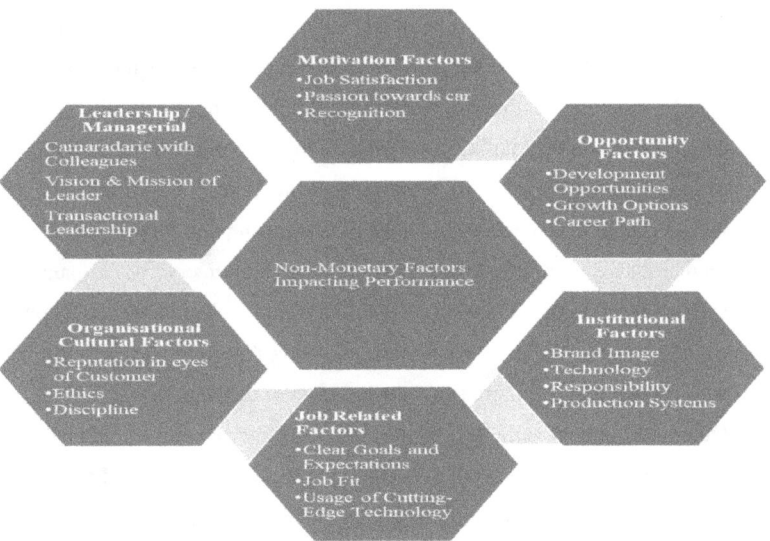

Figure: Conceptual Model based on findings of the study.

Based on the study the author is proposing to have well balanced and synergized combinations of the 6 factors and their Subfactors which will impact employee's performance. Figuring out the right mix is itself a challenge as we are dealing with human beings and not machines, person the person the factors may vary as well.

Finally, it can be demonstrated that "there is in the automobile business, non-monetary factors have a strong and considerable beneficial link with employee performance. The ability and motivation, declarative knowledge, procedural knowledge, motivation to work, attainment of specified goals, staff competence, and established standards all contributed to these performances.

Employment security, decent working circumstances, participation in goal planning and achievement, staff recognition, job expansion, incentives that address social needs, improved working conditions, and fringe benefits were revealed as non-monetary motivations.

Employees have requirements that should be met by their employer to minimize demotivation or distraction from work. As a result, the automobile industry must place a premium on non-monetary motivators in order to maintain, attract, and improve employee performance, satisfaction, and commitment.

Other future research may wish to investigate additional elements affecting employee performance that were not examined or focused on in this study, including employee loyalty, employee emotions, work time flexibility, business culture and values, and employee retention. Another conceivable expansion of this study is to include complete coverage of both companies' other geographical areas. Given that this study did not include enough managers, it would be interesting for future research to include a representative sample of managers and conduct interviews to augment the data collection procedure. If possible, inputs for future publications could come from other sources, such as the outcomes of the companies' performance rating procedures; this would assist assure a more accurate depiction of the data.

Other independent variables, such as the work environment, could be further dissected and analysed in greater detail by focusing on their various facets. For instance, the work environment encompasses office lighting, workstation spacing, office design, and noise levels. Future research may examine the effect of various factors on employee performance by comparing the "before" and "after" effects of these factors. For example, employee performance might be measured before to and following training in order to compare and assign a value to the training received. Additional studies could also look at other demographic aspects and regional trends. Finally, future research may

Further Research Suggestion:

Future studies should examine the influence of non-monetary rewards on employee performance in industries other than the automobile sector. Again, additional research should be conducted to determine the effect of non-monetary rewards on employee job satisfaction, security, work environment, job match, and participative management.

Study is focusing on OEM which further can be expanded to Auto Suppliers as well. Blue Collars are not part of the study as they are governed by law of the land and the benefits are as per the Settlement signed between union and company management. Further Going ahead blue collars can also be included in the scope of study.

A study on Monetary factors can be carried out and merged with findings of current study to create a Holistic and robust model understand impact of both the factors on the employee's performance. Geographical Scale be increased and study and be further expanded to the two wheeler, three wheeler and truck and Tractor manufacturing plant across the geography of india. Also it Can be expanded to manufacturing & IT industries as well to understand the impact of Non-Monetary factors on performance.

Chapter 1

Introduction

This chapter includes:
1. About Automotive Industry
2. Employee performance
3. Taking Charge of Employee Performance (Managing Employee Performance
4. Purpose of an Effective Performance Management Process
5. Significant Factors Affecting Employee Performance
6. Non-Monetary Factors impacting employee performance

1. About Automotive industry

Automotive industry, all those companies and activities involved in the manufacture of motor vehicles, including most components, such as engines and bodies, but excluding tires, batteries, and fuel. The industry's principal products are passenger automobiles and light trucks, including pickups, vans, and sport utility vehicles. Commercial vehicles (i.e., delivery trucks and large transport trucks, often called semis), though important to the industry, are secondary. The design of modern automotive vehicles is discussed in the article's automobile, truck, bus, and motorcycle; automotive engines are described in gasoline engine and diesel engine. The development of the automobile is covered in transportation, **history of: The rise of the automobile**[1].

The history of the automobile industry, though brief compared with that of many other industries, has exceptional interest because of its effects on history from the 20th century. Although the automobile originated in Europe in the late 19th century, the United States completely dominated the world industry for the first half of the 20th century through the invention of mass production techniques. In the second half of the century the situation altered sharply as western European countries and Japan became major producers and exporters.

2 History

Although steam-powered road vehicles were produced earlier, the origins of the automotive industry are rooted in the development of the gasoline engine in the 1860s and '70s, principally in France and Germany. By the beginning of the 20th century,

German and French manufacturers had been joined by British, Italian, and American makers.

Developments before World War I

Most early automobile companies were small shops, hundreds of which each produced a few handmade cars, and nearly all of which abandoned the business soon after going into it. The handful that survived into the era of large-scale production had certain characteristics in common. First, they fell into one of three well-defined categories: they were makers of bicycles, such as Opel in Germany and Morris in Great Britain; builders of horse-drawn vehicles, such as Durant and Studebaker in the United States; or, most frequently, machinery manufacturers. The kinds of machinery included stationary gas engines (Daimler of Germany, Lanchester of Britain, Olds of the United States), marine engines (Vauxhall of Britain), machine tools (Leland of the United States), sheep-shearing machinery (Wolseley of Britain), washing machines (Peerless of the United States), sewing machines (White of the United States), and woodworking and milling machinery (Panhard and Levassor of France). One American company, Pierce, made birdcages, and another, Buick, made plumbing fixtures, including the first enameled cast-iron bathtub. Two notable exceptions to the general pattern were Rolls-Royce in Britain and Ford in the United States, both of which were founded as carmakers by partners who combined engineering talent and business skill.

In the United States almost all of the producers were assemblers who put together components and parts that were manufactured by separate firms. The assembly technique also lent itself to an advantageous method of financing. It was possible to begin building motor vehicles with a minimal investment of capital by buying parts on credit and selling the finished cars for cash; the cash sale from manufacturer to dealer has been integral in the marketing of motor vehicles in the United States ever since. European automotive firms of this period tended to be more self-sufficient.

The pioneer automobile manufacturer not only had to solve the technical and financial problems of getting into production but also had to make a basic decision about what to produce. After the first success of the gasoline engine, there was widespread experimentation with steam and electricity. **For a brief period the electric automobile**[2] actually enjoyed the greatest acceptance because it was quiet and easy to operate, but the limitations imposed by battery capacity proved competitively fatal. Especially popular with women, electric cars remained in limited production well into the 1920s. One of the longest-surviving makers, Detroit Electric Car Company, operated on a regular basis through 1929.

Studebaker electric car, c. 1905.

chapterSteam power, a more serious rival, was aided by the general adoption, after 1900, of the so-called flash boiler, in which steam could be raised rapidly. The steam car was easy to operate because it did not require an elaborate transmission. On the other hand, high steam pressures were needed to make the engine light enough for use in a road vehicle; suitable engines required expensive construction and were difficult to maintain. By 1910 most manufacturers of steam vehicles had turned to gasoline power. The Stanley brothers in the United States, however, continued to manufacture steam automobiles until the early 1920s.

As often happens with a new technology, the automotive industry experienced patent controversies in its early years. Most notable were two long, drawn-out court cases in Britain and the United States, in each of which a promoter sought to gain control of the new industry by filing comprehensive patents. In Britain the claim was rejected by the courts in 1901, five years after the patent application. In the United States there was a legal battle between Ford and the Association of Licensed Automobile Manufacturers over the Selden patent, which the association claimed as a basic patent on the gasoline-powered car. In 1911 the courts held the patent "valid but not infringed" by Ford. The main consequence of the decision was the formation of the predecessor of the Alliance of Automobile Manufacturers to supervise an agreement for cross-licensing patents, which was ratified in 1915.

Mass production[3]

The outstanding contribution of the automotive industry to technological advance was the introduction of full-scale mass production, a process combining precision, standardization, interchangeability, synchronization, and continuity. Mass production was an American innovation. The United States, with its large population, high standard of living, and long distances, was the natural birthplace of the technique, which had been partly explored in the 19th century. Although Europe had shared in the experimentation, the American role was emphasized in the popular description of standardization and interchangeability as "the American system of manufacture." The fundamental techniques were known, but they had not previously been applied to the manufacture of a mechanism as complex as a motor vehicle.

The kind of interchangeability achieved by the "American system" was dramatically demonstrated in 1908 at the British Royal Automobile Club in London: three Cadillac cars were disassembled, the parts were mixed together, 89 parts were removed at random and replaced from dealer's stock, and the cars were reassembled and driven 800 km (500 miles) without trouble. Henry M. Leland, founder of the Cadillac Motor Car Company and the man responsible for this feat of showmanship, later enlisted the aid of a noted electrical engineer, Charles F. Kettering, in developing the electric starter, a significant innovation in promoting the acceptability of the gasoline-powered automobile.

Ford and the assembly line[4]

The mass-produced automobile is generally and correctly attributed to Henry Ford, but he was not alone in seeing the possibilities in a mass market. Ransom E. Olds made the first major bid for the mass market with a famous curved-dash Oldsmobile buggy in 1901. Although the first Oldsmobile was a popular car, it was too lightly built to withstand rough usage. The same defect applied to Olds's imitators. Ford, more successful in realizing his dream of "a car for the great multitude," designed his car first and then considered the problem of producing it cheaply. The car was the so-called Model T, the best-known motor vehicle in history. It was built to be durable for service on the rough American country roads of that period, economical to operate, and easy to maintain and repair. It was first put on the market in 1908, and more than 15 million were built before it was discontinued in 1927.

Ford Motor Company

When the design of the Model T proved successful, Ford and his associates turned to the problem of producing the car in large volume and at a low unit cost. The solution was found in the moving assembly line, a method first tested in assembling magnetos. After more experimentation, in 1913 the Ford Motor Company displayed to the world the complete assembly-line mass production of motor vehicles. The technique consisted of two basic elements: a conveyor system and the limitation of each worker to a single repetitive task. Despite its deceptive simplicity, the technique required elaborate planning and synchronization.

The first Ford assembly line permitted only very minor variations in the basic model, a limitation that was compensated for by the low cost. The price of the Model T touring car dropped from $950 in 1909 to $360 in 1916 and still lower to an incredible $290 in 1926. By that time Ford was producing half of all the motor vehicles in the world.

Spread of mass production
Ford's success inspired imitation and competition, but his primacy remained unchallenged until he lost it in the mid-1920s by refusing to recognize that the Model T had become outmoded. More luxurious and better-styled cars appeared at prices not much higher than that of the Model T, and these were increasingly available to low-income purchasers through a growing used-car market. In Britain, William R. Morris (later Lord Nuffield) undertook to emulate Ford as early as 1912, but he found British engineering firms reluctant to commit themselves to the large-scale manufacture of automotive parts. Morris in fact turned to the United States for his parts, but these early efforts were cut short by World War I. In the 1920s Morris resumed the production of low-priced cars, along with his British competitor Herbert Austin and André-Gustave Citroën and Louis Renault in France. British manufacturers had to face the problem of a tax on horsepower, calculated on a formula based on bore and the number of cylinders. The effect was to encourage the design of small engines that had cylinders with narrow bore and long stroke, in contrast to the wide-bore, short-stroke engines favoured elsewhere. This design handicapped the sale of British cars abroad and kept production from growing. It was not until 1934 that Morris Motors finally felt justified in installing a moving assembly line; the Hillman Company had preceded Morris in this by a year or two.

Large-scale organization
Although the appearance of mass production in the automotive industry coincided with the emergence of large-scale business organization, the two had originated independently. They were related, however, and influenced each other as the industry expanded. Only a large firm could make the heavy investment in plant and tooling that the assembly line required, and Ford was already the largest single American producer when it introduced the technique. The mass producer in turn enjoyed a cost advantage that tended to make it increasingly difficult for smaller competitors to survive. There have been exceptions, but the trend has been consistent.

General Motors[5]

General Motors Corporation (GM), which ultimately became the world's largest automotive firm and the largest privately owned manufacturing enterprise in the world, was founded in 1908 by William C. Durant, a carriage manufacturer of Flint, Michigan. In 1904 he assumed control of the ailing Buick Motor Company and made it one of the principal American producers. Durant developed the idea for a combination that would produce a variety of models and control its own parts producers. As initially formed, General Motors included four major vehicle manufacturers—Buick, Cadillac, Oldsmobile, and Oakland—and an assortment of smaller firms. The combine ran into financial trouble in 1910 and was reorganized by a financial syndicate. A similar combination, the United States Motor Corporation, was formed in 1910, collapsed in 1912, and was reorganized as the Maxwell Motor Company. General Motors survived. A new reorganization took place after Durant, with backing by E.I. du Pont de Nemours and Company, regained control in 1916. Durant, who had previously established the Chevrolet Motor Company, brought Chevrolet into GM in 1918.

At the end of World War I, Ford was the colossus, dominating the automotive scene with the Model T not only in the United States but also through branch plants throughout the world. British Ford was the largest single producer in the United Kingdom. GM was emerging as a potential major competitor in the United States. No other automotive firms of comparable size existed.

During the next decade there was a striking transformation. The depression of 1921 had far-reaching effects on the American automotive industry. GM was plunged into another financial crisis. Alfred P. Sloan became president of the corporation in 1923 and raised it to its unchallenged first place in the industry. Among other steps, he gave GM a staff-and-line organization with autonomous manufacturing divisions, which facilitated management of a large corporate structure and became the model for other major automotive combinations. Henry Ford also went through a crisis because the 1921 crash caught him involved in the construction of a large new plant (River Rouge) and in the process of buying out his stockholders. Ford weathered the storm (though many of his dealers, unable to sell cars and not permitted to return them, went out of business), but the Ford Motor Company had reached its crest.

The third member of the "Big Three" automotive manufacturers in the United States was created at this same time. When the Maxwell Motor Company failed in the 1921 depression, Walter P. Chrysler, formerly of General Motors, was called in to reorganize it. It became the Chrysler Corporation in 1925 and grew to major proportions with the acquisition of the Dodge Brothers company in 1928. When Ford went out of production in 1927 to switch from the Model T to the Model A (a process that took 18 months), Chrysler was able to break into the low-priced-car market with the Plymouth.

The independents

By 1929 the Big Three supplied three-fourths of the American market for motor vehicles; most of the remainder was divided among the five largest independents— Hudson, Nash, Packard, Studebaker, and Willys-Overland. In less than 10 years the number of automobile manufacturers in the United States dropped from 108 to 44. Some of the minor carmakers had technological or personal interests, including Nordyke and Marmon, makers of Marmon luxury cars, and E.L. Cord, who marketed front-wheel-drive cars between 1929 and 1937. The depression years of the 1930s eliminated all but the largest independent manufacturers and increased still further the domination of the Big Three. Motor vehicle production declined from a peak of more than five million in 1929 to a low of just over one million in 1932. It rose again slowly but had not returned to the 1929 figure when World War II broke out.

While these years were difficult economically, they saw some significant developments within the industry. Greater emphasis was placed on style in passenger-car design, with the general trend in the direction of incorporating the body, bumpers, and mudguards into a single pattern of smoothly flowing lines. A number of technical features came into general use: the V-8 engine, introduced by Ford in 1932; three-point engine suspension; freewheeling (permitting the car to coast freely when the accelerator was released); overdrive (a fourth forward speed); and, on a limited scale, automatic transmission.

Growth in Europe[6]

The period from 1919 to 1939 also brought significant growth in automobile manufacturing in Europe, though on a considerably smaller scale than in the United States. The European industry was moving in the same directions as the American industry, toward a mass market for motor vehicles, but it made slower progress for a variety of reasons: lower living standards with less purchasing power, smaller national markets, and more restrictions in tax and tariff policies. Still, the same trend toward concentration was discernible. British automotive production rose from 73,000 in 1922 (both private and commercial vehicles) to 239,000 in 1929, while the number of producers declined from 90 to 41. Three firms—Austin, Morris, and Singer—controlled 75 percent of the British market in 1929.

The apparent analogy to the American experience was temporary. British production had not yet reached the level at which the economies of scale gave the larger firms as commanding a lead as in the United States. There were other factors that created a somewhat different situation. During the 1930s British automotive production continued to increase steadily, in contrast to American production, and so the smaller companies were not forced to compete for a shrinking market. Output reached almost half a million in 1937, and at the end of the decade there were six major British producers instead of three: Morris, Austin, Standard, Rootes, Ford, and Vauxhall. The last two represented entry by American firms. Vauxhall had been bought by GM in 1925; Ford had been in Britain since 1911, had lost ground in the 1920s, and had later recovered. The Rootes Group, based on Hillman and Humber, was a combine formed by a family that had built a large automobile sales concern and then moved from sales to production. The replacement of Singer by Standard was simply the rise of one company and the decline of another, as evidence that open competition could still change the structure of the British automotive industry.

In France three major firms—Peugeot, Renault, and Citroën—emerged in the 1920s. Citroën accounted for 40 percent of French automotive production in 1925 but had reached that dominating position at the cost of financial stability. When André Citroën died before the decade ended, his company came into the hands of Michelin Tire. A new French firm, Simca, rose to prominence in the 1930s. The German automobile industry suffered from the dislocation of World War I and Germany's subsequent economic difficulties. The major developments of the 1920s were the merger of Daimler and Benz in 1926, after the founders of those firms had died (their bitter rivalry for the distinction of being the inventor of the gasoline automobile made any such union during their lifetimes unthinkable), and the entry of General Motors onto the German scene through the acquisition of the Adam Opel company in 1929. The Germans were ardent admirers of Henry Ford and his methods, which they termed Fordismus, but Ford never succeeded in becoming a power in the German automotive world. During the 1930s the Nazi regime sought to emulate Ford by undertaking mass production of a low-priced car, the Volkswagen, but the onset of war interrupted this project. Italian automobile manufacturers gained a reputation for highly engineered sports cars and racing cars, but Italy had no mass market and therefore achieved only small-scale production at that time.

The automotive industry in World War II[7]

During World War I the productive capacity of the automotive industry first demonstrated its military value. Motor vehicles were used extensively for transport and supply. In addition, automotive plants could readily be converted into facilities for manufacturing military equipment, including tanks and aircraft. For all of the belligerents the conversion of automotive facilities was an afterthought, improvised after the beginning of hostilities, and the American industry, involved only for a short time, never fully utilized its capacity.

More preparation was made for using the resources of the various automotive industries as World War II approached. The British government built "shadow factories" adjacent to their automotive plants, equipped to go into military production (principally aircraft) when war came, with managerial and technical personnel drawn from the automotive industry. France attempted conversion, but belatedly and inefficiently. The German automotive industry, which built the military vehicles needed for blitzkrieg, was not fully converted to military production until 1943. In the United States the preparation for industrial mobilization was negligible until 1940; in fact, there was no serious effort even to restrict civilian automobile production until after the attack on Pearl Harbor in December 1941. Still, the American automotive industry represented such a concentration of productive capacity and skill that, once its resources had been harnessed to war production, its contribution was tremendous. Between 1940 and 1945 automotive firms made almost $29 billion worth of military materials, a fifth of the country's entire output. The list included 2,600,000 military trucks and 660,000 jeeps, but production extended well beyond motor vehicles. Automotive firms provided one-half of the machine guns and carbines made in the United States during the war, 60 percent of the tanks, all the armored cars, and 85 percent of the military helmets and aerial bombs.

Jeep

A Willys MB jeep at a training center in California, 1942.

It had been assumed that automotive facilities could be readily converted for aircraft production, but this proved more difficult than anticipated. Automobile assembly plants did not readily accommodate airframes, nor could an automobile engine factory be converted without substantial modification. These problems were eventually resolved, and automobile companies contributed significantly to aircraft production.

Britain was better prepared to use the resources of its automotive industry, at that time the world's second largest. The shadow factories became operative, and Austin, Morris, Standard, Daimler, Ford, and Rootes participated in filling the wartime demand for aircraft and aircraft engines. Leyland Motors and Vauxhall built tanks. Lord Nuffield made a notable contribution to the production effort by establishing a system for repairing aircraft, employing the sales and service organization of Morris Motors, and it was subsequently extended to a large number of small contractors.

The automotive industries of the other belligerents were smaller in scale, and their facilities for armaments manufacture were proportionately greater than in the United States or Great Britain. Consequently, the automotive firms in these countries were concerned chiefly with meeting the insatiable demand for vehicles. The various Ford properties that came under German control, along with Volkswagen, which turned out the German equivalent of the jeep, were employed in this manner. Renault, a tank manufacturer since World War I, built tanks for France and later for Germany.

The automotive industry after 1945

After World War II there was a striking expansion of motor vehicle production. During a 35-year period the total world output increased almost 10-fold. The most significant feature of this increase was that most of it occurred outside the United States. Although American production continued to grow, its share of world automotive production fell from about 80 percent of the total to 20 percent. Among individual countries the United States was the leading producer until the recession of the early 1980s. In 1980 Japan, which had had little automotive manufacturing before the war, became the leading producer, with the European Economic Community (EEC) ranking second. The United States regained the lead in vehicle production in 1994, since by that time Japanese manufacturers were building more of their products in factories in their major overseas markets, such as the United States, in response to economic and political pressures in those markets. However, in the early 21st century, China became the leading manufacturer of cars.

The industry in the United States

At the end of World War II the American automobile industry had intact facilities, somewhat enlarged by construction for military needs. There was also a great demand for automobiles. This situation invited several attempts by newcomers to enter the industry, but all proved unsuccessful. The most promising, Kaiser-Frazer Corporation, lasted some 10 years but lacked the financial, technical, and sales resources to compete when the automobile market returned to normal. By the mid 1950s Kaiser-Frazer had stopped producing everything but Willys Jeeps, an operation that it had acquired by buying Willys-Overland. The manufacture of Jeeps continued as a subsidiary of Kaiser Industries until 1970, when the division was sold to American Motors Corporation (AMC) in a transaction that gave Kaiser financial interest in AMC.

The trend of the automotive industry to mergers and large-scale organization, and to a situation in which each producer could affect but not control the market, continued unchecked. In 1954 Nash and Hudson joined to form AMC. The company enjoyed temporary prosperity in the late 1950s when it introduced the first American compact car, the Rambler, in response to growing imports of small foreign cars. A merger of Studebaker and Packard in 1954 was less successful. The new company stopped production in the United States in 1964 and in Canada two years later.

American Motors Corporation: Rambler

Declining sales and heavy financial losses pushed the Chrysler Corporation close to bankruptcy in the late 1970s. Attempting to avert the company's collapse, the U.S. government granted Chrysler $1.5 billion in loan guarantees. In return Chrysler surrendered supervisory control to the government's Chrysler Loan Guarantee Board. By exercising such control, the U.S. government became a de facto partner of the country's third largest automaker. The government's influence was short-lived as Chrysler, under the leadership of Lee A. Iacocca, returned to profitability and repaid its government loans in 1983, seven years early.

By the early 1980s the automotive industry in the United States was concentrated in four major firms—GM, Ford, Chrysler, and AMC—and one important manufacturer of commercial vehicles, International Harvester Company. A few producers of specialized vehicles remained, along with an assortment of companies that made automotive parts and components.

Increasing competition from imported cars and from new manufacturing operations established by European and Japanese firms continued to reduce the share of the American market controlled by the four domestic manufacturers through the remainder of the 20th century. Germany's Volkswagen opened an assembly operation in the United States in the late 1970s but closed it a decade later. Japan's Nissan Motor Corporation established a plant in the early 1980s to build its popular small pickups and later added car production. Another Japanese automaker, Honda Motor Company, followed with a car manufacturing operation adjacent to its motorcycle plant; it later added a second car facility in the United States and a car plant in Canada. Japan's Toyota Motor Corporation formed a joint venture with GM called New United Motor Manufacturing Incorporated, which built small cars for both Toyota and GM. Toyota also opened two plants of its own in the United States—one for cars and small vans and the other for pickup trucks and sport utility vehicles—and a car-making facility in Canada. A number of other Japanese manufacturers opened plants in the United States as joint-venture operations.

Many of the Japanese-owned American plants were built in response to limitations imposed on exports of cars to the United States by Japan's Ministry of International Trade and Industry. The restrictions followed threats of sanctions by the United States in the wake of Chrysler's near collapse and heavy losses by Ford and GM. Called the Voluntary Restraint Agreement (VRA), it spelled out how many cars each Japanese producer could ship to the United States in a single year. The VRA took effect in 1981 and was renewed annually through the early 1990s. A similar agreement was in effect in Canada during the 1980s.

In 1979 Renault of France acquired a 46 percent interest in AMC to increase its small presence in the United States and gain access to AMC's line of popular Jeep vehicles. Mounting financial pressures, however, prompted Renault to sell its AMC stake to a reinvigorated Chrysler in 1987. Chrysler quickly acquired all outstanding AMC stock and made the company a division. In 1998 Chrysler was merged with Germany's Daimler-Benz AG, which then became DaimlerChrysler AG; the joint venture ended in 2007.

In 2008 the U.S. auto industry seemed close to collapse amid the global financial crisis. Through the Troubled Assets Relief Program (TARP), billions in loans were made available to GM, Chrysler, and Ford; only the last automaker did not accept the government relief. Despite the assistance, GM filed for Chapter 11 bankruptcy protection in June 2009. It emerged from bankruptcy reorganization the following month and went through a period of downsizing that helped it rebound. Chrysler also filed for bankruptcy in 2009, and shortly thereafter the Italian automaker Fiat bought a share of the automaker, eventually becoming a majority shareholder in 2011.

Technically, the initial decades after World War II were marked by improvement and refinement rather than by important innovation. Diesel engines were increasingly used on trucks and buses. Automatic transmissions became virtually standard equipment for passenger cars, and power brakes and power steering found widespread acceptance, as did luxury features such as air-conditioning. In the early 1960s Chrysler experimented with a gas turbine engine for passenger automobiles, but it had too many technical problems for general use. By the early 21st century, automakers were facing new design issues, as growing concerns about climate change had resulted in a push for more fuel-efficient cars, including electric vehicles.

Styling became increasingly important in automotive design as a marketing device. The general trend in styling became established late in the 1920s when cars began to lose their square, boxlike lines and to develop flowing curves. In time the new design encompassed both body and chassis, integrating such formerly separate features as mudguards, running boards, and bumpers. A combination of pressures made American cars of the 1950s high-powered and ornate, with extravagant use of chrome and exaggerated tail fins; these features were abandoned when the public found the simpler lines of imported cars more attractive.

Europe after World War II

In Europe motor vehicles were recognized as an export item that could help restore war-shattered economies. Britain, for example, earmarked more than half of its automotive output for export and restricted domestic purchases for several years after the war. In addition, the horsepower tax was abandoned to enable British manufacturers to build profitably for the world market. The most popular British designs (excluding specialized luxury vehicles such as the Rolls-Royce) continued to be lightweight cars, including several models with an ingenious front-wheel drive. The trend to consolidation led in 1952 to the merger of Morris and Austin to form the British Motor Corporation, Ltd., a combine that accounted for about two-fifths of Britain's motor vehicle production. Another British combine was formed around Leyland Motors, which had grown into the country's largest manufacturer of commercial vehicles and became a power in the passenger-car field by acquiring Standard-Triumph and Sunbeam in the 1950s. Leyland and the British Motor Corporation united in 1968 as the British Leyland Motor Corporation (later British Leyland Ltd. and, after 1978, BL Ltd.); this move, sanctioned by the government, was intended to forestall possible American domination of the British automobile industry. Except for Rolls-Royce, whose automobile production was only a very small part of the company's business, British automobile output was then largely controlled by four firms: British Leyland, Ford, Vauxhall, and Rootes, which came under Chrysler control in 1967 but was sold off to France's Peugeot-Citroën in 1978. When British Leyland had financial difficulties in the early 1970s, it was taken over by the government.

In the 1980s the remaining parts of BL, which by then was focused on building Jaguar, Mini, and Rover cars and Land Rover sport utility vehicles and commercial trucks, became the Rover Group. Eventually Jaguar regained profitability, and the British government sold off the company through a public stock offering. The remaining Rover/Mini operations were acquired by British Aerospace Corporation. Rover then entered into a cooperative venture with Japan's Honda in which cars of Honda design were built at Rover plants for sale in Britain and other European countries under the Rover and Honda brands. A small number also were exported to the United States under the Sterling name. Eventually Honda became dissatisfied with the venture, and British Aerospace sold the Rover/Mini operations to BMW of Germany in 1994. In 2000 BMW sold the Land Rover segment to Ford, which had acquired the stock of Jaguar in 1989, while its Rover cars segment was spun off to a British consortium and became MG Rover Group Ltd. BMW retained the profitable Mini operations. In the late 1990s Britain's Rolls-Royce Motor Cars, then owned by Vickers PLC, became the subject of a bidding war in which Germany's Volkswagen emerged as the owner of the company's Bentley brand and all of its manufacturing facilities; BMW emerged as the owner of the Rolls-Royce brand with respect to cars, effective at the end of 2002. Three years later the ailing MG Rover Group was forced to sell off its assets, and in 2008 Ford sold Jaguar and Land Rover to the Tata Group of India. In addition, GM sold Vauxhall to the French PSA Group in 2017.

The post-World War II revival of the German automobile industry from almost total destruction was a spectacular feat, with most emphasis centering on the Volkswagen. At the end of the war the Volkswagen factory and the city of Wolfsburg were in ruins. Restored to production, in a little more than a decade the plant was producing one-half of West Germany's motor vehicles and had established a strong position in the world market. Breaking away from what had become standard design, the Volkswagen used a four-cylinder air-cooled engine at the rear of the car. It also dispensed with the annual model change that had become customary with other automobile manufacturers. Although the company had been founded by the German government, in the 1960s the government divested itself of 60 percent of its interest by selling stock to the public, an unusual case of denationalization in an era when nationalization of industry was far more common. In the same decade, Volkswagen acquired Auto Union, which evolved into its Audi luxury car segment. In the late 1960s BMW rose from a builder of small, oddly styled Isetta cars and motorcycles into one noted for high-priced passenger vehicles and premium motorcycles. Opel became the base for the European operations of General Motors, and by the 1990s it supplied much of the small-car engineering expertise for GM operations around the world; however, Opel was sold to the PSA Group in 2017. Prior to its merger with Chrysler Corporation in 1998, Daimler-Benz had developed diversified interests ranging from trains to aerospace products. After Daimler and Chrysler split in 2007, Daimler-Benz was renamed Daimler AG.

Fiat (Fabbrica Italiana Automobili Torino), a firm founded in 1899 but without a mass market until the 1950s, dominated Italian automotive production. The French industry was centred on Renault, Peugeot, Citroën, and Simca. Renault was nationalized at the end of World War II, and it became a public corporation in the 1990s. Citroën was acquired in 1976 by independently owned Peugeot to form PSA Peugeot-Citroën (later PSA Group). Simca became a Chrysler property in 1958 but was sold to Peugeot in the late 1970s. Although Sweden was a relatively small producer, Swedish builders Saab and Volvo became important factors in the world market during the 1960s and '70s. Their car operations were acquired in the 1980s and '90s by General Motors and Ford, respectively. However, both Saab and Volvo were sold in 2010, and the former went bankrupt the following year.

Japan
The most spectacular increases in automotive production after World War II occurred in Japan. From a negligible position in 1950, Japan in 30 years moved past West Germany, France, Great Britain, and the United States to become the world's leading automotive producer. Steadily growing export sales of Japan's small, fuel-efficient cars

played a major role in this achievement. During the late 1970s and early '80s, Japan's principal automakers—Toyota, Nissan, Honda, and Tōyō Kōgyō (later Mazda)—enjoyed impressive export gains in North American and western European markets. These companies as well as Mitsubishi, Isuzu, Fuji, and Suzuki later opened manufacturing plants in major markets outside Japan to ease trade tensions and increase their competitiveness as the value of Japan's currency soared. By the 1980s Japan's carmakers were seen as the models for others to emulate, especially for their "just-in-time" method of delivering components to the assembly plants (see Consolidation, below) and the use of statistical process controls for enhancing vehicle quality, which ironically had been developed in the 1950s by an American but rejected at the time by American manufacturers.

In the 1990s the Japanese economy suffered a severe and prolonged recession, and the complicated interlocking relationships and cross-ownerships between Japanese automakers and their major component manufacturers and banks imposed severe financial hardship. At the end of the 20th century, many Japanese automakers and several major component manufacturers were either controlled by or had joint operations with non-Japanese firms. Renault, for example, held a controlling interest in Nissan, and in 2016 Mitsubishi joined the Renault-Nissan alliance.

South Korea

In a span of 20 years beginning in the 1970s, South Korea's automotive industry rose from a small government-controlled parochial industry to a significant place in the world market. Three major companies—Hyundai Motor Company, Kia Motors Corporation, and Daewoo Motor Corporation—accounted for about 90 percent of the South Korean market, while the remainder was split among two minor producers and imports. Hyundai, the country's dominant automaker, produced cars, light trucks, and commercial trucks and buses; it was part of the larger Hyundai Corporation, which had interests ranging from construction to shipbuilding. Kia, South Korea's second largest automaker, was acquired by Hyundai in 1999. Daewoo, owned by the Daewoo Group conglomerate, entered the automobile field on a large scale in the 1980s and had won nearly a fifth of the market before entering into financial receivership and reorganization in 2000. Two years later it was sold to General Motors.

The modern industry[8]

The modern automotive industry is huge. In the United States it is the largest single manufacturing enterprise in terms of total value of products, value added by manufacture, and number of wage earners employed. One of every six American businesses is dependent on the manufacture, distribution, servicing, or use of motor vehicles; sales and receipts of automotive firms represent more than one-fifth of the country's wholesale business and more than one-fourth of its retail trade. For other countries these proportions are somewhat smaller, but Japan, South Korea, and the countries of western Europe have been rapidly approaching the level in the United States.

The trend toward consolidation in the industry has already been traced. In each of the major producing countries the output of motor vehicles is in the hands of a few very large firms, and small independent producers have virtually disappeared. The fundamental cause of this trend is mass production, which requires a heavy investment in equipment and tooling and is therefore feasible only for a large organization. Once the technique is instituted, the resulting economies of scale give the large firm a commanding advantage, provided of course that the market can absorb the number of vehicles that must be built to justify the investment. Although the precise numbers required are difficult to determine, the best calculations, considering both the assembly operation and the stamping of body panels, place the optimum output at between 200,000 and 400,000 cars per year for a single plant. Increasingly stringent and costly regulations aimed at correcting environmental damage due to the rising number of vehicles on the road also have been a factor in the move toward consolidation.

The structural organization of these giant enterprises, despite individual variation, resembles the pattern first adopted by General Motors in the 1920s. There is a central organization with an executive committee responsible for overall policy and planning. The operating divisions are semiautonomous, each reporting directly to the central authority but responsible for its own internal management. In some situations the operating divisions even compete with each other. The Ford Motor Company was consciously reorganized on the GM pattern after World War II; other American automotive firms have similar structures.

In addition, the largest producers decentralize their manufacturing operations by means of regional assembly plants. These permit the central factory to ship frames and components rather than complete automobiles to the areas served by the assembly plants, effecting substantial savings in transportation costs. This system was developed for the Ford company in 1911.

Some alteration of that principle took place in the 1980s and '90s as Japanese firms built new plants around the world and American and European manufacturers adopted, to varying degrees, the Japanese "just-in-time" inventory method. Rather than stockpiling a large number of parts at the assembly plant or shipping all the parts from central locations, automakers have yielded the manufacture of many noncritical components (such as seats and wheel assemblies) to independent suppliers to make the pieces at small facilities close to the assembly plants. The components are often assembled into larger groups of parts or modules (a complete instrument panel, for example) and sent to the assembly plant in the exact sequence and at the exact time needed.

Diversity of products

The automotive industry's immense resources in production facilities and technical and managerial skills have been devoted predominantly to the building of motor vehicles, but there has been a consistent and strong incentive to extend into related products and occasionally into operations whose relationship to automobiles is remote. The Ford Motor Company, for example, once manufactured tractors and made the famous Ford Trimotor all-metal transport airplane in the late 1920s and early '30s. GM manufactured refrigerators and diesel-powered railway locomotives. By the end of the 20th century, however, Ford and GM had divested themselves of most of their nonautomotive operations and had spun off the majority of their automotive component-making divisions into separate stock companies—Delphi Automotive Systems in the case of General Motors and Visteon Automotive in the case of Ford.

In Europe, but to a lesser extent, automakers also divested noncore operations, while depressed economic conditions in Japan forced auto companies there to begin divorcing themselves from nonautomotive and components companies in which they had long held interests. By the late 1990s the trend was toward more international consolidation of core automotive operations.

New car development

The process of putting a new car on the market has become largely standardized. If a completely new model is contemplated, the first step is a market survey. Since there may be an interval of five years between this survey and the appearance of the new car in the dealers' showrooms, there is a distinct element of risk, as illustrated by the Ford Motor Company's Edsel of the late 1950s. (Market research had indicated a demand for a car in a relatively high price range, but by the time the Edsel appeared, both public taste and economic conditions had changed.) Conferences then follow for engineers, stylists, and executives to agree on the basic design. The next stage is a mock-up of the car, on which revisions and refinements can be worked out.

Because of the increasingly competitive and international nature of the industry, manufacturers have employed various means to shorten the time from conception to production to less than three years in many cases. This has been done at GM, for example, by incorporating vehicle engineers, designers, manufacturing engineers, and marketing managers into a single team responsible for the design, engineering, and marketing launch of the new model. Automakers also involve component manufacturers in the design process to eliminate costly time-consuming reengineering later. Often the component maker is given full responsibility for the design and engineering of a part as well as for its manufacture.

Manufacturing processes

The bulk of the world's new cars come from the moving assembly line introduced by Ford, but the process is much more refined and elaborated today. The first requisite of this process is an accurately controlled flow of materials into the assembly plants. No company can afford either the money or the space to stockpile the parts and components needed for any extended period of production. Interruption or confusion in the flow of materials quickly stops production. Ford envisioned an organization in which no item was ever at rest from the time the raw material was extracted until the vehicle was completed—a dream that has not yet been realized.

Volkswagen: manufacturing plant

The need for careful control over the flow of materials is an incentive for automobile firms to manufacture their own components, sometimes directly but more often through subsidiaries. Yet complete integration does not exist, nor is it desirable. Tires, batteries, and dashboard instruments are generally procured from outside sources. In addition, and for the same reasons, the largest companies support outside suppliers even for items of in-house manufacture. First, it may be more economical to buy externally than to provide additional internal facilities for the purpose. Second, the supplier firm may have special equipment and capability. Third, the outside supplier provides a check on the costs of the in-house operation. American companies rely more than others on independent suppliers.

Production of a new model also calls for elaborate tooling, and the larger the output, the more highly specialized the tools in which the manufacturer is willing to invest. For example, it is expensive to install a stamping press exclusively to make a single body panel for a single model, but, if the model run reaches several hundred thousand, the cost is amply justified.

The assembly process itself has a quite uniform pattern throughout the world. As a rule, there are two main assembly lines, body and chassis. On the first the body panels are welded together, the doors and windows are installed, and the body is painted and trimmed (with upholstery, interior hardware, and wiring). On the second line the frame has the springs, wheels, steering gear, and power train (engine, transmission, drive shaft, and differential) installed, plus the brakes and exhaust system. The two lines merge at the point at which the car is finished except for minor items and necessary testing and inspection. A variation on this process is "unitized" construction, whereby the body and frame are assembled as a unit. In this system the undercarriage still goes down the chassis line for the power train, front suspension, and rear axle, to be supported on pedestals until they are joined to the unitized body structure. Most passenger vehicles today are manufactured by the unitized method, and most trucks and commercial vehicles still employ a separate frame.

Automobile assembly line.

Assembly lines have been elaborately refined by automatic control systems, transfer machines, computer-guided welding robots, and other automated equipment, which have replaced many manual operations when volume is high. Austin Motors in Britain pioneered with its automatic transfer machines in 1950. The first large-scale automated installation in the United States was a Ford Motor Company engine plant that went into production in 1951. A universal form of automatic control has used computers to schedule assembly operations so that a variety of styles can be programmed along the same assembly line. Customers can be offered wide choices in body styles, wheel patterns, and colour combinations.

Sales and service organization[9]

Mass production implies mass consumption, which in turn requires an elaborate distributive organization to sell the cars and to develop confidence among customers that adequate service will be available. In the early days of the industry, cars were sold directly from the factory or through independent dealers, who might handle several different makes. Many bicycle manufacturers simply used their existing sales outlets when they added horseless carriages to their line. When sales in large quantities became the objective, however, more elaborate and better organized techniques of distribution became essential.

In the United States the restricted franchise dealership became the uniform and almost exclusive method of selling new cars. In this system, dealers may sell only the particular make of new car specified in their franchise, must accept a quota of cars specified by the manufacturer, and must pay cash on delivery. In return the dealers receive some guarantee of sales territory and may be assisted in various ways by the manufacturer—financing or aid in advertising, for example. Contracts also specify that dealers must maintain service facilities according to standards approved by the manufacturer.

Seemingly weighted in favour of the manufacturer, the system has been subjected to periodic dealer complaints, producing state legislation and a federal statute in 1956 to protect dealers from arbitrary actions by manufacturers. Yet dealers have never been united in these attitudes, and no effective substitute for the restricted franchise has yet been found. On the contrary, it is becoming the general practice in other parts of the world where large-scale markets for motor vehicles have developed.

Attempts by automakers in the 1990s to move away from the traditional franchised dealer network to direct selling via the Internet met strong resistance in the United States. American dealers enlisted the help of state governments in enacting prohibitions of this practice (and in blocking attempts by automakers to own dealers through subsidiary corporations). In markets outside the United States, principally in Europe and South America, manufacturers sell directly to consumers via the Internet in limited quantities.

The market in used cars is an important part of the distribution system for motor vehicles in all countries with a substantial motor vehicle industry because it affects the sale and styling of new cars. The institution of the annual model was adopted in the United States during the 1920s to promote new-car sales in the face of used-car competition. The new model must have enough changes in styling or engineering to persuade prospective buyers that it is indeed an improvement. At the same time, it must not be so radically different from its predecessors as to give the buyer doubts about its resale potential.

Like all machinery, motor vehicles wear out. Some become scrap metal to feed steel furnaces; some go to wrecking yards where usable parts are salvaged. Throughout the world, however, the disposal of discarded motor vehicles has become a problem without a completely satisfactory solution. In many areas, landscapes are disfigured by abandoned wrecks or unsightly automobile graveyards. Spurred by European legislation requiring automakers to take back all of their end-of-life-cycle vehicles beginning in 2007, manufacturers worldwide have begun engineering new products with the complete recycling of components in mind. At the same time, they have used more and different recycled material in new vehicles. For example, old bumper covers have been recycled into fender liners or battery trays for new cars.

International operations

Although the automotive industry has long been multinational in its organization and operation, beginning in the 1980s and accelerating in the late 1990s, it established a trend toward international consolidation. Larger, more financially secure firms bought controlling interest in financially troubled ones, usually because the weaker firm manufactured a highly prized product, had access to markets that the larger company did not, or both. However, the results were mixed. For example, Chrysler, as discussed above, acquired AMC in 1987 for access to AMC's Jeep vehicles and in 1998 was itself merged with Daimler-Benz, which sought Chrysler's expertise in high-volume manufacturing and design techniques. Recognizing its need to penetrate closed markets in Japan and South Korea, DaimlerChrysler in 2000 took a controlling 34 percent interest in Mitsubishi Motors Corporation and signed a cooperative venture in trucks with Hyundai Motor Company. Such deals failed to help the struggling DaimlerChrysler, and in 2007 Chrysler was sold to an American private equity firm. Seven years later Chrysler became a subsidiary of Fiat.

In 1989 General Motors bought a 50 percent interest in Sweden's Saab and acquired the remainder 10 years later; in 2000 it took a 20 percent stake in Japan's Fuji Heavy Industries (renamed Subaru in 2017) to have access to the all-wheel-drive technology used in Fuji's Subaru vehicles. Amid financial troubles, however, Saab was sold in 2010, and it went bankrupt the following year. In addition, in 2020 Toyota reached a deal to acquire Subaru. In 1999 Ford bought the passenger car operations of Sweden's AB Volvo, and in 2000 it bought Britain's Land Rover operations from BMW. However, the latter was sold to the Tata Group of India in 2008, and two years later Ford sold Volvo to a Chinese firm.

The most promising markets for motor vehicles have traditionally been developed countries with the purchasing power to create a demand for automobiles; these have included North American and European countries as well as Australia, New Zealand, South Africa, and Japan. Since 1950 there has been a significant shift in market prospects, however, as less-developed countries have shown greater growth in vehicle registrations than the highly developed countries. Consequently, there has been an intensification of both assembly and distribution in parts of the world not previously important in the automotive industry.

The great bulk of this production is assembly, done in plants affiliated with and usually operated by Chinese, American, European, Japanese, or South Korean automotive firms. In order to stimulate their own automotive industries, most developing countries have tariff policies that make imported cars prohibitively expensive and, in addition, have requirements that a substantial portion of the components used in local assembly plants be of domestic origin. A certain percentage of local ownership, public or private, is also a normal requirement. The rest of the financing and most of the initial managerial and technical skill come from the parent company.

In the 1990s China attracted the attention of the world's major automotive companies. Somewhat relaxed governmental controls on private ownership and the consequent rise of entrepreneurial enterprises provided a burgeoning market in China for automobile ownership by individuals. This potential, plus local-component requirements, led to the establishment by automakers and component manufacturers of complete manufacturing facilities in China rather than limited local assembly operations. In addition, Chinese firms—several of which were state owned—increasingly manufactured their own line of vehicles, and in the early 21st century the country's car sales became among the highest in the world.

Economic and social significance

The automotive industry has become a vital element in the economy of the industrialized countries—motor vehicle production and sales are one of the major indexes of the state of the economy in those countries. For such countries as the United

Kingdom, Japan, France, Italy, Sweden, Germany, and South Korea, motor vehicle exports are essential to the maintenance of healthy international trade balances.

The effect of motor vehicle manufacturing on other industries is very great. Almost one-fifth of American steel production and nearly three-fifths of its rubber output go to the automotive industry, which is also the largest single consumer of machine tools. Moreover, the special requirements of automotive mass production have had a profound influence on the design and development of highly specialized machine tools and have stimulated technological advances in petroleum refining, steelmaking, paint and plate-glass manufacturing, and other industrial processes.

The indirect effects are also considerable through the many auto-related businesses, such as motor freight operators and highway construction firms. In addition, truck transportation has grown steadily throughout the world.

Highway development[10]

Before the advent of the motor vehicle, roads in most parts of the world were generally poor. The available methods of road transport were so costly and inefficient that, unless there were special considerations such as military movements, it was not worthwhile to maintain roads for other than local traffic. The general use of automobiles created a strong demand for better highways. The first response was to provide for the improvement of existing road networks. Experience subsequently demonstrated that roads for automobile traffic needed to be differentiated functionally, depending on whether they were intended for through traffic or local traffic. Main arteries are best designed as freeways (motorways, autostrade, or Autobahnen)—i.e., divided highways with complete control of access and no intersections at grade.

Social effects

A historian has said that Henry Ford freed common people from the limitations of their geography. The statement cogently summarizes the social transformations still proceeding throughout the world as a result of the motor vehicle. It has created mobility on a scale never known before, and the total effect on living habits and social customs is still incalculable.

The automobile has radically changed urban life by accelerating the outward expansion of population into the suburbs and beyond. As with other automobile-related phenomena, the trend is most conspicuous in the United States but is rapidly appearing elsewhere. The decentralizing trend is accentuated by the fact that highway transportation encourages business and industry to move outward to sites where land is cheaper, where access by car and truck is easier than in crowded cities, and where space is available for the one-story structures that permit optimum use of modern materials-handling techniques. Yet the effect on rural life has been, if anything, more pronounced than the effect on cities. In the days of horse-drawn transport, the economical limit of wagon transportation was 15–25 km (about 10–15 miles); any community or individual farm more than 25 km from a railroad or navigable waterway was isolated from the mainstream of economic and social life. Motor vehicles and paved roads have narrowed much of the gap between rural and urban life. Farmers can ship easily and economically by truck and can drive to town when convenient. In addition, such institutions as regional schools and hospitals are now accessible by bus and car.

It would be impossible to list all of the specific effects of motor vehicle production, but two are especially illustrative. First, the marketing of automobiles has stimulated a great expansion in the use of credit. Installment buying existed before the automobile but in a limited scope. The technique was introduced into the American automobile industry in 1916 by manufacturers of medium-priced cars to help meet the competition of the low-priced Model T. It became a universal practice in nearly all countries in the purchase of motor vehicles, and it accustomed people to buying other durable consumer goods in the same way. Second, there has been a striking development of businesses such as drive-in and drive-through eating establishments and of commercial developments, such as shopping malls, that are designed to be accessed primarily by car.

In both urban and rural areas after World War II, the automobile is credited with having caused drastic changes in the sexual values of young people, who found in it a privacy not formerly attainable.

Recreational travel

One of the conspicuous effects of the automobile has been to permit nearly everyone in the automotive countries to travel for recreation. The motor vehicle allows for such auxiliary devices as trailers (called caravans in Europe), campers, trailers for boats and off-road vehicles, and bicycle and ski racks, which broaden the scope of recreational opportunities.

Adverse effects

The mass use of motor vehicles was bound to have some unforeseen and undesirable consequences, of which three can be singled out: traffic congestion, air pollution, and highway accidents. The approach to each of these problems illustrates a common propensity to blame the technology, rather than the way in which the technology has been used.

City streets were congested long before the automobile existed, but the problem has been compounded enormously by the masses of motor vehicles that enter or leave cities at peak traffic hours. The constantly growing number of automobiles throughout the world adds to the difficulty of finding remedies for congestion. The heart of the problem is that few city street systems have been designed for automobile traffic. Reliable estimates are that some two-thirds of the vehicles in central business districts are only passing through and should have been routed on circumferential highways. Remedying this situation is difficult and expensive. It calls for modern highways to provide both ready access into downtown areas and ways to avoid them. Programs for this purpose encounter vigorous opposition, frequently justified, on the ground that building freeways in cities disrupts neighborhoods and destroys scenic or historic areas.

The widespread use of automobiles for business travel has also led in many cities to a decline in public transit systems, and the need to develop and use mass transit has been much discussed. Given the trend toward dispersal of people and businesses in urban areas, it seems doubtful that mass transit will appreciably diminish motor vehicle traffic. Still, in most cities, bus systems can provide the needed capacity for public transportation and are the most economical way of doing so.

Atmospheric pollution antedates the automobile, but the concentration of many thousands of motor vehicles in large cities has given the problem a new dimension. Automobile exhaust commonly contributes half the atmospheric pollutants in large cities and even more in cities where atmospheric and topographic conditions are peculiarly conducive to smog formation. In the 1960s federal and state legislation in the United States required the installation of controls on motor vehicles to restrict the emission of pollutants (see emission-control systems). By the end of the 20th century, most scientists believed that emissions from motor vehicles, industrial processes, and power plants were leading to a buildup of carbon dioxide in the atmosphere, thus trapping additional heat and raising Earth's temperature with potentially disastrous long-term results (see greenhouse effect). This led governments in many major automotive countries to enact legislation requiring a significant increase in motor vehicle fuel economy, thereby reducing the output of carbon dioxide. Many automobile manufacturers also have undertaken development of alternative, less-polluting power sources, such as fuel cells that convert hydrogen (derived from gasoline, natural gas, methanol, or other sources) and oxygen into electricity to power an electric motor, to enhance their competitive positions even in countries without strong requirements that they do so.

Highway accidents create a distressing toll of fatalities and injuries wherever there is widespread use of automobiles. Each year there are hundreds of thousands of motor vehicle fatalities worldwide and about 40,000 in the United States alone. The social and economic cost of such accidents is incalculable. Efforts to improve highway safety have been successful in most countries, but a reduction in the ratio of fatalities and injuries per distance traveled is often offset by increases in numbers of accidents because of the ever-growing use of motor vehicles.

Safety features such as seat belts and air bags that inflate on impact have become standard features in cars and passenger trucks since the 1960s (see vehicular safety devices). Today many vehicles are equipped with multiple air bags to protect occupants in side-impact and rollover accidents as well as frontal crashes.

The desire to reduce fatalities and to conserve fuel has led policy makers to focus on speed limits. Most countries of the world have set speed limits ranging from about 65 km (40 miles) per hour in some island nations to 120–130 km (75–80 miles) per hour in many European countries. In some parts of the world, such as areas of Germany, India, and the Philippines, speed limits traditionally are not prescribed. In the early 21st century, the United Kingdom and the European Union supported a controversial proposal to equip new cars with a speed-control device that would use global positioning satellites to track a vehicle's location and, in conjunction with an onboard digital road map, cut off the car's fuel supply if local speed limits were exceeded.

Employee performance[11]
Definition of Employee Performance

Employee performance refers to your employees' behaviour in the workplace and their ability to accomplish the job obligations you've assigned to them. Typically, your firm establishes performance goals for individual employees and the organisation as a whole in order to ensure that your business provides value to consumers, minimises waste, and functions efficiently.

Performance can refer to the efficacy, quality, and efficiency of an individual employee's work at the task level. For example, your salesperson may be expected to make a particular number of calls to potential leads every hour, with a certain percentage of those calls resulting in closed sales. On the other side, a production worker may be required to meet performance standards for product quality and hourly production.

Individual performance has an effect on the performance of your team and company. If you have staff that are unable to keep up or who perform mediocre work, this may need other employees to pick up the slack or require work to be redone. When employees perform poorly, they may be unable to satisfy clients, resulting in negative effects on profits, corporate reputation, and sales.

Employee Performance Metrics That Are Frequently Used
The measures used to evaluate employee performance will ultimately depend on the sort of work performed by your organisation. However, there are some measurements that are universally applicable.

Businesses should check work quality, individual employee objectives, training efficacy, and staff efficiency. Evaluating work quality and efficiency helps you avoid costly mistakes, increases the likelihood that your employees will meet deadlines, and minimises wasted time, materials, and effort. Evaluating the success of training and individual employee work goals will assist you in determining if employees are adequately prepared to do their duties and in providing necessary guidance.

Depending on the nature of your firm, you may wish to employ additional particular performance measures such as the following:
- **Achievement of Goals / KRA**
- **Production Efficiency - Number of units produced per day or per months based on efficiency of setup/plant.**
- **The quantity of defective products**

- The total number of errors
- The quantity of sales
- The quantity of units manufactured
- The duration of the call
- Initial contact resolution
- Rate of absenteeism

Performance Evaluation of Employees

Your firm has numerous ways for evaluating employee performance, and you may find it beneficial to combine them to obtain a more full picture of individual, team, and organizational performance. Among these are the following:

Management according to objectives: This approach of reviewing employee performance relies on goal setting between managers and employees. It has the advantage of setting clear expectations for how people should execute their jobs and tracking progress toward these goals through the use of deadlines.

360-degree feedback: This strategy entails soliciting feedback on an employee's performance from a variety of individuals with whom the employee interacts. Along with having a direct supervisor assess work-performance measures such as effectiveness and efficiency, coworkers, other managers, and anybody else to whom the employee reports can offer insight about the person's abilities and character.

Scale and rating methods: There are numerous employee performance assessment choices that assess an employee using lists or scales of desired attributes. Employees may be ranked according to their performance from best to worst in order to quickly discover individuals who may be desirable for higher-level positions as well as those who require additional training.

Self-evaluation of employees: Often used in conjunction with another review approach, self-evaluation allows employees to reflect on their own work performance and identify their strengths and faults. However, this strategy has the disadvantage of making it difficult for employees to be subjective about themselves.

Increasing Employee Productivity

Along with conducting frequent performance evaluations, you'll need an employee performance improvement strategy to address your results. It's beneficial to begin by determining why your staff fall short of performance objectives. Perhaps they lack enough training, motivation, morale, or a grasp of performance objectives.

Once the root reason has been identified, it is time to take action by providing more training, developing an effective reward system, changing the work atmosphere, empowering your employees, and integrating relevant technologies.

Taking Charge of Employee Performance (Managing Employee Performance)[12]

Managing employee performance is a critical component of organisational success in the current environment of organisations attempting to embrace a resource-centered organisational vision. As previously demonstrated, integrating human resource management methods with organisational goals and strategy boosts a firm's competitive edge. Similarly, firms that value people as a vital asset must manage employee performance within the context of organisational goals. As previously stated, organisations in the service sector that place a high premium on people must guarantee that employee performance is handled holistically.

A Two-Way Road

When we discuss employee performance, we must keep in mind that it is a two-way street that connects the manager and the employee, with the HR manager acting as a mediator. For example, any discussion of employee performance must include both the management and the employee, or the manager and those who are managed. As a result, it is critical that both parties to this transaction understand their respective obligations and collaborate to ensure that the process runs well. The next sections describe the manager's and employee's roles, as well as how an organisational focus on controlling employee performance can play a role.

The Manager's Function

The manager owes it to his or her staff to ensure that their management is devoid of biases and prejudices. It has been documented across industries and verticals that employees feel discriminated against, resulting in turnover, decreased employee morale, and, in extreme circumstances, lawsuits against the organisation. As a result, the manager must "walk the walk" and not simply pay lip service to the company's performance policies. While operating as a team, there are certain to be occasions of friction between the management and the team, as well as within the team. The manager's responsibility is to ensure that this does not deteriorate into a corrosive effect that threatens the team's very existence.

The Employee's Role

The preceding section discussed the manager's role. The manager has a responsibility to manage the team effectively, and each employee also has comparable responsibilities. Absenteeism, Disappeared Work, negative attitudes and a casual attitude toward work are two characteristics that the employee must avoid. It is beneficial for the employee to understand that once classified as having an attitude problem, it will be tough to overcome the perception and function well. This is not to say that the employee must accept whatever is thrown his or her way. The notion is that the employee must pursue remedy through accessible avenues rather than sulking at work if he or she has issues against the manager.

Organizational Objectives

Though the HR manager's and organization's roles appear to be little, it is a reality that organisational goals and culture play a critical role in ensuring that employee performance is managed to the organization's benefit. The majority of us have read or heard about the perks of working for multinational corporations (MNCs) in India. The reason they are so well-known is that potential and aspiring employees have a positive image of how these organisations handle their staff. Though the purpose of this section is not to disparage Indian businesses, it does emphasise the ways in which organisations can influence how people are treated in theory and reality.

> As a result, human resource management has a considerable impact on performance. [13]

The performance of an organisation may be traced back to the actions of its employees on the shop floor. Employees work in a given way or act in a certain way in order to contribute to the organization's (objective). [14]

Employee behaviour can present itself in three distinct ways in relation to organisational performance.[15]

Execution of tasks

Behaviour centered on completing the task. Task performance is frequently seen as the most critical part of job behaviour and is frequently used interchangeably with overall job performance.

Behaviour of Organizational Citizenship

This is sometimes referred to as 'soft performance'. In a nutshell, this occurs when individuals perform duties that are not directly related to their immediate area of responsibility or job description, thereby contributing to the organization's objectives.

Deviant Behaviour in the Workplace

This is behaviour in which an employee breaches an organization's standards, thereby endangering the organisation or his coworkers. Spreading false rumours, insulting coworkers, stealing, and sabotage are just a few examples. Employees that are actively disengaged exhibit this behaviour. Employees must receive feedback on their behaviour and performance. If such is not the case, they will use their prior performance as a benchmark to determine:

Which activities they will perform[16]
how much work they will exert[17]
how motivated they are[18]
to what extent they will recognise and rectify errors

The critical nature of performance

If your organisation or organisational unit does not add value, it has no reason to exist. This may include value for customers, society, and shareholders, as well as value for employees within the organisation.

Each person offers a unique contribution to the organisational unit's performance, and consequently to the overall success of your organisation. If an organisational unit or individual employee's performance lags over an extended period of time, reorganisation or redundancy are likely. The necessity of ongoing performance is growing, even more so in a context where competition is fiercer than ever.

What Is the Purpose of an Effective Performance Management Process (PMP)?[19]

A dependable and stable Employee Performance Management Process, along with all of its associated strategies, tools, and ratings, contribute significantly to improving the performance of employees and supervisors throughout the firm. An efficient employee

performance management programme contributes to the following benefits for the organisation:
- Produces efficacy, adaptability, and equality
- The objectives established are precise, reasonable, and quantifiable.
- Enhances employee productivity, engagement, and development
- Encourages both proactive and ongoing succession planning
- Consistency throughout the organization's departments to foster development and talent usage
- Develops a more capable staff
- Develops, moulds, and engages employees in all circumstances
- Prior performance is taken into account when setting new targets.
- Additionally, a future viewpoint is examined to aid in the creation of development chances.
- Enhances communication by ensuring that everyone respects the rules
- Reduced stress among coworkers as a result of communication
- Employee education and development

The entire performance management process revolves around four pillars: developing, recognizing, planning, and assessing. All of this is accomplished with the assistance of supervisors. The primary tools used throughout the procedure are as follows:

Individual Development Plan (IDP): This is a tool that assists managers and employees in developing annual personal development plans. IDP and the department share a common aim of success.

Dialogue in Performance (PD): The team develops the PD in order to evaluate their current and previous updates.

How Should Employee Performance Be Measured?

Any business owner is always reliant on his staff' efficiency. To motivate their personnel to achieve at their peak levels, they must work diligently. They will constantly require someone who can strive to elevate their firm and also track the performance of their personnel. Certain tools aid in the evaluation of employee performance.

The following tools are used to evaluate employee performance:

Productivity Evaluations

Productivity measurement demonstrates how well your employees are meeting expectations. These tests are fairly prevalent in factories where output is quantified.

Management by Objectives

The assessment process evaluates employees' performance in technical, skilled, communicative, and motivational domains. Certain employees' performance is evaluated based on their annual percentage of goal achievement.

Performance Evaluations

This is one of the most critical, comprehensive, and successful methods of evaluating your employees' business performance. Annual evaluations ensure that the results are correct.

360° Feedback

This input enables the organization's management sector to be quantified. It benefits supervisors, trainers, and human resource management leaders, among others.

As a result of all of this, we may infer that performance management is important in order to establish a more efficient organisation.

Significant Factors Affecting Employee Performance[20]

Have you ever pondered why certain employees perform above and above the call of duty while others fall short? Employees are a business's primary contributors, and its growth and success are highly dependent on their performance. Learn how to manage employee performance strategically and determine whether to promote or terminate personnel. The following are the most often cited elements affecting employee performance.

Environment of Work

At work, an individual who is subjected to repetitive movements and static postures is at a greater risk of developing musculoskeletal ailments. A healthy work environment incorporates ergonomic measures to reduce the chance of damage. The following practices will help you maintain a safe workplace:

- Employees should be trained on ergonomic principles to foster an awareness of physical limitations.
- Provide ergonomic workspaces and make necessary modifications to existing equipment to prevent awkward positions.

- Enhance work procedures to assist employees in avoiding excessive overtime that contributes to weariness and stress.
- Maintain a safe and secure workplace to avoid mishaps and provide a comfortable working environment for employees.
- Assign the appropriate amount of people to each task to minimise individual workload.
- Encourage staff to take micro-breaks to avoid being in a static position for extended amounts of time.
- Adjust furniture and peripherals to the height of employees to encourage appropriate body posture.
- A safe and healthy work environment helps safeguard employees against illness and workplace injuries. Additionally, it helps raise employee morale and productivity.

Colleagues and Leaders

Collaborating with diverse individuals has an effect on employee performance, which can be either favorable or negative. The ability to discuss ideas and viewpoints with others allows an employee to work without feeling pressed, which enables them to meet their targets and be more productive. Employees must maintain a positive attitude in order to operate successfully and amicably with others.

Collaborating with a variety of people helps employees enhance their collaboration abilities and enables them to deliver the best solutions for their projects. Additionally, it aids in the collection of diverse thoughts and information, which builds a sense of unity among employees and enables them to work together toward a single goal.

Leaders are critical to the success of any team. A strong leader's impact encourages and motivates their subordinates to maintain a positive attitude and work together. Your team should be led by an individual who understands how to listen to others. Ascertain that leaders can supply their subordinates with the essential assistance, information, and training to further develop employee skills. Assuring that your employees' skills are current enables them to operate at their best and contribute to the achievement of corporate goals.

Competencies and Workloads

When it comes to your employees, there are a few questions you should ask yourself: Are these employees qualified for the job/role they've been assigned? Are they qualified to accomplish their assigned duties? Is it necessary for them to receive more training? Is the company providing them with the tools they need to do their job efficiently, comfortably, and safely? If you responded no to at least one of these questions, your company need change.

Prior to assigning workloads, it is critical to understand employees' skill sets and capacities. You cannot expect the accounting department to provide adequate medical care or the IT department to provide correct balance sheets. Employees' skill sets and training should complement one another in order for them to complete duties efficiently. While skill training will vary according to employee needs, it is vital, especially if there are clear skill gaps.

Training in skills development can aid in the development of two distinct types of abilities:

1) soft skills — communication, critical thinking, leadership, adaptability, and work ethics are all examples of soft skills.

2) technical, programming, in-house procedures, financial, and data analysis skills. In some instances, skill development may be necessary to assist personnel in achieving their objectives.

How do you decide the talents that your staff require?

Conduct employee gap studies to determine staff skill gaps and develop corrective action plans. This contributes to overall job quality improvement and ensures staff are qualified for their given roles.

Feedback

Employees cannot better themselves if they do not know the aspects of their job performance to enhance. Giving feedback is an effective method of identifying positive outcomes, constructive criticism, and places for improvement in order to gain a better understanding of an employee's position within the firm.

Feedback is an effective method of motivating employees because it establishes a channel of communication between you and them. It promotes an attitude of candour and transparency within the organisation and aids in the elimination of misunderstandings. Open communication enables the identification of opportunities for employees to improve their overall performance.

Giving employees pertinent & positive feedback enables them to continuously learn and improve, establish new tactics, and improve service. Additionally, it assists in streamlining processes that assist personnel in accomplishing their objectives.

Positive comments can significantly enhance staff morale, which has a beneficial effect on their performance. This demonstrates to them that their efforts have been recognized and appreciated by the organisation.

Incentives

Employees are motivated to perform at their best in order to meet their targets through incentive and reward schemes. Rewards serve as a means of validating and recognising their contribution to the business. Additionally, it informs them if they are continuously meeting their targets and doing well.

Implement reward programmes to motivate your finest staff to go above and beyond the call of duty. This encourages other employees to continue their exceptional work, as they are aware that their efforts are being recognised by the organisation.

You can provide your staff **two types of incentives:**

Monetary (Financial) Incentives — these are monetary rewards such as pay appraisals, cash bonuses, and profit sharing.

Non-monetary incentives — these are perks granted to employees, such as flexible work schedules, remote work access, and increased vacation time. Additionally, it encompasses acknowledgment that results in professional advancement, such as promotions and other job chances.

Organizational Culture

Employees that share similar views and are committed to the organization's goal are more productive. A corporation that adheres to mandated laws and rules, respects employee rights, and fosters camaraderie earns the trust and boosts employee morale of its personnel.

The company culture reflects the mission, values, and ethics of the corporation. It should be reflected in employees' activities and perspectives on the company's objectives. Employees that fit the corporate culture are more likely to be optimistic and efficient, completing assignments on schedule.

Adopt an employee-centered culture that values and inspires employees. Provide the resources necessary to assist people in reaching their full potential and never fail to recognise a job well done. Conduct regular employee evaluation and feedback sessions to ensure that you have a written record of their performance. This will assist you in determining whether an employee requires career growth, additional appraisal, or termination.

The Most Important Factors Affecting Employee Performance[21]

Worker performance is not solely determined by their level of proficiency - however proficiency certainly play a factor.

Employee experience, work environment, coworkers, management, and a variety of other elements all interact to influence performance.

Employers seeking to boost employee performance should conduct in-depth analyses within their organizations. These assessments can assist in identifying both problems and solutions.

Several elements to consider when doing those assessments include the following:

MANAGEMENT STYLE

Effective management contributes to the enhancement of motivation, engagement, and performance. Ineffective management has the opposite effect, diminishing employee satisfaction, productivity, and performance. Numerous studies support this assertion, indicating that employee performance is highly dependent on management. Gallup and Udemy, for example, have performed polls establishing a correlation between ineffective management and low performance. Thus, one strategy to boost performance is to identify and resolve management issues.

Employee surveys can provide immediate insight into a company's management status, identify potential concerns, and recommend ways to resolve those issues.

THE BUSINESS CULTURE

The organisational culture is made up of attitudes and assumptions that influence employee behaviour in part.

Certain characteristics and actions have a beneficial effect on employee performance, while others have a detrimental effect.

For instance, the following characteristics can aid in improving employee performance:
- A culture centred on lifelong learning and progress

- A conviction in the importance of digital literacy and dexterity
- Adaptability to change and fresh ideas

There is no single feature or notion that can overnight influence employee behaviour - cultural revolutions, on the other hand, are difficult and require time.

However, instilling the appropriate principles in a workplace can help shift people' perspectives on work... and, more significantly, their performance.

THE DIGITAL WORKPLACE

The digital workplace consists of the following:
- Employees' digital tools
- The manner in which those digital technologies are utilized
- Training and development of digital skills
- Workflows digitals

A fluid, seamless, and user-friendly digital work environment is possible.

Alternatively, it could be scattered and disjointed.

The more a firm invests in its digital component, the happier and more productive its people will be.

THE WORK ENVIRONMENT IN PERSON

Additionally, the physical work environment influences critical employee KPIs such as engagement, contentment, and performance. A good work environment should be suited to the culture and demands of the organization and its employees.

For example, fast-paced creative companies frequently build work spaces that reflect their culture, beliefs, and mission. Numerous them incorporate engaging décor, recreational areas, and games.

The same work environment, on the other hand, would not work for a company with a distinct culture operating in a distinct industry.

Regardless of sector or culture, however, the physical environment does influence performance.

By and large, the more favorable the work environment – from workstations to décor – the more satisfied people will be with their jobs.

JOB DUTIES AND WORKFLOWS ON A DAILY BASIS

Actual job duties also have an effect on employee performance.

After all, employees who find their occupations fascinating, engaging, and meaningful will work harder.

However, when employees are disengaged or bored, their performance can easily decrease.

In some circumstances, it is possible to make changes that will promote engagement, motivation, and the meaning of work.

Consider the following:

Automation can eliminate time-consuming, monotonous jobs from a worker's to-do list. Demonstrating how a worker's responsibilities benefit the client can help provide significance to daily job routines.

Offering skills training and professional development opportunities can help employees better their career prospects, thereby enhancing their engagement – and, at the same time, their organizational worth.

For disengaged and bored employees, implementing these steps can assist improve performance, as well as engagement, longevity, and other critical indicators.

AN EMPLOYEE'S PERSPECTIVE

Employee experience encompasses all stages of the employee journey, including the following:

Employer-Employee Onboarding Engagement Post-Exit Interactions

That experience is contingent upon a variety of elements, some of which are listed below.

Several benefits accrue from fostering a great employee experience:

- Increased performance
- Increased employee motivation and engagement
- Increased participation
- Reduced friction

Today, many businesses recognise that the employee experience is more than "icing on the cake" — it has a direct impact on the amount of value individuals add to the firm.

ONBOARDING OF NEW EMPLOYEES

Onboarding, a critical stage in the employment journey, shapes how employees view and engage with a business.

After all, first impressions are critical.

To maximize the effectiveness of an onboarding programme, firms should adhere to a checklist that covers all bases:

Integration of operations, which ensures that personnel have the tools, skills, and resources necessary to succeed in their tasks.

Integration with coworkers and supervisors

Integration on a strategic level, to guarantee that employees are committed to and supportive of the company's mission

The correct onboarding strategy can have a significant impact on the bottom line.

After all, employees who integrate quickly and efficiently will be more productive, engaged, and satisfied... and will be less likely to seek other employment.

Non-Monetary Factors impacting employee performance

Satisfaction with one's job performance

It is natural to begin with defining work performance, as this study's objective is to determine the effect of various factors on it. Job performance is a multidimensional concept that encompasses how well employees accomplish their assigned jobs, their initiative, and their ingenuity in resolving difficulties. Additionally, it reveals the degree to which they finish tasks, the manner in which they utilize existing resources, and the amount of time and energy they devote to their work **(Boshoff, & Arnolds, 1995)**[22]. Job performance can be influenced by both situational and dispositional elements, such as the job's features, the organisation, and coworkers. Dispositional factors include personality traits, wants, attitudes, preferences, and motives that influence one's proclivity to behave in a particular way to situations **(Strümpfer, Danana, Gouws, & Viviers, 1998)**[23]. In this case, we define performance improvement as a decrease in absenteeism, a decrease in human error, adherence to deadlines, organisation and prioritization, successful teamwork, a decrease in turnover, an increase in impactful creativity, an increase in task efficiency, a decrease in task postponement, and a faster pace of communication between members and departments of the organisation.

Job satisfaction is simply how people feel about their work and various aspects of their jobs. It refers to the degree to which individuals like (satisfaction) or despise (dissatisfaction) their jobs **(Spector, 2000)**[24] Employment satisfaction is also a psychological concept that refers to attitudes and traits associated to one's job, such as compensation and benefits, policies, leadership practices, management styles, and relationships with coworkers **(Amponsah-Tawiah, & Darteh-Baah, 2010)[25]**. **Armstrong (2010)[26]** notes that job satisfaction is related to people's attitudes and sentiments toward their work. This indicates that good or favourable attitudes toward work indicate employment satisfaction, and negative or unfavorable attitudes toward work indicate job discontent. Employee morale is interdependent.

In relation to job satisfaction, it is defined as the degree to which an individual believes his or her level of satisfaction is a result of his or her work position (Armstrong, 2010).Job happiness is influenced by a variety of elements, including personal expectations, career options, workplace influence, team and job challenges, supervisor quality, social interactions with coworkers, and the degree to which individuals succeed or fail at work **(Wilson, 2010)[27]** Wilson (2010) further asserts that discretionary employee behaviour that contributes to the firm's performance is most likely to occur when employees are content and motivated. According to the study's findings, the primary elements determining job satisfaction were rewards and motivation.

Employee happiness contributes to the organization's overall productivity through influencing job performance, absenteeism, organisational citizenship, organisational commitment, and turnover. Additionally, it was discovered that leadership has a considerable impact on employee satisfaction **(Sarah, Nik, & Pranav, 2012)[28]**.

Empowerment, participation, and engagement of employees

Carless (2004)[29] defines employee empowerment as the extent to which employees are empowered to make decisions in their daily operations. Employee empowerment is associated with motivation and an increased sense of self-confidence among employees. According to **Cheryl (1999)[30]**, organisational success is a result of employee empowerment for the following reasons:

Employees' performance on the job mirrors their personal success.

The organization's personnel accomplish the organization's aims and objectives; as a result, the organisation achieves success.

The organization's employees have a mutually beneficial and rewarding work experience that satisfies their social and personal growth goals.

Employee empowerment can also be described as the degree to which employees can make decisions on their own without consulting their supervisors **(Michailova, 2002)**[31]. Here, management delegated responsibility and autonomy to employees to perform their assigned jobs. This type of delegated empowerment benefits employees by allowing them to make independent decisions because they are able to follow their own procedures without intervention **(Ampofo-Boateng, Merican, & Wiegan, 1997)**[32].

Empowerment was found to have substantial positive associations with both performance and happiness in a study conducted by **Bartram and Casimir (2007)**[33]. More precisely, empowerment was found to be more strongly connected with follower performance than with leader satisfaction. **Chen and Tjosvold (2006)**[34] demonstrated that participation management is about involving employees in the decision-making process by creating an environment in which employees believe they have the opportunity to debate issues and have an impact on organisational decisions. Participation has a measurable effect on employee work performance and retention.

Perrin (2003) defines employee engagement as people who are prepared and skilled enough to contribute to their company's success by making a sustained effort toward that goal. Additionally, his study found that involvement is influenced by emotional and cognitive aspects associated with work and the work experience. Employee engagement, as defined by **Dernovsek (2008)**[35], is the enthusiastic involvement of employees in their work. Establishing a positive mental connection and dedication among employees to their organisation. **Robinson, Perryman, and Hayday (2004)**[36] substantiate this claim with their definition of an employee's favourable perception of the company and its value. This is the situation in which a motivated employee will:

Collaborate with other members of the company to boost performance for the greater good of the organisation.

Encourage teamwork and take part in it. Assist other employees in their growth and development. Assist him when necessary.

The Institute of Employment Studies **(Robinson et al., 2004)**[37] discovered that the primary cause for employee engagement is the employee's sense of being appreciated and involved. This includes including employees in decision-making, allowing employees to be heard within the company, providing opportunities for employees to advance their careers, and demonstrating the organization's concern for its employees' health and well-being.

Employee engagement benefits employee performance in three significant ways **(Baumruk, & Gorman et al., 2006)**[38]:

(1) The employee acts on behalf of and supports the organisation.
(2) Despite possibilities to work elsewhere, the person maintains a deep connection to the organisation.
(3) The individual is willing to provide additional time, effort, and initiative to the organization's success.

Enrichment of employment

Employees may be more satisfied if managers enrich their jobs. This is accomplished by increasing the quantity or variety of tasks assigned to staff. As a result, their level of performance will improve. To accomplish these goals, jobs should be changed and employees should be given increased responsibility (horizontal and vertical job expansion). Additionally, by involving employees in the planning, organisation, and design of their own jobs, they can meet their esteem and self-actualization goals while increasing their performance **(Ekerman, 2006)**[39].

Employment Security

Senol (2011) determined that job security is the most essential factor among a number of factors that operate as a motivator for employees. It altered and improved their negative attitudes toward job termination. Another study **(Miller, Erickson, & Yust, 2001)**[40] discovered a favourable correlation between job security as a motivator and job performance. Additionally, job security has a substantial effect on worker performance, and when job security is inadequate, people are less motivated to work.

Promotion

According **to Herzberg (1986)**[41], providing employees with prospects for advancement within their firm through internal promotions serves as a work-related motivator. Additionally, he adds that providing employees with opportunities for progress and promotion is one of the most effective ways to encourage them. **Harrison and Novak (2006)**[42]**'s** research demonstrates that when managers attempt to generate staff advancement chances, there is a positive motivating effect on employee satisfaction and levels.

The work environment

The workplace environment refers to the physical location of the job, such as an office or construction site, where employees conduct their daily tasks and obligations. Additional variables such as fresh air, refreshment, noise level, and other amenities like as child care also contribute to the workplace environment. Depending on the nature of the work environment, the workplace environment can have a positive or negative effect on employee satisfaction. Employees perform better in a positive work environment. Poor working conditions may result in damage to company property and accidents that involve injury or death; this will have a severe negative effect on staff morale. Thus, organisations must provide supportive working environments. Examples of performance-enhancing work settings include those that are secure, quiet, well-lit, and at an appropriate temperature **(Weil, & Woodall, 2005)**[43]**.**

Numerous aspects of the work environment contribute to employee satisfaction.

The work environment is divided into two components that can influence employee behaviour:

(1) Physical – this refers to the ease with which office personnel interact with their work environment.
(2) Behavioural – this is the way that good employees interact with one another in the office. Barry's (2008) work is evaluated in order to expand on the two components of the work environment. It explains why there are two subcategories of the physical environment: (1) Office layout — open-plan

offices versus closed cellular or cubic offices (2) Office comfort - this refers to the degree to which the office environment and work procedures are compatible. Additionally, the behavioural environment is divided into two subcategories: (1) Interaction—how well-behaved individuals cooperate with one another in the workplace; (2) Distraction—possibilities or incidents in the workplace that detract from interaction.

Office design is a critical component of the office work environment; Business Dictionary (2008) defines office design as "realizing the possibility of accomplishing work most efficiently through the organisation of the work area." Additionally, office design plays a significant role on employee satisfaction. It has an effect on how employees work; for example, several firms have implemented open-plan workplaces to foster collaboration. Additionally, office design considers workflow, in which the work to be done is first analyzed, and then the offices are configured to guarantee that the task is completed efficiently.

According to the American Society of Interior Designers (1999), physical workplace design is one of the top three elements affecting performance and job satisfaction. According to the study's findings, 31% of participants were content with their jobs and enjoyed pleasant work surroundings. 50% of participants were seeking for work and stated that they would want to work in a company with a nice physical environment. Gensler Designs (2006) conducted another study on the US employment environment, examining workplace design, job satisfaction, and productivity. 89 percent of respondents ranked design as important or extremely important. Nearly 90% of senior executives indicated that effective office design is critical for increasing staff productivity. The result was that businesses can increase productivity by optimizing their workplace designs. According to CEO estimates, a well-designed office may boost a company's performance by over 22%. **Brill, Margulis, Konar, and Bosti (1984)**[44] classified factors affecting productivity according to their relative importance. The following factors are listed in order of importance: furniture, noise, adaptability, comfort, communication, lighting, temperature, and air quality. **Leaman (1995)**[45] performed another poll to determine the association between the indoor work environment and employee satisfaction and productivity. Employees were unsatisfied with their work environment, which had a detrimental effect on their productivity.

Job stress and pressure

According to **French (1975)**[46], job stress occurs when an individual's personal qualities are insufficient to meet the available resources and job needs. He goes on to explain that workplace stress is a result of a perilous work environment. Organizations will require a specific volume and quality of work from their employees, but their employees will be unable to meet these standards with their allocated jobs. In other words, the organization's demand surpasses the capacity of its personnel, who, in the eyes of management, are unable to perform their duties.

Stress is an emotional state brought on by pressure or demands placed on an individual, impairing that individual's ability to cope with the pressure or obligations. Workplace stress occurs when job demands need the use of additional resources and capabilities accessible to employees **(Ricardo, Amy, & Rohit, 2007)**[47].

Job stress can have a detrimental influence on health, resulting in heart disease, gastroenteritis, sleep difficulties, and other accidents, lowering job performance and increasing absenteeism and job quitting rates **(McVicar, 2003)**.

Another study conducted by **Jamal (2007)** examined the relationship between a stressful work environment and its effect on an employee's performance; the findings indicated that in 90% of firms, a negative relationship existed between a stressful work environment and job performance.

It is critical to discuss the sources of stress, and busyness is the primary source of work-related stress. However, there are additional relevant elements that contribute to stress, including downsizing and de-cluttering, organisational change, long hours, bullying, shift work, and sexual or racial harassment (Ricardo, Amy, & Rohit, 2007).

According to **Amanda and Jonathan (2006)**[48], there are six potential sources of stress:

(1) Demands: job-related difficulties such as working conditions (temperature, lighting, ventilation, and noise), long hours, workload, and shift work.
(2) Control: the degree to which an employee is autonomous in carrying out his or her work and assigned tasks. Low job control is associated with high levels of stress.

(3) Relationships: stress can be induced by referring to relationships with all members of the organisation (managers, subordinates, and colleagues). For instance, poor levels of trust and support, conflict among organisation members, and harassment and bullying all contribute to increased work stress.

(4) Change: The manner in which management implements and communicates change to employees can induce stress. When events are poorly planned or communicated, they contribute to increased stress.

(5) Function: When employees lack a clear sense of their role within the organisation, stress can result from uncertainty or conflict about positions or degrees of responsibility.

(6) Support: How well-managed organisations support their employees by providing them with the resources and training they need to do their tasks. Low levels of encouragement, sponsorship, and support among the organization's members will result in increased stress.

(7) Non-Monetary Factors Impacting Employee's Performance The following diagram illustrates the factors that contribute to workplace stress.

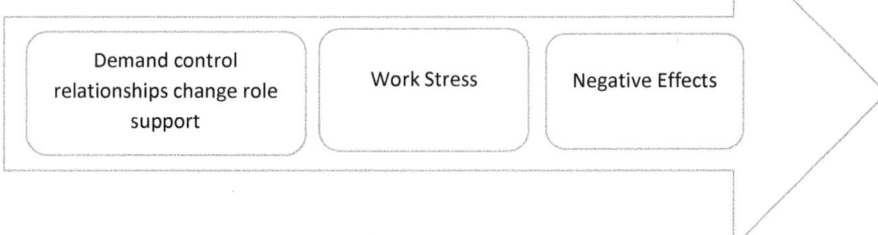

Motive

DeCenzo and Robbins (1996)[49] define motivation as the extent to which an individual is willing to execute a task in order to meet his or her requirements. Another definition of motivation is the process that propels an individual with zeal and determination in the direction of achieving a goal **(Page, 2008)**[50]. Motivation has ramifications for both the psychological and managerial realms **(Tosi, Mero, & Rizzo, 2000)**[51]. The psychological component is made up of the individual's own mental state. This mental state dictates the onset, direction, persistence, intensity, and end of behaviour. The managerial component of motivation refers to managers' and leaders' strategies for influencing personnel to obtain desired results. At this point, management must determine precisely what motivates people in order to ensure that resources are used efficiently and not misallocated. Motivation enhances job engagement by making work more relevant and engaging, as well as by keeping people more productive and improving job performance (Ekerman, 2006).

Motivation at work is a delicate issue that affects every individual and their level of contribution and effectiveness inside the firm. Thus, motivation in either of its two manifestations (intrinsic or extrinsic) adds to employee happiness and has the potential to boost performance and productivity **(Bhattacharyya, 2007)**[52]. **Shah and Shah (2010)**[53] defined motivation as the process of enticing others to collaborate in order to achieve the best results. To elaborate on this notion, motivation occurs when managers meet their employees' desires and motivations in order to encourage them to perform in a desirable manner.

Palmer (2005)[54] asserts that the motivation approach in affect must be motivating during the actual process of goal attainment. This means that the implementation step must be motivating in its own right that individuals do not feel disheartened and quit. To do this, a process must be skillfully created with the purpose of attaining the objectives and controlling the motivating approach in mind. This method is critical for carrying out everyday activities and inspiring employees of the organisation to work toward common goals. In terms of the organisation, motivation must follow a set of procedures that must be examined and renewed on a regular basis. As a result, the organization's members remain motivated.

According to **Hackman and Oldham (1980)**[55], significant intrinsic motivation occurs when three psychological states are induced:
1. The employee is aware of the significance of his task.

2. The employee bears responsibility for the outcome of his or her Labour.

3. The employee is aware of the actual effects of his or her effort.

Additionally, Hackman and Oldham (1980) believe that businesses should foster intrinsic drive by:

1. Increasing task diversity and significance; this contributes to the work's meaning.

2. By increasing workers' work autonomy, employers increase employees' obligations.

3. Facilitating feedback to ensure that staff are aware of the outcome of their job.

Motivation is achievable when the relationship between performance and outcome is well defined. This outcome must also meet the requirements of organisational members. In other words, the Labour that employees perform must be repaid to them in the form of a reward, and this reward must be sufficient to compensate for the effort involved in performing the work. This fact explains why intrinsic motivation derived from one's work can be a more powerful and effective element than extrinsic drive. Intrinsic motivation enables employees to use their prior experiences to determine how beneficial or worthwhile the results are in exchange for their behaviour or effort **(Lawler, 2003).**

There are two interesting ideas that examine "needs." The first is **David (1987)**, often known as "The Learned Wants Theory," which asserts that an individual acquires unique needs throughout his or her life. Additionally, the idea says that everyone has three primary motivators (success, affiliation, and power), with one of these motivators being the most essential. These three motivators may have an effect on how employees perform their jobs. Individuals who prioritize achievement are efficient workers who have a strong desire to accomplish difficult goals and seek feedback on their work. On the other hand, individuals with a low demand for achievement do better when motivated by money. Individuals that have affiliation as their primary motivator do better with other individuals when they are in agreeable relationships. They desire to be a part of a group and to be accepted and liked, and hence will work diligently to accomplish whatever the group decides. Additionally, this personality type values collaboration above rivalry, making them ideal for developing long-term, stable, and productive relationships. Due to these Employee happiness and enjoyment are derived from the work itself, which takes place in an atmosphere with frequent interpersonal contacts. For those motivated by power, whether directly or indirectly, they would seek to dominate or affect the behaviour of others. They thrive in a competitive environment, aspire to status and leadership positions, and relish the opportunity to win fights and be acknowledged for their efforts. Individuals who use their powers to assist others have socialized power, and leaders who crave socialized power are likely to be more effective than those who have a strong need for individualized power **(Vredenburgh, & Brender, 1998)**[56].

The second theory to consider is Abraham Maslow's needs hierarchy hypothesis of motivation, which categorizes human wants according to their priority. Maslow argues that human wants may be organized in a way that demonstrates which individuals' needs will be met first. Maslow identified five basic needs: physiological, safety, social, esteem, and self-actualization **(Maslow, 1987)**[57]. Two interpretations for this Needs theory are as follows: (1) people will always desire what they lack and

(2) Satisfied needs will no longer provide motivation for behaviour. According to this hierarchy, after lesser wants are met, people will move on to higher ones.

The following diagram depicts the five most basic human requirements.

Figure 1: Maslow's theory of needs

Source: Author's own elaboration based on Maslow (1987).

1. Physiological needs: the first level of the pyramid, the most fundamental, which comprises hunger, thirst, sleep, and shelter. For instance, if an employee is hungry, he or she will be unconcerned with work performance.

2. Safety requirements: This section emphasizes emotional and physical safety, as well as stability. In times of economic distress, when jobs are few, the majority of people desire a stable job. Additionally, if a person is threatened or afraid for his or her well-being, he or she will not proceed to meet higher levels of requirements.

3. Social/Belonging needs: This level is concerned with the social facets of an individual's existence. It encompasses such concepts as friendship, love, and the desire to belong to or relate to a certain group. Social acceptance is an example of this need. Through interactions with coworkers, employees can create a social support network and a sense of belonging, which can result in increased job satisfaction and performance.

4. Esteem needs: This level contains the highest aspirations for achievement and status. These desires are motivated by a need for acknowledgment from others. Esteem demands can be met by purchasing a larger home or a more luxurious car, which contributes to a sense of success, as well as through on-the-job benefits such as praise from the boss, a promotion, a nicer view from the office, or a designated parking space.

5. Self-actualization: This is the most fundamental of all human needs. Employees must have opportunities for progress in order to satisfy their drive for self-actualization. For instance, no matter how high the compensation, a monotonous and dull job would not satisfy the self-actualization desire.

According to Maslow's hierarchy of needs, if an employee does not respond to economic incentives, management must examine other forms of employee motivation.

Maslow (1987) concluded that allowing employees to make work-related decisions satisfies their desire for autonomy and enables managers to use it as a motivator for enhancing employee productivity. **Across (2005)** concurs, stating that people perform poorly in environments where they lack autonomy, even more so after acquiring the ability to operate autonomously.

Another idea to consider is the equity theory, which emphasizes that people are concerned not just with the amount of rewards they obtain for their efforts, but also with the relationship between their rewards and those of others **(Armstrong, 2010)**[58]. Individuals can compare outcomes such as levels, increases, recognition, and other factors based on their own perceptions of effort, experience, education, and competence. When individuals perceive an imbalance in their output-to-input ratio in comparison to others, tension develops. This conflict can serve as a motivator, as individuals desire what they perceive to be equitable and just.

Communication
Communication is described as the act of making contact or interacting with another person in order to convey information, meanings, and comprehensions **(Fisher, 1980)**[59]. Effective communication inside an organisation helps work teams to work together effectively, whereas ineffective communication results in problems and conflicts between organisational members and customers. Individuals involved in the communication process must possess the fundamental skills and abilities necessary for information transmission. Otherwise, the Information may be overlooked or misinterpreted. Additionally, the organization's facilities and tools, as well as the managers' behaviors, must be capable of accurately accepting and delivering information. Through the communication process, managers must demonstrate their initiative in developing and giving opportunities for their staff to gain new skills. The timing of information receipt and delivery is also critical in communications **(Cole, 2002)**[60].

Workplace emotions
Human emotions are complicated; their control reflects corporate trust and occupational stress. When both parties have a high level of trust in their relationship, workplace emotions are better regulated and stress levels are lowered **(Zeynep, 2013)**[61]. Thus, organisational trust is critical to workplace efficiency. According to Zeynep (2013), people perceive others through the lens of their own mental components and emotions;

they also select how much risk to take when interacting with others, which lays the groundwork for trust in the work environment.

Employee Education

Employee training is used in the field of human resource management to improve the performance of organisational personnel. Employee development, human resource development, and learning and development are all terms that are occasionally used to refer to employee training **(Aguinis, & Kraiger, 2009)**[62]. Employee training has a beneficial effect on their productivity and satisfaction. Employees that have been trained are more capable of completing their responsibilities and report greater job satisfaction **(Sutermeister, 1976)**[63]. According to **Wheelan (2010)**[64], educating and training employees on the technical aspects of their jobs and the importance of successful teamwork will improve team performance.

Herzberg (1986)[65] argued in his Two Factor Theory that providing employees with training and development opportunities motivates and enables them to pursue the positions they desire within the firm. **Kress, Norris, Schoenholz, Elias, and Seigle (2004)**[66] all concur that providing employees with opportunities for learning and training is a motivating element for job performance improvement. In another study, **Roca, Chiu, and Martinez (2006)**[67] discovered a significant beneficial association between training and job performance in international businesses.

Employee training benefits both employees and employers by enhancing their knowledge, competences, behaviors, as well as their skills and talents. As a result, employee performance improves, which benefits the organisation **(Wright, & Geroy, 2001)**[68] Additionally, Cole (2002) lists the following benefits of employee training:

1) Higher morale: trained employees have increased confidence and motivation.

2) Lower production costs: training mitigates risk by enabling trained employees to make more effective and efficient use of materials and equipment, hence decreasing waste.

3) Reduced turnover: training fosters a sense of security at work, reducing employee turnover and absenteeism.

4) Change management: training aids in the facilitation of change by enhancing employee understanding and involvement in the process, as well as equipping employees with the skills and talents necessary to adapt to new situations.

5) Training fosters self-esteem, a sense of responsibility, and the prospect of greater compensation and promotion.

6) Training increases employee availability and quality.

Loyalty to One's Employer

Becker, Randal, and Riegel (1995)[69] define loyalty as a strong desire to stay a member of an organisation, the organization's willingness to establish a high level of effort on behalf of the organisation, and a clear belief and acceptance of the organization's values and goals. As such, classify as a belief that contributes positively to the organization's member retention. Job satisfaction is a prelude to organisational loyalty. Employee satisfaction, loyalty, and organisational performance are all positively correlated **(Fletcher, & Williams, 1996)[70]**.

Employee happiness was strongly connected with employee loyalty to their organisation, according to **Martensen and Gronholdt (2001)[71]**. Additionally, studies such as **(Wu, & Norman, 2006)[72]** demonstrate a high association between employee organisational loyalty and job happiness. Additionally, it is claimed that job dissatisfaction results in low morale and organisational loyalty.

Relationships between management and subordinates

According to **Northouse (2007)[73]**, leadership is a notion in which an individual may influence a group of individuals to change their behaviour in order to accomplish a common goal. The sort of leadership process used inside an organisation has a significant impact on whether or not employee performance is aided or harmed **(Armstrong, & Murlis, 2004)[74]**. As a result, leaders and managers are critical to the organization's success. Effective managers will leverage their employees' interpersonal relationships to increase employee loyalty and morale.

Carrell, Kuzmits, and Elbert (1989)[75] argue that mutual trust between subordinates and managers is necessary, and that employees should be empowered to participate in organisational decision-making. This enables the organisation to be more adaptable and innovative. In other words, organisational planning should be done with the people, not for the people. When such a positive relationship exists, established employees are less likely to strike or stop working without first attempting to resolve the issue through channels of contact with management. Additionally, employees are

They are less likely to be counter-productive, and will gradually improve their performance and help the organisation achieve its goals. When employees are heard and involved in decision-making, they become motivated because management views them as partners rather than subordinates in contributing to the organization's success. Innovative human resource management practices that promote employee engagement and job flexibility, as well as decentralization of managerial functions and responsibilities, will result in improved employee performance **(Ichniowski, Shaw, & Prennushi, 1997)**[76].

According to **Caruth and Handlogten (2002)**[77], reward systems are the bedrock of employee motivation. Employee knowledge, skills, and abilities are critical components of every organization's success. As a result, management should always encourage employees' efforts, loyalty, commitment, and contribution by discovering effective ways to recognise their efforts, loyalty, dedication, and input.

Personality characteristics

To study the effect of various personality qualities on performance, **Costa and McCrae's (1992)**[78] five-factor model of personality dimensions is used. Neuroticism, Extraversion, Openness, Agreeableness, and Conscientiousness are the five personality constructs included in the model.

1. Neuroticism refers to an individual's proclivity for negative emotions such as fear, sadness, embarrassment, rage, guilt, or disgust. A high Neuroticism score indicates that an individual is more prone to have irrational thoughts, has less control over his impulses, and reacts poorly to stress. While a low Neuroticism score indicates that an individual is emotionally stable, calm, and relaxed, and capable of coping with stressful situations without becoming upset **(Hough, Eaton, Dunnette, Kamp, & McCloy, 1990)**[79]. Neuroticism is adversely associated to job performance, as **Judge, Higgins, Thoresen, and Barrick (1999)**[80] discovered.

2. Extraversion: characteristics of the personality such as sociability, activity, talkativeness, vitality, and optimism. Extraversion is associated with happy emotions and experiences and is regarded positively **(Clark, & Watson, 1991)**. **Johnson (1997)**[81] discovered a positive connection between Extraversion and police officer performance.

3. Susceptibility to experience: comprises active imagination, sympathy, sensitivity, awareness of inferred feelings, acceptance of variation, intellectual curiosity, and independent judgement. Individuals with a poor receptivity to experience tend to be conservative in their behaviour and outlook. They value familiarity above novelty and change, and they are also emotionally reserved. Individuals that achieve high scores are unusual, challenge authority, and are willing to consider new social, political, and even ethical standards. These individuals are naturally curious and receptive to change and novel ideas; they are also more susceptible to both negative and pleasant emotions.

According to research, an openness to experience is associated with success in consulting, training, and adjusting to change **(Raudsepp, 1990)**[82].

4. Agreeableness: An agreeable person is cooperative, altruistic, compassionate toward others, and helpful, and believes that others will reciprocate. On the other hand, an unpleasant individual is cynical and competitive. The agreeable person's cooperative characteristics may help him or her succeed in jobs that need teamwork and customer service **(Judge et al., 1999)**.

5. Conscientiousness: encompasses personality characteristics such as self-control, planning, organisation, and task completion (Barrick, & Mount, 1993). Conscientious individuals are determined, possess a strong will, and are goal-oriented. Individuals that are highly conscientious are goal-oriented, diligent and persistent, trustworthy and responsible, and organized. However, excessive conscientiousness can manifest as an obsession with neatness and organisation, as well as workaholic behaviour. While poor conscientiousness might result in persons being disorganized and dispersed in their efforts to complete their work. **Borman, White, Pulkos, and Oppler (1991)**[83] and Hough et al. (1990) discovered that conscientiousness and job performance are positively correlated.

organization's culture

An organization's culture is made up of a set of fundamental beliefs, assumptions, understandings, and standards that are shared among its members and taught to new members. A strong organisational culture is critical for increasing employee performance, which results in the achievement of objectives and an increase in the organization's overall performance **(Kotrba, Gillespie, Schmidt, Smerek, Ritchie, & Denison, 2012)**[84]. An organization's culture is multi-layered, with clear declared values and implicit values or assumptions, as well as a degree of adaptability or rigidity. For instance, culture can be classified as either adaptive or purely bureaucratic and hierarchical. According to **Abu-Jarad, Yusof, and Nikbin (2010)**, the organization's norms and ideals have a major impact on all of its members. These standards and values are invisible or implicit, but they have an effect on employee performance. Thus, a flexible corporate culture can facilitate change and adaptability while motivating employees to work together toward a single objective. Additionally, the adaptable organisational culture enables managers to moulds and change employee behaviour more easily in order to accomplish organisational goals.

Rotation of jobs and transfers

Position rotation and transfers are a method of broadening the abilities and knowledge of an organization's personnel by transferring them from one formal responsibility or job to another. For instance, climbing up the organisational ladder, or from one branch to another, or from one department to another. When it comes to larger, worldwide organisations Transfers could be accomplished by relocating staff between countries. These work rotations and transfers enable employees to obtain fresh knowledge about the organization's various activities and processes. Additionally, this newly gained information will enhance employee performance and provide the firm with a competitive edge (**McCourt, & Derek, 2003**)[85].

CONCLUSION:

It is evident from the review that many factors contribute to employee performance in the organization. The organizations have to implement those factors which are relevant to the industry and the organization for its success or failure to which, the results can be terrible.

Reference :

1. https://www.britannica.com/technology/automotive-industry/Ford-and-the-assembly-line
2. https://www.britannica.com/technology/electric-automobile
3. https://www.britannica.com/technology/mass-production
4. https://www.britannica.com/technology/assembly-line
5. https://www.britannica.com/topic/General-Motors-Corporation

6. https://www.britannica.com/technology/automotive-industry/Growth-in-Europe
7. https://www.britannica.com/technology/automotive-industry/Europe-after-World-War-II
8. https://www.britannica.com/technology/automotive-industry/The-modern-industry
9. https://www.britannica.com/technology/automotive-industry/Sales-and-service-organization
10. https://www.britannica.com/technology/automotive-industry/Highway-development
11. https://bizfluent.com/how-6885971-measure-employee-performance-production-metrics.html
12. https://www.managementstudyguide.com/managing-employee-performance.htm
13. Patterson, M.G. et al (1998), Impact of People Management Practices on Business Performance, Institute of Personnel and Development, London, 1-27
14. Viswesvaran, C. and Ones, D.S. (2000), Perspectives on Models of Job Performance, International Journal of Selection and Assesment, 8, 216-226
15. Dunlop, P.D. and Lee, K. (2004), Workplace Deviance, Organizational Citizenship Behavior and Business Unit Performance: the Bad Apples do spoil the whole Barrel, Journal of Organizational Behavior, 25, 67-80
16. Greenwald, A.G. (1980), The Totalitarian Ego: Fabrication and Revision of Personal History, American Psychologist, 35, 603-618
17. Felson, R.B. (1984), The Effect of Self-Appraisals of Ability, on Academic Performance, Journal of Personality and Social Psychology, 47, 944-952
18. McFarlin, D.B. and Blascovich, J. (1981), Effects of Self-Esteem and Performance Feedback on Future Affective Preferences and Cognitive Expectations, Journal of Personality and Social Psychology, 40, 521-531
19. http://studylecturenotes.com/employee-performance-management-system-and-process/
20. *Jona Tarlengco is a content writer for SafetyCulture, a software company that enables businesses to perform inspections using digital checklists.*
21. https://www.digital-adoption.com/employee-performance/

22. (Boshoff, & Arnolds, 1995). Boshoff, C., & Arnolds, C. (1995). Some antecedents of employee commitment and their influence on job performance. South African Journal of Business Management, 26 (4), 125-135.
23. (Strümpfer, Danana, Gouws, & Viviers, 1998). Boshoff, C., & Arnolds, C. (1995). Some antecedents of employee commitment and their influence on job performance. South African Journal of Business Management, 26 (4), 125-135.
24. Spector, 2000) Boshoff, C., & Arnolds, C. (1995). Some antecedents of employee commitment and their influence on job performance. South African Journal of Business Management, 26 (4), 125-135.
25. (Amponsah-Tawiah, & Darteh-Baah, 2010). Boshoff, C., & Arnolds, C. (1995). Some antecedents of employee commitment and their influence on job performance. South African Journal of Business Management, 26 (4), 125-135.
26. (Armstrong, 2010). Boshoff, C., & Arnolds, C. (1995). Some antecedents of employee commitment and their influence on job performance. South African Journal of Business Management, 26 (4), 125-135.
27. Wilson (2010) Wilson, G. (2010). The effects of external rewards on intrinsic motivation. Available at: http://www.abcbodybuilding.com/rewards.pdf
28. (Sarah, Nik, & Pranav, 2012). Sarah, Y., Nik, K., Pranav, K., (2012) Factors Affecting Employee Satisfaction among Nonteaching Staff in Higher Educational Institutions in Malaysia. American Journal of Economics, Special issue, 93-96.
29. Carless (2004) Sarah, Y., Nik, K., Pranav, K., (2012) Factors Affecting Employee Satisfaction among Nonteaching Staff in Higher Educational Institutions in Malaysia. American Journal of Economics, Special issue, 93-96.
30. Cheryl (1999), Sarah, Y., Nik, K., Pranav, K., (2012) Factors Affecting Employee Satisfaction among Nonteaching Staff in Higher Educational Institutions in Malaysia. American Journal of Economics, Special issue, 93-96.
31. (Michailova, 2002) Sarah, Y., Nik, K., Pranav, K., (2012) Factors Affecting Employee Satisfaction among Nonteaching Staff in Higher Educational Institutions in Malaysia. American Journal of Economics, Special issue, 93-96.
32. Ampofo-Boateng, Merican, & Wiegan, 1997). Ampofo-Boateng, K., Merican, W.R.A., Jamil, A., & Wiegand, B. (1997), Employees adaptation to technological changes in a multinational corporation in Malaysia, innovation in

technology management – the key to global leadership. PICMET'97- Portland. International Conference on Management and Technology

33. Bartram and Casimir (2007) Ampofo-Boateng, K., Merican, W.R.A., Jamil, A., & Wiegand, B. (1997), Employees adaptation to technological changes in a multinational corporation in Malaysia, innovation in technology management – the key to global leadership. PICMET'97- Portland. International Conference on Management and Technology

34. Chen and Tjosvold (2006) Ampofo-Boateng, K., Merican, W.R.A., Jamil, A., & Wiegand, B. (1997), Employees adaptation to technological changes in a multinational corporation in Malaysia, innovation in technology management – the key to global leadership. PICMET'97- Portland. International Conference on Management and Technology

35. Dernovsek (2008), Ampofo-Boateng, K., Merican, W.R.A., Jamil, A., & Wiegand, B. (1997), Employees adaptation to technological changes in a multinational corporation in Malaysia, innovation in technology management – the key to global leadership. PICMET'97- Portland. International Conference on Management and Technology

36. **Robinson**, Perryman, and Hayday (2004) Robinson, D., Perryman, S., & Hayday, S. (2004). The Drivers of Employee Engagement Report 408, Institute for Employment Studies, UK.

37. (Robinson et al., 2004) Robinson, D., Perryman, S., & Hayday, S. (2004). The Drivers of Employee Engagement Report 408, Institute for Employment Studies, UK.

38. (Baumruk, & Gorman et al., 2006): Baumruk, R., & Gorman, B. (2006). Why managers are crucial to increasing engagement. Melcrum Publishing.

39. (Ekerman, 2006). Baumruk, R., & Gorman, B. (2006). Why managers are crucial to increasing engagement. Melcrum Publishing.

40. (Miller, Erickson, & Yust, 2001) Miller, N. G., Erickson, A., & Yust, B. L. (2001). Sense of place in the workplace: The relationship between personal objects and job satisfaction and motivation. Journal of Interior Design, 27(1), 35-44.

41. Herzberg (1986), Herzberg, F. (1986). One more time: How do you motivate employees? Harvard Business Review, 65(5), 433-448.

42. Harrison and Novak (2006) Harrison, L. L., & Novak, D. (2006). Evaluation of a gerontological nursing continuing education programme: Effect on nurses' knowledge and attitudes and on patients' perceptions and satisfaction. Journal of Advanced Nursing, 13(6), 684-692.
43. (Weil, & Woodall, 2005). Harrison, L. L., & Novak, D. (2006). Evaluation of a gerontological nursing continuing education programme: Effect on nurses' knowledge and attitudes and on patients' perceptions and satisfaction. Journal of Advanced Nursing, 13(6), 684-692.
44. Brill, Margulis, Konar, and Bosti (1984) Harrison, L. L., & Novak, D. (2006). Evaluation of a gerontological nursing continuing education programme: Effect on nurses' knowledge and attitudes and on patients' perceptions and satisfaction. Journal of Advanced Nursing, 13(6), 684-692.
45. Leaman (1995) Leaman, A. (1995). Dissatisfaction and office productivity. Journal of Facilities Management, 13(2), 3-19.
46. French (1975), French, J. R. (1975). A comparative look at stress and strain in policemen. New York: Elsevier.
47. (Ricardo, Amy, & Rohit, 2007). French, J. R. (1975). A comparative look at stress and strain in policemen. New York: Elsevier.
48. Amanda and Jonathan (2006), Amanda, G., & Jonathan, H. (2006). Defining a case of work-related stress. Health & Safety Executive Report (449). HSE Books.
49. DeCenzo and Robbins (1996) DeCenzo, D. A., & Robbins, S. P. (1996). Human resources management. New York: John Wiley & Sons, Inc.
50. (Page, 2008). Page, L. (2008). Do not show me the money? The growing popularity of non-monetary incentives in the workplace. American Journal of Economics, 93-96.
51. (Tosi, Mero, & Rizzo, 2000). Tosi, H.L., Mero, N.P., & Rizzo, J.R. (2000). Managing Organizational Behavior. Cambridge, Massachusetts: Blackwell.
52. (Bhattacharyya, 2007). Bhattacharyya, D.K. (2007). Human Resource Research Methods. New Delhi: Oxford University Press.
53. Shah and Shah (2010) Bhattacharyya, D.K. (2007). Human Resource Research Methods. New Delhi: Oxford University Press.
54. Palmer (2005) Palmer, B. (2005). Practical Advice for HR Professionals: Create individualized Motivation Strategies. Melcrum Publishing Ltd.

55. Hackman and Oldham (1980), Hackman, J.R., & Oldham, G.R. (1980). Work redesign. Readings, MA: Addison-Wesley
56. (Vredenburgh, & Brender, 1998). Vredenburgh, D., & Brender, Y. (1998). The Hierarchical Abuse of Power in Work Organizations. Journal of Business Ethics, 17(12), 1337-1347.
57. (Maslow, 1987). Maslow, A.H. (1987). Motivation and Personality, 3rd Ed. New York, NY: Harper & Row.
58. (Armstrong, 2010). Maslow, A.H. (1987). Motivation and Personality, 3rd Ed. New York, NY: Harper & Row.
59. (Fisher, 1980). Fisher, B. A. (1980). Small group decision making: Communication and the group process 2nd Ed. New York, NY: McGraw-Hill.
60. Cole (2002) Cole, G.A. (2002). Personnel and human resource management, 5th Ed. Continuum London: York Publishers.
61. (Zeynep, 2013). Zeynep, O. (2013). Managing emotions in the workplace: It's mediating effect on the relationship between organizational trust and occupational stress. International Business Research, 6, 81- 88.
62. (Aguinis, & Kraiger, 2009). Aguinis, H., & Kraiger, K. (2009). Benefits of training and development for individuals and teams, organizations, and society. Annual review of psychology, 60, 451-459.
63. Sutermeister, 1976). Sutermeister, R.A. (1976) People and Productivity, 3rd Ed, New York McGraw-Hill.
64. Wheelan (2010) Wheelan, S.A. (2010). Creating effective teams - A guide for members and leaders. Thousand Oaks, USA: Sage Publications.
65. Herzberg (1986) Herzberg, F. (1986). One more time: How do you motivate employees? Harvard Business Review, 65(5), 433-448.
66. Kress, Norris, Schoenholz, Elias, and Seigle (2004) Kress, J. S., Norris, J. A., Schoenholz, D. A., Elias, M. J., & Seigle, P. (2004). Bringing together educational standards and social and emotional learning: Making the case for educators. American Journal of Education, 111(1), 68-89.
67. Roca, Chiu, and Martinez (2006) Roca, J. C., Chiu, C. M., & Martínez, F. J. (2006). Understanding e-learning continuance intention: An extension of the

Technology Acceptance Model. International Journal of Human-Computer Studies, 64(8), 683-696.
68. (Wright, & Geroy, 2001). Wright, P. C., & Geroy, G. D. (2001). Human competency engineering and world class performance: a cross-cultural approach, Cross Cultural Management. An International Journal, 8(2), 25-46.
69. Becker, Randal, and Riegel (1995) Becker, T.E., Randal, D.M., & Riegel, C.D. (1995). The multidimensional view of commitment and theory of reasoned action: a comparative evaluation. Journal of Management, 21(4), 617-638.
70. (Fletcher, & Williams, 1996). Fletcher, C., & Williams, R. (1996). Performance management, job satisfaction and organizational commitment. British Journal of Management, 7(2), 169-179.
71. Martensen and Gronholdt (2001). Fletcher, C., & Williams, R. (1996). Performance management, job satisfaction and organizational commitment. British Journal of Management, 7(2), 169-179.
72. (Wu, & Norman, 2006) Wu, L., & Norman, I.J. (2006). An investigation of job satisfaction, organizational commitment and role conflict and ambiguity in a sample of Chinese undergraduate nursing students. Nurse Education Today, 26, 304-314.
73. Northouse (2007), Northouse, P. G. (2007). Leadership Theory and Practice, 7th Ed. London: Sage Publications.
74. (Armstrong, & Murlis, 2004) Armstrong, & Murlis, H. (2004). Reward management: A handbook of remuneration strategy and practice. 5th Ed. Kogan Page: London.
75. Carrell, Kuzmits, and Elbert (1989) Armstrong, & Murlis, H. (2004). Reward management: A handbook of remuneration strategy and practice. 5th Ed. Kogan Page: London.
76. (Ichniowski, Shaw, & Prennushi, 1997). Ichniowski, C., Shaw, K., & Prennushi, G. (1997). The effects of human resource management practices on productivity: a study of steel finishing lines. American Economic Review, 87(3), 291-313.
77. Caruth and Handlogten (2002), Caruth, D.L., & Handlogten, G.D. (2002). Compensating Sales Personnel. The American Salesman, 47(4), 6-15.

78. Costa and McCrae's (1992) Costa, P.T. & McCrae, R.R. (1992). Revised NEO Personality Inventory (NEO-PI-R) and NEO Five Factor Model (NEO-FFI) professional manual. Odessa, FL: Psychological Assessment Resources.
79. Hough, Eaton, Dunnette, Kamp, & McCloy, 1990) Hough, L.M., Eaton, N.K., Dunnette, M.D., Kamp, J.D., & McCloy, R.A. (1990). Criterion-related validities of personality constructs and the effect of response distortion on those validities. Journal of Applied Psychology, 75, 581-595.
80. Judge, Higgins, Thoresen, and Barrick (1999) Judge. T.A., Higgins, C.A., Thoresen, C.J., & Barrick, M.R. (1999). The big five personality traits, general mental ability, and career success across the life span. Personnel Psychology, 52, 621-652.
81. (Clark, & Watson, 1991). Clark, L.A., & Watson, D. (1991). General affective dispositions in physical and psychological health. In C.R. Snyder & D.R. Forsyth (Eds.) Handbook of social and clinical psychology: The health perspective. New York: Pergamon
82. Raudsepp, 1990 Raudsepp, E. (1990). Are you flexible enough to succeed? Manage, 42(90), 6-10.
83. Borman, White, Pulkos, and Oppler (1991) and Hough et al. (1990) Borman, W.C., White, L.A., Pulkos, E.D., & Oppler, S.H. (1991). Models of supervisor job performance ratings. Journal of Applied Psychology, 76, 863-872.
84. (Kotrba, Gillespie, Schmidt, Smerek, Ritchie, & Denison, 2012). Kotrba, L. M., Gillespie, M. A., Schmidt, A. M., Smerek, R. E., Ritchie, S. A., & Denison, D. R. (2012). Do consistent corporate cultures have better business performance? Exploring the interaction effects. Human Relations, 65(2), 241-262.
85. (McCourt, & Derek, 2003). Kotrba, L. M., Gillespie, M. A., Schmidt, A. M., Smerek, R. E., Ritchie, S. A., & Denison, D. R. (2012). Do consistent corporate cultures have better business performance? Exploring the interaction effects. Human Relations, 65(2), 241-262.

Chapter 2

Literature review

Anna Mokhniuk and Larysa Yushchyshyna (2018)[1] in their research paper titled **"The Impact of Monetary and Non-Monetary Factors of Motivation on Employee Productivity"** concluded as Our research, as described in this paper, sought to ascertain the elements that inspire various personnel groups and to investigate their effect on labour productivity. The findings indicate that a successful motivation system should incorporate a variety of rewards for various staff groups. The findings corroborate Maslow's (1954) theory of motivation by indicating that the top two elements employees value most are their base income and bonuses.

Thus, the base income plays a critical role in enhancing employee motivation. To begin, it satisfies fundamental human wants. Second, it serves as a barometer of one's profession's status and one's standing inside a corporation. Thirdly, it provides a backdrop for further motivational techniques. It is obvious that all nonmonetary motivational approaches appear to lose effectiveness unless they are complemented by enough cash remuneration. In other words, when employees are content with their compensation, they are far more sensitive to additional forms of stimulation such as recognition, flexible work hours, and autonomy. Regrettably, in Ukraine's current unfavorable business environment, numerous intangible motivating tactics are adopted in place of monetary incentives, primarily due to a scarcity of cash resources. Bonuses and profit-sharing arrangements are examples of secondary motivation approaches. They recognise and reward the efforts and accomplishments of individual employees.

There is a high chance that monetary incentives improve employee motivation and motivate employees to follow their superiors' orders. We believe that employees regard base pay and bonuses as a form of compensation and that they must compensate for this by enhancing their performance.

However, compensation and bonus considerations alone cannot achieve the long-term goals of promoting creativity and invention, or of developing foresight and the ability to make successful judgments in tough situations.

It is critical to note the major disparities in how different groups of employees perceived motivational elements. These variables have been ranked according to their significance to the influence, beginning with the most significant.

The following factors are advocated for top-level managers: involvement in decision-making, recognition, public appreciation, base pay, bonuses, competitive spirit, autonomy, flexible hours, profit sharing opportunities, public criticism, and on/off the job training.

Bonuses, recognition, profit sharing, autonomy, competitive spirit, basic salary, demanding work, flexible hours, participation in decision-making, job happiness, and the availability of free cell phones are all recommended motivator incentives for middle-level managers.

Low-level managers will benefit the most from bonuses, recognition, job satisfaction, autonomy, competitive spirit, flexible hours, on-the-job training, profit sharing, gym membership, demanding work, and a life insurance plan.

Pradorn Sureephong, Winai Dahlan, Suepphong Chernbumroong, and Yootthapong Tongpaeng[2] in their research paper titled "The Effect of Non-Monetary Rewards on Employee Performance in Massive Open Online Courses" concluded as this study described and illustrated the effect of several non-monetary rewards on employee performance (tangible, social, and job-related). This study enrolled ninety volunteer employees from a food manufacturing company in Chiang Mai, Thailand. Two field studies were done to assess staff motivation and performance. In field study 1, a questionnaire evaluating Valence, Instrumentality, and Expectancy was used to assess employee motivation for three distinct non-monetary reward categories. The results suggested that the group of non-monetary physical rewards had the greatest valence score.

Employees tended to value physical things more highly than social and job-related benefits. As a result, experts believe that individuals who receive physical non-monetary benefits are more motivated to participate in the online training programme. In field research 2, the same set of participants as in field study 1 was divided into three non-monetary reward groups and assigned to enroll in an online curriculum called

"HSC MOOC." Only those participants who met the prerequisites for MOOCs got incentives, which varied by group. The results suggested that about 63% of participants in the group receiving tangible non-monetary rewards completed the MOOC curriculum.

According to the researchers, physical rewards have a beneficial effect on participants' learning performance.

Ruth Kanini Bosire and Dr. James Muya(2019)[3] in their research paper titled "NON-MONETARY COMPENSATION PRACTICES AND EMPLOYEE OUTPUT: A CRITICAL REVIEW OF LITERATURE" focused on This research tried to establish some critical non-monetary remuneration practises and their impact on employee output. The research established through a review of the theoretical and empirical literature that non-monetary remuneration systems have a direct effect on motivation levels and, eventually, on productivity. Various organisations have implemented a variety of non-monetary remuneration techniques, including medical plans, work-hour flexibility, staff training, and employee recognition and development opportunities. The study argues that in order for a business to excel in terms of quality and quantity of production, as well as retention of competent individuals, it is critical that they implement non-monetary pay strategies to boost employee morale and demonstrate appreciation. Finally, the report advises that governments, Labour unions, and regulatory agencies responsible for salaries and remunerations enact rules that encourage firms to use non-monetary pay to drive employees to perform better.

Tavonga Gilson Gudo[4] in his paper titled "An analysis on the impact of non monetary incentives on employee performance" concluded as Due to the diversity of inferences that may be drawn from the findings of this study, the conclusion of the research study on the impact of non-monetary incentives on employee performance at TelOne can be summarized as follows:

1. TelOne, the postal and telecommunications firm, operates a functional nonmonetary incentive structure. The findings indicate that the Institution has a functional non-monetary incentive structure that is well understood by its personnel. According to research findings, the existence of a functional non-monetary incentive system contributes significantly to improving employee performance, as evidenced by

TelOne's sustained profitability growth over the years, which the researcher attributes to the non-monetary incentive strategy among a variety of other strategies.

2. Employees assert that non-monetary incentives have had a significant impact on their performance at work, both positively and negatively, depending on the incentive's use. Non-monetary incentives like as career progression opportunities, on-the-job training, promotion, paid time off, vacation, job stability, good communication, work rotation, health care, and goal setting and rewards have all had a favourable effect on employee performance. According to the data, this has resulted in personnel exhibiting increased performance in order to accomplish their assigned tasks. However, it is the unethical and unfair employment practices based on nepotism that have had a detrimental effect on employee performance. The awarding of these non-monetary incentives based on management's personal preferences has hindered efforts to reform the system, as employees are demotivated to perform better as a result of the injustice.

TelOne standards for providing non-monetary rewards should be predicated on transparency, fairness and merit, nepotism and favoritism should not play a crucial part in this regard. Thus, their use must be continuously managed to ensure that they have a beneficial effect on staff performance.

3. TelOne has used non-monetary incentives such as career growth opportunities, on-the-job training, promotion, paid time off, vacation, job stability, effective communication, work rotation, health care, and goal setting and rewards. These non-monetary incentives have been well received by employees and, according to research findings, have contributed to increased employee performance. The most popular initiatives identified in the report were the payment of dependents' school tuition, health care, and subsidising telephone expenses. These initiatives have increased employee loyalty, which has a positive effect on their performance.

4. That there is a positive linear link between employee performance and non-monetary incentives that must be maintained. There is a significant linear association between employee performance and non-monetary relationships. To be effective, managers must have a working knowledge of the linear relationship between employee performance and non-monetary incentives, as well as motivation and the various motivational theories that attempt to explain motivation. According to the study's findings, when employees are assured non-monetary rewards, they work at their maximum ability.

5. The existing economic environment precludes the use of non-monetary incentives, as institutions struggle to allocate money for motivation in such an economy. According to the study's findings, some institutions have eliminated non-monetary incentives from their strategies in response to the present economic climate, which has seen the majority of businesses running on shoestring budgets and earning the barest of profits. Due to the existing state of the economy, it is impossible to apply nonmonetary incentives. While non-monetary incentives may have a beneficial effect on employee performance, the current economic climate makes their employment nearly impossible.

In light of the foregoing conclusions drawn from the investigation, one can confidently conclude that the research issues addressed by the study were adequately addressed. The conclusions achieved do, in fact, fully address the research issues.

ErajesvariePillay and Dr.Shamila Singh[5] in their research paper "The Impact of employee engagement on organisational performance – a case of an Insurance Brokerage company in Gauteng" concluded as The purpose of this study was to determine the effect of employee engagement on the performance of a short-term insurance brokerage. Employee engagement does have an effect on organisational performance, as evidenced by both the literature and the study conducted. Second, communications, work design, incentives and rewards, leadership, employee involvement, culture, and career development have all been highlighted as critical elements in employee engagement. The study's shortcomings include the fact that it was done in a single organisation and was not equally representative of both genders due to the organization's two male employees. Second, while purposive sampling is meant to identify participants with extensive knowledge and expertise in the topic area, the researcher was unable to determine which employees were more informed about employee engagement due to the sample size being insufficient. In light of this study, additional research in the short-term industry is needed to acquire a better knowledge of the impact of employee engagement on organisational success.

Zafar, Marium and Karim, Emadul and Abbas, Omair(April 2017)[6] in their paper "Factors of Workplace Environment that Affects Employee Performance in an Organization": A study on Greenwich University of Karachi concluded as For enterprises, employee performance is a critical aspect in their success, as it enables them to stay ahead of the competition, accomplish their objectives, and make profits.

The goal of this study was to examine the many elements that influence employee performance at Greenwich University in Karachi. Multiple Linear Regression was used to test the hypothesis, which was done using the SPSS software. Leadership, training and development, and stress had the most impact on the performance of Greenwich University staff, indicating that these independent variables had the greatest effect on the dependent variable.

Saharuddin1 , Sulaiman (Oct 2016)[7] The Effect Of Promotion And Compensation Toward Working Productivity Through Job Satisfaction And Working Motivation Of Employees, In The Department Of Water And Mineral Resources Energy North Aceh District concluded as The findings of this study can be interpreted in practice as indicating that variable compensation, promotion, and job satisfaction all have an effect on employee productivity, either directly or indirectly. This demonstrates the critical role of promotion and remuneration as fringe benefits in an organization's continual improvement of productivity, as well as the need of providing capacity building and growth to employees. Career stagnation (no promotion) results in sloth and unhappiness; also, the salary earned by employees does not match their performance, posing a danger of employee dissatisfaction, which results in decreasing work productivity. On the other hand, promotion and compensation serve as a magnet for capable and qualified employees within the organisation, encouraging employees to remain motivated and qualified to remain loyal, ensure fairness, control costs, adhere to the rule of law, improve efficiency and effectiveness, and maintain and/or increase employee productivity.

Daniel Njoya Ndungu(2017)[8] The Effects of Rewards and Recognition on Employee Performance in Public Educational Institutions: A Case of Kenyatta University, Kenya focused on The findings of this study reveal that employees at Kenyatta University are less motivated by money and recognition rewards, and that variables only contribute slightly to job performance improvement. This indicates that if Kenyatta University's management places a greater emphasis on reward and recognition, it may have a favourable effect on university workers, resulting in increased job performance.

The findings, however, may be unique to Kenyatta University and may not be generalizable to other universities in Kenya.

Nonetheless, Kenyatta University's administration may use the research findings to evaluate its current incentive and recognition programmes. This will be especially effective if the focus is on the requirements of all employees, regardless of their working status: whether casual, permanent, contract, or any other. According to the research, cash and recognition awards had the lowest mean values. This demonstrates that employees are less motivated by money benefits and frequently overlook aspects of acknowledgment. On the other hand, when the work atmosphere is conducive, employees are nice, they are compensated fairly for their efforts, their jobs are secure, and they have opportunities to advance within Kenyatta University, their motivation remains high.

Employees at Kenya University regard prizes and recognition for their efforts as a means of motivating them to continue working for the institution. This demonstrates that employees desire recognition for their efforts in order to be motivated to repeat the behaviour that results in increased performance levels. The study's findings indicated that few personnel had worked for the institution for an extended period of time, implying that Kenyatta University has a high rate of staff attrition. The majority of staff had spent less than five years at the organisation. According to respondents, awards and recognition should be based on objective performance criteria that are seen to be fair. Low-level employees, the majority of whom were casual workers, saw disparities in wage, benefits, and other characteristics as demotivating. Lack of communication was also identified as a significant impediment to respondents' motivation, which impacted performance. It is therefore essential to communicate incentives and recognition in a timely manner and with appropriate ceremony to ensure that staff are prepared and motivated.

Iqbal N, Anwar S and Haider N[9], Effect of Leadership Style on Employee Performance explored on According to Myron Rush and Cole, participatory leadership has a more beneficial effect on employee performance when employees feel empowered and confident in their ability to execute their jobs and make alternative judgments. And in an autocratic approach, leaders have the right to make decisions that make employees feel inferior in their ability to do tasks and make decisions. Employees in a democratic style have some discretionary authority over their work, which results in higher performance than in an autocratic style.

- The authoritative tone is suitable.

- When new employees are unfamiliar with their duties and lack appropriate knowledge about them
- If an employee abuses their authority on a consistent basis
- When employees breach business policies
- When a single individual is accountable for decision-making and implementation
- Appropriate consultative style
- When a business need innovative issue solving
- When an organisation has planning meetings to improve a department's operations
- When a company prepares individuals for leadership responsibilities
- When you want competent and effective completion of routine organisational chores
- It is appropriate to use a participative style.
- When an organization's team members are skilled and talented
- When a corporation or department has meetings to discuss ways to improve
- When a business has evaluation sessions
- When encouraging an organization's top performers
- When you require inventive and imaginative work.

ASAMU Festus Femi(Aug. 2014)[10], "The Impact of Communication on Workers' Performance in Selected Organisations in Lagos State" concluded as According to the study's findings, good communication fosters mutual understanding between management and employees, resulting in the development of true relationships between both sides within businesses. Additionally, this study demonstrates that poor communication might have a negative effect on worker performance. As a result, firms should communicate their policies, aims, and objectives to their employees on a frequent basis in order to boost job performance. That is, communication is the process through which the task and resources required to complete an assignment, the roles and responsibilities, and the expected results are communicated to subordinates, making work easier and resulting in improved performance. Additionally, managers must contact with employees on a frequent basis to solicit feedback and make suggestions for future task assignments; this will help enhance employee performance and organisational productivity. Additionally, top managers should interact directly with their direct reports on critical concerns. Organizations should remove communication barriers and establish efficient, participatory, and transparent communication channels to increase employee commitment.

Parkash Vir Khatri* and Jyoti Behl (June 2013)[11], "IMPACT OF WORK-LIFE BALANCE ON PERFORMANCE OF EMPLOYEES IN THE ORGANISATIONS" elaborated on To end, this article has shed some light on staff perceptions of work-life balance. Additionally, it recommended several areas for improvement and policies enabling flexible work arrangements for further development. Employees want their employers to be sympathetic to their demands by providing a work-life balance approach. It has the potential to sway employees' employment decisions. From a company perspective, it makes sense to promote a work-life balance approach not just to recruit and retain people, but also because employees believe that a work-life balance strategy enables them to work more effectively.

Miss Somrudee Somsa-ard Mr. Tosaporn Mahamud (May 2016)[12], "MOTIVATION FACTORS AFFECTING EMPLOYEES' PERFORMANCE: A CASE STUDY OF TGT CONSTRUCTION PARTNERSHIP LIMITED" focused on Motivating elements: The study's findings indicate that job achievement factors are consistent with Kamolrat Bamrungsri's (2012) observation that the majority of operational level employees work well with colleagues. On the basis of career progression, the study findings were consistent with those of Kamolrat Bamrungsri (2012), namely that the majority of operational level personnel receive organisation assistance for skill development. In terms of responsibility, the research findings parallel those of Theeranand Phanit (2012), who discovered a high level of significance for the responsibility aspect.

Supporting Factors: In terms of interpersonal relationships, the research findings corroborate those of Kamolrat Bamrungsri (2012), who discovered that the majority of employees were satisfied with their coworkers. In terms of work security, the research produced a similar outcome to Theeranand Phanit's (2012) study, namely that job security was of moderate relevance. The study's findings are consistent with those of Kamolrat Bamrungsri (2012), who recommended maintaining a clean work environment. In terms of compensation and fringe benefits, the findings are consistent with those of Kamolrat Bamrungsri (2012), who discovered that the majority of employees require an annual health examination, annual leave, and a salary commensurate with their job.

The data on work motivation elements reveal a high overall mean, beginning with job performance, career advancement, work environment, compensation and fringe benefits, interpersonal relationships, responsibility, and job security.

Employees require confidence in the company, security, as well as appreciation and respect from the organisation, according to data gathered through interviews. Annual or quarterly seminars should be organized to educate staff about the organization's policies.

Dr. KIRAN KUMAR THOTI, G.N.SRINIVAS CHAKRI and B. PAVANI[13] " A STUDY ON EFFECTIVE TRAINING PROGRAMMES IN AUTO MOBILE INDUSTRY" concluded as the purpose of this study is to determine the efficiency of a training programme offered by DAESUNG AUTO PARTS INDIA PVT.LTD. From the in-depth analysis of the study's data. The effectiveness of the training programme is demonstrated by a considerable improvement in the employees' knowledge and skill levels as a result of continuous and periodic evaluation of training needs and subsequent trainings.

Several recommendations have been made based on the study's findings for further improving the effectiveness of trainings. If these are adopted, the employee's contribution to job performance will be significant, which will benefit both the organisation and the individual.

R. Anitha and Dr. M. Ashok Kumar (August 2016) [14]**, "THE IMPACT OF TRAINING ON EMPLOYEE PERFORMANCE IN PRIVATE INSURANCE SECTOR, COIMBATORE DISTRICT"** concluded as Human resource refers to the workforce, which affects organisations and must be managed for the organization's welfare. Their needs and growth should be addressed specifically by management. Employees will be productive and devoted to their jobs only if they have the necessary inputs, whether they are machines, materials, or skill sets. Training is a tool that enhances the skill sets and knowledge of employees, hence increasing the organization's productivity and profitability. This study examined the effect of training on employee performance in the private insurance sector in the Coimbatore district using a sample of 75 respondents. The survey was conducted through questionnaire. The data were examined using the t-test and Chi-square.

The findings indicate that good training boosts employee performance. The efficiency of the training should be enhanced by properly arranging it on a regular basis, selecting qualified trainers, and adopting the most effective training methods. Both new hires and existing personnel should receive training. Their feedback should be sought, and their performance should be evaluated following the training programme, in order to improve the training's effectiveness. Additionally, it assesses employee performance following training.

Norida Abdullah, Olurotimi A. Shonubi, Rahman Hashim, and ,Norhidayu Hamid, (Sept 2016) [15]**, "Recognition and Appreciation and its Psychological Effect on Job Satisfaction and Performance in a Malaysia IT Company: Systematic Review"** focused to investigate and assess employees' perceptions of recognition and appreciation, as well as to determine the most effective ways favoured by employees in TM Melaka-Malaysian firms. The purpose of this study was to determine whether the findings could serve as guidelines for developing an appropriate reward and recognition system for information technology organisations in general, as well as literature for future researchers, particularly those interested in employee intrinsic motivational factors.

Subha Imtiaz* & Shakil Ahmad(2009)[16]**," Impact Of Stress On Employee Productivity, Performance And Turnover; An Important Managerial Issue"** elaborated on According to the survey results, the overarching population in the study's universe suffers from a lack of span of control over the work environment, low acceptance for the work performed, rigid organisational structure, high unpredictability in job patterns, departmental variation in administrator support, insufficient monetary reward, and personal gratification. And the significant perspective was that employers; indeed, the entire organisational management is not responding to these factors, and the Punjab government's financial reforms are not being implemented.

Long-term consequences can be devastating, lowering the already deplorable state of government hospitals; however, private organisations provided a better environment, but employees expressed increased desperation due to a lack of field exposure, jeopardizing their career development; this area can be further researched. The management hospital must implement quick adjustments to maximize the value of their assets.

These findings illustrate the overall conduct of managers and administrators, as well as the rationale for their concern about low staff performance and high employee stress. Effective management must be practiced by managers, or else the potential of efficient personnel would be squandered, posing a serious danger to organisational goals and diminishing overall performance.

Counseling is an undiscovered method of stress management that can be used in conjunction with monetary, non-monetary, and structural reforms by management to successfully manage stress and retain high-performing employees by reducing turnover and discontent.

ALKHALIEL ADEEB ABDULLAH and HOOI LAI WAN (Dec 2013) [17], "Relationships of Non-Monetary Incentives, Job Satisfaction and Employee Job Performance" concluded as The study addresses the link between independent and dependent variables philosophically. Numerous studies have explored the relationship empirically, and as demonstrated in the paper's research, non-monetary incentives and job satisfaction have a direct effect on employee job performance. Non-monetary incentives, on the other hand, were expected to have a favourable effect on job satisfaction as well. Three propositions were recommended for testing in the study. In practical terms, examining these links would aid in supplementing methods of enhancing employee job performance.

J., Anitha(Nov 2014) [18], "Determinants of employee engagement and their impact on employee performance" concluded as While all of the listed characteristics were proven to be predictors of employee engagement, the variables with the greatest impact were the working environment and team and coworker relationships. Employee involvement was found to have a considerable effect on employee performance. Practical implications Dedicated attention and effort are required to the elements working environment and team and coworker relationships, since they have been found to have a substantially greater impact on employee engagement and thus employee performance. Organizations should prioritise creating a positive work environment for their employees and promoting programmers who foster peer relationships. Social implications. The drivers of employee engagement imply a positive work environment that reflects the organization's social effect. Employees would receive significant attention in terms of the determinants under consideration. The research demonstrates the growing importance and necessity of crystallizing the concept of employee engagement. The research is unusual in that it develops and validates a full model.

SUDHAMSETTI NAVEEN1 , PRASADARAO YENUGULA(May 2-17)[19], "The Impact of Monetary and Non-Monetary Incentives on Performance of Employees: A Research Study on Beverage Industry, A.P, In India", concluded as According to the study's findings, it can be concluded that the organization's level of nonmonetary incentive application is appropriate, based on employee perceptions in the beverage industry. It may be recognised that this organisation benefited significantly from nonmonetary incentives in motivating staff. As mentioned in the expectation theory of motivation, the employees' incentive practices also have a role in determining the level of motivation. Some employees are dissatisfied with their wages in general, which is reflected in their first rating of a fulfilling wage as a critical element contributing to their job competence. In terms of incentive preferences, it appears as though monetary incentives take precedence over nonmonetary rewards. However, this does not mean that non-monetary incentives will have no effect on employees. According to the answers analysis, employees regard nonmonetary incentives highly, even in the absence of monetary incentives.

Among non-monetary incentives, job-related non-monetary incentives are favored since they are most likely to improve employees' interest in their jobs. This could imply that the majority of employees in the business value meaningful work with increased responsibility, variety of tasks and opportunities to apply a variety of talents, autonomy over one's job, participation in decision-making, and advancement, among other things.

Himanshu Kushwaha in his research paper[20] "IMPACT OF FINANCIAL AND NON-FINANCIAL INCENTIVES ON EMPLOYEE PRODUCTIVITY" concluded as On the basis of the examined literature, it is possible to conclude that incentives and productivity are positively related. The majority of employees are pleased with their monetary compensation. While financial incentives have been shown to have a significant impact on employee productivity, the importance of non-monetary incentives cannot be underestimated, as employees also want acknowledgment and recognition for their work. Motivated employees are more committed to their jobs and are less inclined to leave the company.

The study concludes that a financial incentive for increased productivity and profitability should be increased. Other non-monetary motivations, such as growth opportunities and a higher quality of work life, should also be considered. Businesses should employ both financial and non-financial incentives to accomplish organisational and individual goals. Employee input should be sought while developing incentive policies. Additionally, the research suggests that the corporation establish a distinct entity to address pay package difficulties.

Olake, Oni, Babalola, and Ojelabi (2017)[21] investigated the effect of incentive compensation packages on employee productivity in Nigerian real estate enterprises. To ascertain which firms use incentive packages, a panel survey approach was used. They discovered a high correlation between employee incentives and productivity. Additionally, they said that a sizable proportion of employees are dissatisfied with the incentives supplied by the bulk of real estate organisations. Incentives packages alone are not sufficient to predict performance in real estate enterprises. They found that real estate corporations should reintroduce incentive programmes to boost potential employees' productivity. Additionally, the opinion of employees should be sought regarding incentive programmes.

Khan, Waqas, and Muneer (2017)[22] conducted a study on the effect of intrinsic and extrinsic rewards on employee job performance. Employees' perspectives and experiences were gathered via questionnaire, and data analysis was performed using SPSS. The study's target demographic was courier company employees, and respondents were recruited via stratified convenient sampling. The study examined both inner and extrinsic motivations. They noted that these benefits have a significant impact on employees' personalities and inspire them to be loyal and perform better. Additionally, they indicated that there is a clear positive correlation between these types of awards and employee performance.

Achie and Kurah (2016)[23] conducted a study on employees of Nigerian electricity distribution businesses to determine the effect of non-monetary factors as a motivator for employee productivity. The population size was set at 65, and 45 staff members were randomly picked as a sample. The data collected via questionnaires demonstrated that financial incentives have a significant impact on staff productivity and can be used to gain an advantage over competitors, as they result in increased productivity and overall profitability for the organisation. Additionally, they indicated that in addition to financial incentives and compensation, other factors influence employee productivity, enabling them to perform at their best for the organisation. They advised that financial incentives should be raised in addition to other motivational variables in order to boost productivity and profitability.

Ravi (2015)[24] claimed in his study that in order to achieve organisational performance and strong employee morale, management should build a sound employee incentive structure. A well-designed incentive programme results in job satisfaction. He continued by stating that entrepreneurs in the manufacturing industry must provide both monetary and non-monetary incentives to their employees in order to raise their morale and productivity, which will ultimately increase the firm's total profitability. He concluded that both monetary and nonmonetary incentives, as well as a better work-life balance, should be provided to employees in order to increase productivity.

Yousaf, Latif, Aslam, and Siddiqui (2014)[25] listed a variety of financial and non-financial incentives that influence an employee's motivational level in their article. They discussed not only the relevance of incentives, but also the importance of retaining them within the organisation. The survey was conducted using a qualitative research methodology. To elicit employees' perspectives on motivation, a questionnaire and semi-structured interview were employed. They discovered that various elements contribute to employee motivation, which may be classified as financial and non-financial incentives. While financial incentives are critical for developing countries with high living costs, one cannot ignore the role of non-monetary incentives. Salary, bonus, health insurance, and fringe benefits were identified as financial motivators, whereas appreciation and recognition were identified as non-financial motivators. Money was placed first among the many motivating elements by the researchers because it enables employees to meet their basic necessities. Non-monetary incentives are also critical for staff morale improvement. They found that the organisation should consider a variety of incentive-related concerns and place equal emphasis on monetary and non-monetary components of motivation in order to retain and motivate personnel.

Safiullah (2014)[26] did a study to ascertain the relationship between extrinsic and intrinsic rewards, as well as their impact on employee performance and motivation. To accomplish their purpose, data was analyzed using mean values and percentage tables of frequency. Their study revealed that when people advance in their professional paths, salary levels, and ages, intrinsic incentives become a more significant motivator. Additionally, they discovered that employees must be driven by the aspects that contribute to the job's substance. It is critical to link employee success to compensation, as money is a powerful motivator.

Ahiabor (2013)[27] did research on the effect of incentives on employee productivity in Ghanaian enterprises. To collect data, an objective-based questionnaire was created. The data was analyzed and processed using basic percentage and frequency calculations. According to the study, there is a favourable correlation between rewards and production. Additional than monetary incentives, other factors should be considered while attempting to increase productivity and achieve organisational effectiveness. He also concluded that non-monetary variables such as recognition, respect, appreciation, health, and equipment use trump monetary incentives. He advocated the establishment of a new entity to address concerns relating to productivity incentives. The purpose of such a unit would be to encourage, monitor, and raise employee morale inside the organisation. Additionally, this unit will perform a study on employee welfare, the results of which will be used to create a more effective incentive scheme. The business should constantly seek out bright people to recognise, as this serves as an incentive for others.

Sajuyigbe, Olaoye, and Adeyemi (2013)[28] conducted a study in Ibadan, Oyo State, Nigeria to determine the effect of encouragements on employee performance in manufacturing businesses. The study collected data from 100 employees using a structured questionnaire and a purposive sampling strategy. With the assistance of SPSS, data were analyzed using regression analysis. They determined that incentives have a considerable effect on employee performance. Additionally, they suggested that rewards such as recognition, appreciation, and bonuses should be used to inspire employees to enhance their performance. The study concluded that both management and staff should be worried about incentive programmes. They advocate that organisations use both inner and extrinsic incentives to inspire employees to attain individual and organisational goals. Management must tailor compensation programmes to the unique needs of each employee. Employees' compensation structures should be set in conjunction with them.

Reddy and Karim (2013)[29] did an empirical study to determine the effect of incentives on factors affecting employees' ability to meet their objectives. Employees were categorized into three categories: supervisory personnel, clerical personnel, and workers, and data were analyzed using the mean score and the z-test. Their study indicated that incentive programmes had a favourable effect on attendance, job loyalty, employee productivity, teamwork, rewarding efficient workers, and other performance-related characteristics. Additionally, they noted that as a result of incentives, employees frequently work extra, contributing to health problems. The overall analysis concluded that incentive programmes can be made more effective by providing incentives on a weekly rather than fortnightly basis and by basing them on the team's shift average production in order to promote teamwork.

Srivastava and Barmola (2011)[30] conducted a study to determine the relationship between employee motivating tactics and their commitment to increasing productivity. They did a conceptual investigation to provide a plausible explanation for how motivation results in increased productivity. They argued that an employee will perform well and be motivated only if they believe their work is meaningful and that they are accountable for the outcomes of the tasks allocated to them.

Dr.P.GURUSAMY and J. PRIYADHARSHINI (Jan 2019)[31] , **"ENHANCING THE IMPORTANCE OF NON-MONETARY APPRECIATION ON EMPLOYEES PERFORMANCE IN BANKING SECTOR"** concluded as Non-monetary incentives are efficient at rewarding employees for their efforts by providing additional opportunities for training, flexible work schedules, enhanced work environments, and sabbaticals. When deciding on incentives, companies must consider the recruits for whom the enticements are intended. Choosing a proper balance of non-monetary and monetary incentives is intended to result in a more acceptable curriculum that can address the diverse benefits and desires of human resources.

Though money is not the primary motivator. When fundamentals such as reasonable and adequate compensation are in place, the additional performance enhancement achieved through pecuniary incentives is negligible, and non-pecuniary incentives thus prove to be a superior stimulus. These may include "accomplishment, acknowledgment, the inherent character of the work, autonomy, and opportunities for growth and advancement." For instance, 3M and Google provide free time to their human resources departments in order to encourage employees to spend their office time on a particular project they are fanatical about pursuing.

Garba Bala Bello et al. (2017)[32], a study on the relationship between monetary rewards and teacher performance in a sample of public schools in Kano State, Nigeria. The study examined the relationship between monetary rewards and teacher performance in selected public schools in Kano state, Nigeria, using three categories of monetary reward: pay, allowances, and benefit. The study demonstrates that teachers prioritized allowances because they account for more volatility, particularly in teacher performance. Additionally, it concludes that monetary incentives have a considerable effect on teacher performance.

(2017) Md. Nurun Nabi[33] et al. A case study of the impact of motivation on employee performance at Karmasangsthan Bank Limited in Bangladesh demonstrates that for any business to work efficiently and without interruption, there must be positive relationships between employees and senior management, as well as among employees. Extrinsic motivation, job enrichment and performance appraisal, relationships and security, decision-making authority, and growth potential and prospects were also evaluated in the study. It concludes that when people are motivated positively, their performance improves. The researchers omitted to include the importance of the employee's motivation aspect, which is taken into account in the study.

Dr.Janes O Samuel's (2017)[34] study on the effect of employee motivation on the productivity of mining businesses in Tanazia's Geita Gold mine discovered that monetary motivation is used and is regarded as the primary employee motivator. It advocated placing a greater emphasis on staff motivation. One of the explanation's shortcomings is that it focused exclusively on monetary motive. It could have been more illustrative to widen the scope of the study to include non-monetary motivations rather than focusing just on monetary motivations. It concludes that the correct motivation of employees might result in increased output in mining firms.

Elumah Lucas O et al. (2016)[35] examined the impact of financial and moral incentives on organisational performance at Nigerian universities and discovered that adequate incentives are provided to staff, resulting in high organisational performance. The study suggests that employees prioritise money incentives over moral motives.

Hasan Salih Suliman Al-Qudah (2016)[36], on the impact of moral and material incentives on employee performance, demonstrates that while incentives provided to employees in hospitals are lacking, the study demonstrates that there is no difference in approach to moral and material incentives for employees to improve their performance based on variables such as gender, age, and educational qualifications. He concludes that the hospital should design a robust incentive programme.

According to Syeda Ayat-e-Zainab et al. (2016)[37], tangible incentives are benefits that have monetary worth for employees, such as bonuses, salary increases, and promotions.
Intangible incentives are prizes given in exchange for a certain achievement, such as respect, public recognition, lunches, and dinners. The data collected were analyzed using a statistical software for the social sciences (SPSS). The study concludes that both tangible and intangible incentives contribute to worker happiness. The researcher omitted to mention worker precedence.

Mary E. Davis and Medford (2016)[38] shown that piece rate systems are widely used to motivate people to be more productive on the workplace through a case study of the piece rate and health in the developing world. According to the study, piece rate payment is a more effective technique in poor countries than in rich countries. However, the analysis indicates that employees paid on a piece rate had poorer physical and emotional health. The findings might be more applicable if the explanation incorporated both the good and negative aspects of the piece rate system. The entire remark neglected to emphasise the piece rate's positive side.

Prakash Kumar Sen et al. (2016)[39] Employees are satisfied with the independence granted by management, and the majority of employees view performance appraisal as a motivator. The study concludes that employees prefer non-monetary compensation methods.

Belly Onanda (2015)[40] examines the effect of motivation on job performance at seven Kenya Commercial Bank branches located in Mombasa county. His research demonstrates that protection, interpersonal relationships, and a lack of fear and anxiety at work all contribute to the creation of an environment conducive to maximum performance. Additionally, it suggests that combining monetary rewards with intrinsic, self-actualization requirements may be the most effective employee motivator.

Ola Kvaloya and Anja Schottnerb's (2015)[41] study on motivators to motivate employees. It examines the scenarios in which monetary incentives and motivational efforts can be used in place of one another. Additionally, it demonstrates that motivating effort may exceed the degree of efficiency.

Kwesi Ampnash-Tawaiah and Elizabeth Boye kuranchie-menash (2015)[42] A comparative study of employee motivation and performance in Ghana's mining industry demonstrates that employee happiness results in improved performance. It concludes that while both extrinsic and intrinsic factors inspire employees, the emphasis is on compensation or recompense. They determined that competitive compensation is the most driving element for mining industry personnel.

Chukwuma Edwin Maduka and Dr. Obiefuna Okafor (2014)[43] discovered that workers are unmotivated, resulting in reduced production. The sample size is 400 employees, including management and junior employees. Additionally, the analysis revealed that the salary paid to junior staff was significantly less than the amount agreed upon by the Nigerian joint industry council. Financial incentives are preferred by junior personnel over non-monetary incentives. The main implication is that businesses must encourage employees in order to boost productivity and decrease employee turnover. However, the study did not discover why junior employees place a higher premium on financial incentives than on non-financial incentives. Additionally, the study is silent on the parameters employed for both financial and non-financial incentives.

According to Dr. Ashraf and Dr. Md. Shabieb (2014)[44], the function of incentives and reward systems in boosting employee performance for employees of Jordanian tourism and travel organisations is dependent on four factors: moral incentives, rewards, reward system efficiency, and promotions. They conclude that the greatest significant influence on employee performance is the rewards system, with promotion coming in last. Their study, however, was limited in scope due to the fact that they chose a sample size of 44 respondents.

Falola et al. (2014)[45] discovered that employees placed a high premium on the various incentives offered by their employer. This demonstrates that government personnel can perform better if their incentive package is enhanced. However, the survey falls short of determining which incentive package is most chosen by employees in the firm. It concludes that the more desirable the incentive system, the more favourable an employee's attitude about work will be.

Sarah Maslen and Andrew Hopkin (2014)[46], A qualitative study of manager motivation in hazardous industries" examines the extent to which current senior managers are driven by incentives. He finds that senior management and executive management select to evaluate performance and are compensated accordingly. If incentives are to remain a strategy for motivating financial and commercial performance, safety – particularly as it relates to major accident prevention – must also be rewarded.

Kongala Ramprasad (2013)[47] argues that some managers do not believe that effective motivation of workers results in high performance and achievement of the organization's goals, and thus suggests that understanding the critical importance of people in the organisation requires recognising that the human element and the organisation are inextricably linked. He stated that India's existing economic and Labour market conditions indicate that Labour supply exceeds demand. As a result, some managers assume that workers may be retained without being appropriately motivated, given the market's scarcity of jobs. However, the study's usefulness was limited because he did not identify sample size or industry. He concludes that motivation is one of the tactics for improving worker performance.

Pankaj Chaudhary (2012)[48], in his study on the Effects of Employee Motivation on Organizational Success, accurately states that motivation is critical for boosting employee job satisfaction, productivity, and organisational performance.

It is recommended that motivation will work if the proper person is assigned the right job; else, resources and time will be wasted. The researcher's conclusions might have been more useful had he ascertained the sorts of motivation used in the organisation. He concludes that the majority of respondents report having a positive relationship with their superiors.

Quratul-Ain Manzoor (2012)[49], Employee Motivation and Organizational Effectiveness: A Study. The researcher discovered that acknowledgment and empowerment are critical components of increasing employee motivation for organisational tasks. He concludes that corporate effectiveness and employee motivation are inextricably linked.

The impact of reward and recognition on job satisfaction and motivation was studied by **Rizwan Qaiser Danish and Ali Usman (2010)[50]**. They discovered a strong correlation between the various characteristics of job motivation and satisfaction. It demonstrates employee appreciation and engagement in decision-making, which motivates employees. Financial motivation, on the other hand, is the primary drive for employees in a firm.

Ian Kessler and Stephen Bach (2009)[51] conducted a study on the citizen-consumer as an industrial relations actor: new modes of Labour and the end-user in social care. The study demonstrates how the end-user becomes a critical actor in social care, particularly in employment relationships. Conclusions reached by social care organisations about the end user's role as an actor in Labour relations. To begin, just as unions and employers require differentiation in order to comprehend their industrial roles, end users do as well. The second type of end-user involvement is system- and context-dependent. Finally, the study concludes that the evidence is insufficient and warrants further investigation. Additionally, it finds that the end user will continue to be a critical factor in public service Labour relations.

K.k. Jain et al. (2007)[52], a case study of Indian oil and the effect of organisational climate and occupational stress on job satisfaction. The study's sample size is 158 management personnel of Indian oil corporation Ltd. The findings indicated that low-income managers are less satisfied than high-income managers, with the primary cause being monetary compensation. It is the primary motivational factor for employees. The manager's age has little effect on motivation or job satisfaction. The most significant finding is that employees' emotions and attitudes toward the organisation have a significant impact on performance.

R. D. Banker et al. (1996)[53] conducted a field study to determine the effect of a performance-based incentive strategy. The authors' analysis of data from 15 retail locations over 66 months demonstrates that when a strategy is executed, sales grow and staff performance also improves. The author made no attempt to ascertain the organization's overall performance.

H. Barum et al (1995)[54]. Study on incentives and provider payment techniques established that there is no single best strategy for compensating providers and that the acceptability of a given approach is context-dependent. They argue that in order to increase efficiency incentives, global budgets must be performance-based.

Iqbal N, Anwar S and Haider N[55] "Effect of Leadership Style on Employee Performance" elaborated as According to Myron Rush and Cole, participatory leadership has a more beneficial effect on employee performance when employees feel empowered and confident in their ability to execute their jobs and make alternative judgments. And in an autocratic approach, leaders have the right to make decisions that make employees feel inferior in their ability to do tasks and make decisions. Employees in a democratic style have some discretionary authority over their work, which results in higher performance than in an autocratic style.

- The authoritative tone is suitable.
- When new employees are unfamiliar with their duties and lack appropriate knowledge about them
- If an employee abuses their authority on a consistent basis
- When employees breach business policies

- When a single individual is accountable for decision-making and implementation
- Appropriate consultative style
- When a business need innovative issue solving
- When an organisation has planning meetings to improve a department's operations
- When a company prepares individuals for leadership responsibilities
- When you want competent and effective completion of routine organisational chores
- It is appropriate to use a participative style.
- When an organization's team members are skilled and talented
- When a corporation or department has meetings to discuss ways to improve
- When a business has evaluation sessions

Marium Zafar and Emadul Karim and Omair Abbas[56] in their research paper "Factors of Workplace Environment that Affects Employee Performance in anrganization": A study on Greenwich" concluded as For enterprises, employee performance is a critical aspect in their success, as it enables them to stay ahead of the competition, accomplish their objectives, and make profits. The goal of this study was to examine the many elements that influence employee performance at Greenwich University in Karachi. Multiple Linear Regression was used to test the hypothesis, which was done using the SPSS software. Leadership, training and development, and stress had the most impact on the performance of Greenwich University staff, indicating that these independent variables had the greatest effect on the dependent variable.

Hassan Hijry a , Asif Haleem b (2017)[57] in their research paper "Study the Factors That Influence Employees Performance in the Steel Factory, Saudi Arabia" focused on Six critical elements affecting employee performance at the SS Factory were found in the study. The qualities of an organization's structure are highly agreed upon by 70.98 percent of respondents, while those with a negative attitude are represented by 10.1 percent. Flexible, structure, innovation, social integration, and standard operating procedures were all variables. The second most important aspect was work atmosphere, with more than 66% strongly agreeing and agreeing, and less than 9%

having an unfavourable attitude. The total percentages for agreed and strongly agreed upon attitude traits

Over 60% agree, while 10% disagree. Around 70% of reward factors are strongly agreed upon or agreed upon, and those with a negative attitude account for more than 10%. Sixty-six percent of knowledge factor combined qualities are positive, while twelve percent are negative. Finally, 65 percent of skill factors are firmly agreed upon, and more than 15% are agreed upon for a negative opinion. The study established that organisational structure has an impact on employee performance.

Similarly, the work environment and employee attitudes have an effect on performance. Similarly, and salary have a substantial impact on employee performance. Additionally, employee performance based on knowledge.

The availability of opportunity to develop and use skills has an effect on employee performance.

Hassan M. E. Aboazoum, Umar Nimran and, Mochammad Al Musadieq (2015)[58], "Analysis Factors Affecting Employees Job Performance in Libya", explored The purpose of this study was to ascertain the elements that influence employee performance in Libya. To build the model for this research, an extensive review of the literature was undertaken. A questionnaire was used to evaluate the model. As a result, this study takes a quantitative approach. The study's findings indicate an inverse association between employee performance and corporate culture, job satisfaction, and training and development. Similarly, the findings indicate a negative correlation between employee performance and workplace stress. A series of recommendations has been produced in response to the study's findings. Libyan decision makers must be concerned with employee performance and create an environment in which people may enjoy their work and have a sense of belonging. Additionally, the company must promote the importance of teamwork. Pay and benefits are critical for employees, and as such, they must be based on their performance and contribution. Continuous motivation combined with a just and equitable work environment can help employees perform better and motivate them to repeat the desired behaviour. Additionally, decision makers must discuss with employees the training and development plan that will enable them to perform their jobs more effectively and eliminate any barriers that may contribute to a stressful work environment.

6Le Tran Thach Thao and Chiou-shu J. Hwang[59] , "FACTORS AFFECTING EMPLOYEE PERFORMANCE–EVIDENCE FROM PETROVIETNAM ENGINEERING CONSULTANCY J.S.C"

Employee performance is thought to be one of the most critical factors determining an organization's overall performance and success in today's competitive market. The primary objective of this thesis is to examine the factors affecting employee performance at PVE. The researcher arrived at the following general conclusions through the data analysis described in the preceding chapters:

To begin, there are three primary elements that influence employee performance at the case company – PVE. These factors include leadership, motivation, and training. The study established that a leader's style has an effect on employee performance.

Employees will undoubtedly perform better as a result of leadership coaching, empowerment, or more employee participation.

Motivating people to improve their performance is critical. Especially in the case of PVE, an organisation that places a premium on employees' education, knowledge, qualifications, abilities, and experience, the best employee performs best when they are motivated. The researcher emphasises the high correlation between training and employee performance in this study. Using the scenario of a company that provides technical consulting services to the oil and gas industry, training is a proven method for improving employee performance. In practise, training employees to approach new technologies and enhance their abilities in order to be certified for high-technical and worldwide projects has become a critical factor in strengthening the company's competitive edge and ensuring its long-term viability.

Second, the results of Chapter IV indicate that the three elements (leadership, motivation, and training) are interdependent. They have an effect on employee performance directly and indirectly. For instance, training is intended to serve as a non-monetary motivation by rewarding employees for their superior performance.

Leaders' coaching and empowerment assist in motivating their subordinates to perform better. Employees that receive on-the-job training from direct supervisors perform better and participate more actively in their jobs.

Heydy Jimenez, Toni Didona (2015)[60], "Perceived Job Security and its Effects on Job Performance: Unionized VS. NonUnionized Organizations" concluded as The findings of this study corroborated the predictions made in the original theory. Between work security perception and job performance, there is a statistically significant positive association. This suggests that the more secure an employee feels in his or her position, the higher the individual's performance will be. These findings may be beneficial for forecasting individual performance once employees are provided with an appropriate sense of job security. Additionally, unionized employees report feeling more comfortable than non-unionized employees, although this does not appear to be related to pay, as there is no pay differential between the two groups. Numerous limitations existed in the study. The researcher designed the instrument and it had not been validated for validity or reliability previously. Because this study used personnel from Miami International Airport as a convenience sample, no generalizations to the larger population can be made. The survey was originally intended to be posted on the airline's Facebook page, but owing to a shortage of time, approval from the airline was not obtained. As a result, contestants were asked to respond to the survey via text messages from the researcher and other participants. Data gathering was impeded by access restrictions and other time constraints. Although the study's conclusions cannot be generalized, they may provide important information for businesses. A business does not have to be unionized to provide job security. A competitive benefit package, a high probability of advancement, employee involvement in the provision and status of employment, and opportunities for personal growth and development can all contribute significantly to an employee's perception of job security, which can affect their overall performance. Additional research on the subject should be conducted.

Rashid Saeed, Shireen Mussawar, Rab Nawaz Lodhi, Anam Iqbal, Hafiza Hafsa Nayab and Somia Yaseen (2013)[61], "Factors Affecting the Performance of Employees at Work Place in the Banking Sector of Pakistan" concluded as the results of this study present a novel attempt at studying a clear yet disregarded link there is a favourable relationship between the manager's attitude and employees' performance in the Banking sector of Pakistan. The organisations with friendly manager's attitude have greater favourable impact on employees' performance. The results also reveal that there is a positive association between the Organization's culture and employees' performance in the Banking industry of Pakistan. The value of Cronbach Alpha is 0.79 which demonstrates that the association is substantial. There is a relationship between the Personal difficulties and employees' performance in the Banking sector of Pakistan which is further investigated by employing regression analysis. The major result demonstrates a between them. There is a positive association between There's no place like home? The contributions of the Job content and employees' performance in the job and nonwork creative support to Banking industry of Pakistan which is examined and confirmed by statistical analysis. With the help of substantial results of regression, it was proven that there is a positive your managers good coaches? association between financial awards and employees' performance in the Banking industry of Pakistan. Even MBA employment choices for the 21 Century. though the data indicate that the hypotheses tested offered substantial result and it is apparent that the full directed hypotheses are correct and gave favourable results. Furthermore, there is a margin to check the relationship learning on staff motivation in Greek small firms: the among independent factors like job content, Employees' Perspective. corporate culture, personal difficulties, manager's attitude and financial benefits of the corporation.

Shaju. M and Subhashini. D (2017)[62], "A study on the impact of Job Satisfaction on Job Performance of Employees working in Automobile Industry, Punjab, India" focused on Organizations frequently overlook the importance of job happiness in determining an employee's success. The purpose of this study is to demonstrate how multiple variables of job satisfaction are evaluated and then associated with job performance of employees in various groups within the Automobile industry. There is a substantial association between an employee's job satisfaction and performance in both the Supervisor and Worker groups within the Automobile Industry. Job satisfaction was shown to be higher among managers than among employees. Additionally, it reveals that individuals with more job experience are more satisfied with their jobs than those with less job experience in Punjab's Automobile Industry.

Because the primary purpose of this study is to determine the effect of respondents' job satisfaction on their performance level, it is discovered that the former has a greater influence on the latter in the supervisor group with higher ranks. Additionally, people with more job experience report a broader spectrum of job satisfaction than those with less experience. Additionally, the study will examine the relationship between job satisfaction indicators and respondents' performance evaluation findings. In this regard, employees who are more satisfied with their jobs have reported a higher performance evaluation score. Thus, increasing job happiness among an organization's employees would assist them improve their performance as well.

Eventually, the measures can be implemented to improve the organization's performance management system and can be integrated with these particular for future compliance. The purpose of this study is to educate enterprises about the importance of job satisfaction in relation to employee performance and how it can be exploited to achieve desired objectives. As a result, the findings of this study may be applied to various types of organisations.

Hamdan Rasheed Al-Jammal and Akif Lutfi Al-Khasawneh and Mohammad Hasan Hamadat(2015)[63], "The impact of the delegation of authority on employees' performance at great Irbid municipality: case study" concluded as At Great Irbid Municipality, there is a statistically significant effect of authority delegation on developing employee performance (GIM). Delegation fosters positive relationships between individuals who were formerly in the first rank. Final ranking for delegation's capacity to improve an employee's performance level.

At Great Irbid Municipality, there is a statistically significant effect of authority delegation on improving employee performance efficiency (GIM). The extent to which employees accepted overtime was ranked #1. The extent of delegating enhances the perspective from boss to final-ranked employee.

At the Great Irbid Municipality, there is a statistically significant effect of authority delegation on employee empowerment (GIM). The extent to which delegating eliminates central power in decision-making ensures that the firm is not hampered by the absence of the administrative leader ranked final.

Thevanes, N and Mangaleswaran. T (2018)[64], "Relationship between Work-Life Balance and Job Performance of Employees" concluded as The researcher examines the relationship between work-life balance and job success in Sri Lanka, one of the world's fastest growing economies. According to the study's empirical findings, work-life balance, as a critical component of human resource management, does have an effect on employee performance. Generally speaking, the better the work-life balance in a certain organisation, the better the job performance of its people. This study is significant since Sri Lanka has implemented a variety of work-life policies in recent years. Empirical findings should aid practitioners in comprehending how work-life balance affects job performance.

Dr. KIRAN KUMAR THOTI, G.N. SRINIVAS CHAKRI and B. PAVAN [65] "A STUDY ON EFFECTIVE TRAINING PROGRAMMES IN AUTO MOBILE INDUSTRY" concluded as the purpose of this study is to determine the efficiency of a training programme offered by DAESUNG AUTO PARTS INDIA PVT.LTD. From the in-depth analysis of the study's data. The effectiveness of the training programme is demonstrated by a considerable improvement in the employees' knowledge and skill levels as a result of continuous and periodic evaluation of training needs and subsequent trainings.

Several recommendations have been made based on the study's findings for further improving the effectiveness of trainings. If these are adopted, the employee's contribution to job performance will be significant, which will benefit both the organisation and the individual.

Research Gap:

LR GAP

Author	Paper Title	Literature review GAP/ Takeaway from the paper
Alfie Kohn	Why incentives plan do not work Year- 2003	The majority of managers believe that people will perform better if they are promised some sort of incentive. However, this type of incentive does not foster long-term commitment and only serves to motivate employees temporarily, which can have a negative effect on their productivity in the long run.

Harvard Business Review (2013) – case studies	Impact of Employee Engagement on Performance Harvard Business Review- Case Studies	Employee engagement helps businesses achieve key performance indicators such as greater customer satisfaction or market share. Engagement was a high priority for certain businesses since engaged employees perform more successfully and efficiently.
Marium (2017)	Factors of Workplace Environment that Affects Employee Performance in an Organization	Environmental factors do have an effect on employee performance, as more productive work cultures exist.
Dr.Shamila Singh	Impact of Employee Engagement on Performance	Employee engagement helps businesses achieve key performance indicators such as greater customer satisfaction or market share. Engagement was a high priority for certain businesses, as engaged staff perform more successfully and efficiently.
Mr.Marium Zafar	Factors of Workplace Environment that Affects	"Employee performance is affected by environmental

	Employee Performance in an Organization	influences, as positive work cultures are more productive. Employee performance is a critical aspect in an organization's success, since it enables it to stay ahead of the competition, accomplish its objectives, and make profits. The study's objective was to examine the numerous variables that influence employee performance. Multiple Linear Regression, done on the SPSS software, was used to test the hypothesis."
Miss. Somrudee Somsaard	Motivational factors affecting employees performance	The significance of aspects determining employee motivation was demonstrated by a high overall mean beginning with job performance, career advancement, work environment, remuneration and fringe benefits, interpersonal relationships, responsibility, and job security. The hypothesis test suggests that factors such as career

			advancement and responsibility have an effect on an employee's motivation to work. Additionally, researchers made the most effective use of Herzberg's two-factor theory, which encompasses motivational and hygienic theories.
Iqbal, Anwar Haider		Effect of Leadership Style on Employee Performance	When new employees are inexperienced with their jobs and lack adequate knowledge of them, the authoritative manner is suitable. If an employee abuses their authority on a regular basis When employees disobey the company's policies When a single individual is accountable for making and implementing decisions. When a company requires creative issue solution, a consultative style is acceptable. When an organization has meetings to discuss how to improve the department's operations,

		When an organization develops individuals for leadership positions When you require a high level of performance and efficiency in your organization's day-to-day operations When an organisation has competent and talented team members, a participatory style is appropriate. When a business or agency has meetings to discuss ways to improve When a business conducts audits When encouraging an organization's highest performers When inventive and imaginative work is required
Heydy Jimenez	Job security and its effect on job performance	There is an inverse relationship between job security perception and job performance. This indicates that the more secure an employee feels in his or her position, the higher his or her performance will be. These findings may be

		beneficial in forecasting individual performance once employees are provided with an appropriate sense of job security. Additionally, unionized employees report feeling more secure than nonunionized employees, although this does not appear to be related to compensation, as the two groups earn the same.
Saharuddin, Sulaiman	The Effect Of Promotion And Compensation Toward Working Productivity Through Job Satisfaction And Working Motivation Of Employees	Employee productivity is affected directly or indirectly by compensation, promotion, and job satisfaction. This demonstrates the critical role of promotion and remuneration as fringe benefits in an organization's continual improvement of productivity, as well as the need of providing capacity building and development for employees. Career stagnation (no promotion) results in

		sloth and dissatisfaction; also, the salary received by employees does not match their performance, posing a danger of employee dissatisfaction, which results in decreasing work productivity.
Festus Femi (Ph.D.)	Impact of Communication on employees performance	According to the study's findings, good communication fosters mutual understanding between management and employees, resulting in the development of true relationships between both sides within businesses. Additionally, this study demonstrates that poor communication might have a negative effect on worker performance. As a result, firms should communicate their policies, aims, and objectives to their employees on a frequent basis in order to boost job performance. That is, communication is the process through which

		the task and resources required to complete an assignment, the roles and responsibilities, and the expected results are communicated to subordinates, making work easier and resulting in improved performance. Additionally, managers must contact with employees on a frequent basis to solicit feedback and make suggestions for future task assignments; this will help enhance employee performance and organisational productivity. Additionally, top managers should interact directly with their direct reports on critical concerns. Organizations should remove communication barriers and establish an efficient, participatory, and transparent communication channel.
Daniel Njoya Ndungu	The Effects of Rewards and Recognition on	This study examined the notion of employee

| | | Employee Performance published by Global Journal of Management and Business Research: A Administration and Management | recognition and incentive programmes, as well as their effect on employee motivation and performance. Additionally, the contribution of these programmes to the overall achievement of organisational goals has been considered. The purpose of this study was to ascertain the influence of compensation and recognition on employee work performance. Additionally, using employee responses, the association between other performance-related elements (working environment and leadership styles) and performance was examined. The impacts of incentives and recognition on employee performance were investigated using a descriptive research methodology. The sample design consisted of stratified random |

		sampling and purposive random sampling. Attitudes, compensation, productivity, recognition, performance, and motivation are some of the terms used to describe these phenomena.
Parkash Vir Khatri, Jyoti Behl	IMPACT OF WORK-LIFE BALANCE ON PERFORMANCE OF EMPLOYEES IN THE ORGANISATIONS	To summarize, this article has presented some clear signs of employee attitudes about work-life balance. Additionally, it suggested several areas for improvement and policies enabling flexible work arrangements that may be expanded. Employees want their employers to demonstrate empathy for their needs by implementing a work-life balance strategy. It has the potential to impact employees' employment decisions. From an organisational standpoint, it makes sense to promote a work-life balance approach not just to attract and retain people, but also because employees believe that a

		work-life balance strategy enables them to work more effectively.
Rashmi Ranjan, Dr umesh Mishra	Impact of Rewards on Employee Performance: A Case of Indian Oil Corporation, Patna Region	It has been observed that many employees were dissatisfied with the company's monetary compensation. According to them, bonuses were not allocated equally among staff.
Norida Abdullah, Olurotimi A. Shonubi, Rahman Hashim, Norhidayu Hamid	Recognition and Appreciation and its Psychological Effect on Job Satisfaction and Performance in a Malaysia IT Company: Systematic Review	This study can serve as a guide for establishing an effective reward and recognition system, with a focus on intrinsic motivational elements of employees.
Anitha, Dr Ashok Kumar	A STUDY ON THE IMPACT OF TRAINING ON EMPLOYEE PERFORMANCE IN PRIVATE INSURANCE SECTOR, COIMBATORE DISTRICT	".Efficient training improves an employee's performance. Training effectiveness should be enhanced by maintaining a consistent schedule, selecting qualified trainers, and utilizing the most effective training tools. Coverage should be universal. Age, educational attainment,

		and professional experience all have an effect on an organization's performance. The return on investment (ROI) can be calculated by evaluating the organization's viability (future area of study)."
Zahid H Bhat	Impact of Training on Employee Performance: A Study of Retail Banking Sector in India	"Although training improves performance, it is not the single factor; rather, a number of factors contribute to this improvement. The leadership style has an effect on the training's effectiveness and impact. Subfactors such as TNI and training design also contribute to the effectiveness of training."
Dr Kiran Kumar Thoti, D N Srinivas Chakri, B Pavani	A STUDY ON EFFECTIVE TRAINING PROGRAMMES IN AUTO MOBILE INDUSTRY	The effectiveness of the training programme is demonstrated by a considerable improvement in the employees' knowledge and skill levels as a result of continuous and periodic evaluation of

		training needs and subsequent trainings.
Walid Al Salman, Zubair Hassan	Impact of Effective Teamwork on Employee Performance	Interpersonal skills and employee performance have a significant and beneficial association. Leadership has a beneficial effect on employee performance. Leadership is a critical component of the organization's design; leadership can be the deciding factor between failure and success.
Ashraf M. Attia, Earl D. Honeycutt Jr	Measuring Sales Training Effectiveness at the Behaviour and Results Levels using Self- and Supervisor Evaluations	This work presents novel and distinctive findings, and to the authors' knowledge, this is one of the few studies examining the impact of market orientation's internal and external subdimensions on performance in the local public sector. The outcomes of this study corroborate the recent emphasis on disaggregated approaches to the (internal and external) market

		orientation performance connection.
Marco Guerci, Marco Vinante	Perspective on Practice: Training Evaluation: An analysis of the stakeholders' Evaluation Needs	The emergent model's purpose is to give academics and practitioners with a new framework for consideration that is informed by both early and contemporary theories of engagement. The emergent model may serve as the foundation for new engagement development methods and structures, as well as provide fresh insight on how employees interpret their work-related engagement experiences. This is the first qualitative study on employee engagement in the human resource development literature, trailing only Kahn's original qualitative research.
Antonio Giangrco, Andrea Carugati,	Are We Doing the Right Thing ? A Food for thought on Training Evaluation and Its context	The primary findings of the literature assessment indicate that the Kirkpatrick model's principal objections,

		while rigorous, are irrelevant in today's postindustrial economy. Complexity, accuracy, and refinement are all issues that must be reconsidered in the current economic reality.
Antonio Sebastiano, Sheryl Kline, Kimberly Harris	ROI is MIA: Why are hoteliers failing to demand the ROI of Training	The study demonstrates the hotel industry's inconsistent approach to corporate spending and training tracking. It delves into hoteliers' inability to hold themselves accountable for staff development investments. Because this is an exploratory study, its findings cannot be extrapolated to the full population of human resources and training departments in the hotel business. This article examines motel managers' particular perspective on the topic of return on investment in training. There is scant study on this aspect of training's return on

		investment in the hotel business.
Ian Roffe	E-Learning Engagement, Enhancement and Execution	The course examines the practical and theoretical difficulties associated with evaluating, ensuring the quality of, and engaging with the operation of an elearning programme as a distance learning service for persons in employment on an international scale. The article discusses the experiences of delivering elearning in a case study at the University of Wales, Lampeter, which was modified from a pilot experiment to mainstream service. Suggestion that the current emphasis on the prefix "e" in educational applications should be shifted away from electronic and toward more supportive definitions of student participation, enhancement, and execution. Current quality assurance

		recommendations for elearning are discussed. Concludes with evidence from Lampeter's specific case of elearning offering and the program's primary results.
Jonathan Passmore, Maria Velez	A Training Evaluation Model for HR	The objective of this article is to conduct a critical analysis of existing models for evaluating organisational human resource (HR) interventions and to design a practical yet robust model for practitioners and researchers to use. According to the research, many existing models are either out of date or lack a practical emphasis. The SOAPM model provides five evaluation levels, four of which are appropriate for human resource professionals and one of which is appropriate for researchers.

Gordon Wills, Carol Oliver	Measuring The ROI from Management Action Learning	Too few management development programmes focus on the enterprise's hard return on investment. Describes how the focus on company-specific difficulties inherent in action learning makes this more viable. Reports on a four-year impact review of MBA programmes, demonstrating that employers benefited significantly and that individual managers benefited from a variety of soft benefits. The endemic issues of action learning are also discussed, but once again, the Set's contribution (fellow members of a small learning cell) is highlighted as the most critical.
Carool Hooi	Relationships of Non-Monetary Incentives, Job satisfaction & Employee Job Performance. Year-2013	The article explains the link between independent and dependent variables from a conceptual standpoint. Numerous empirical research have

			been conducted, and as demonstrated in the paper's literature, non-monetary incentives and job satisfaction have a direct effect on employee job performance. According to Errikson and Villeval, many people are swayed more by non-monetary considerations than by monetary ones. Satisfaction of higher and meta-needs
M.Moses, Rajendran, Kidanu Mulgeta		Effects of non-monetary benefits on Employees performance Year-2017	To gain a better understanding of the situation regarding the effects of non-monetary benefits, a sample of 150 employees was chosen and interviews with human resources were conducted using a variety of methods, including questionnaires, descriptive methods, correlation analysis, and regression analysis. The study's findings reveal that there are correlations between non-monetary

			perks and employee performance.
J.Anitha		Determinants of Employee Engagement and their impact on employee performance Year-2014	The research paper was written to gain a basic understanding of the impact of employee engagement on employee performance, the working environment, and team coworker relationships, all of which have been shown to have a significantly greater effect on employee engagement and thus employee performance. Organizations must prioritize creating a positive work environment for their employees and promoting programmes that foster peer relationships.
Alf Crossman, Bassem Abou-Zaki		Job Satisfaction and Job Performance of Lebanese Banking. Year-2003	The paper examines the findings of a study conducted on a Lebanese bank regarding the relationship between job happiness, individual job features, sociodemographic

		characteristics, and job performance in the banking sector. The findings demonstrate that job happiness is not mutually exclusive across all job dimensions and that pleasure with one may result in satisfaction with another. It was discovered that tenure increases self-reported work performance.
Subha Imtiaz & Shakil Ahmad	Impact of Stress on Employee Productivity, Performance & Turnover, An Important Managerial Issue. Year-2009	The review of how the organisation handles stress and the level of stress that is tolerated. Employees, without a doubt, are assisting in understanding because it affects the working environment, etc. This has an effect on job performance as well. Counseling is an unexplored option for stress management. Many employees express that their job is a significant cause of stress in their lives, however reducing workload, improving management

		and supervision, improving pay, perks, and vacation time can all help reduce employee stress. Management can be used in conjunction with monetary, non-monetary, and structural reforms to successfully manage employee stress and sustain high performance by minimizing staff turnover and unhappiness.
Martha Harunavamwe & Herbert kanengoni	The Impact of Monetary & Non-Monetary Rewards on Motivation among lower level Emloyees in selected Retail shops Year- October 2013	The research findings indicated that non-monetary benefits were prioritized by lower level employees in particular. These findings are consistent with Nelson's (2004) analysis of Herzberg's two-factor theory of motivation, which found that 78% of employees rated it as very or extremely important to be recognised by their managers for good work, but contradict popular perceptions. For example, in a widely publicized study, Gupta

		and her colleagues analyzed thirty-nine studies conducted over a five-year period.
Sudhamsetti Naveen, Prasadrao Yengula	The Impact of Monetary & Non-Monetary Incentives on Performance of Employees	"According to the study's findings, the level of non-monetary incentive use in businesses is adequate, based on employee attitudes in industry. It may be acknowledged that this firm benefited significantly from non-monetary incentives in motivating employees, as indicated in the expectation theory of motivation. Additionally, the employees' incentive practices are a factor in determining the motivational level. Certain employees are likewise concerned with determining their degree of motivation. Certain employees are dissatisfied with their salary in general, which is reflected in their incentive pay. According to the answers analysis, employees regard

		nonmonetary incentives highly, even in the absence of monetary incentives. Among non-monetary incentives, job-related non-monetary incentives are favored since they are most likely to improve employees' interest in their jobs. This could imply that the majority of employees in the firm value meaningful work with increased responsibility, variety of tasks and opportunities to apply a variety of talents, autonomy over one's job, participation in decision-making, and advancement, among other things."
Thevanes, N , Mangaleswaran.T	Relationship between Work-Life Balance and Job Performance of Employees	According to the study's empirical findings, work-life balance, as a critical component of human resource management, does have an effect on employee performance. Generally speaking, the better the work-life balance in a certain organisation, the better

		the job performance of its people. This study is significant since Sri Lanka has implemented a variety of work-life policies in recent years. Empirical findings should aid practitioners in comprehending how work-life balance affects job performance.
Hassan Hijry, Asif Haleem	Study the Factors That Influence Employees Performance in the Steel Factory, Saudi Arabia	Employee performance is influenced by three distinct factors: leadership, motivation, and training. The study established that a leader's style has an effect on employee performance. The three variables (leadership, motivation, and training) are interdependent. They have an effect on employee performance directly and indirectly.
Razi Afif Aqel	Identifying non-monetary factors that affect employee performance in the Palestinian telecommunications sector	"Their managers' excellent relationships and motivation do have a good effect on their performance. The office environment does have a

		favourable effect on its employees' performance. Recognizing employees' efforts has a huge positive effect on their performance. Training has a major detrimental effect on staff performance. Job rotation has been shown to boost employee performance."
Rashid Saeed, Shireen Mussawar, Rab Nawaz Lodhi, Anam Iqbal, Hafiza Hafsa Nayab and Somia Yaseen	Factors Affecting the Performance of Employees at Work Place in the Banking Sector of Pakistan	Businesses with a hospitable manager attitude have a greater favourable effect on staff performance. Additionally, the findings indicate that there is a positive correlation between an organization's culture and its employees' performance in Pakistan's banking sector. Cronbach Alpha equals 0.79, indicating that the link is significant.
Hassan M. E. Aboazoum, Umar Nimran, Mochammad Al Musadieq	Analysis Factors Affecting Employees Job Performance in Libya	The purpose of this study was to ascertain the elements that influence employee performance in Libya. To build the model for this research, an

		extensive review of the literature was undertaken. A questionnaire was used to evaluate the model. As a result, this study takes a quantitative approach. The study's findings indicate an inverse association between employee performance and corporate culture, job satisfaction, and training and development. Similarly, the findings indicate a negative correlation between employee performance and workplace stress.

Numerous studies have discovered a direct correlation between Non-Monetary Factors Affecting Employee Performance and employee performance. Numerous studies have established a direct association between non-monetary elements and job performance. Though excellent results and enhanced performance have been achieved in numerous institutions as a result of motivation, obstacles and similar Non-Monetary Factors continue to exist in critical areas. While the studies made significant contributions to various aspects of their countries and organisations, they were conducted in disparate geographical contexts and failed to address how non-monetary factors influenced employees' performance in the auto industry, resulting in a dearth of literature in the area. This is the research gap that the research seeks to fill by examining the relationship between nonmonetary incentive and employee performance in the automobile sector.

References:

1. Anna MokhniukLarysa Yushchyshyna (April 2018), The Impact of Monetary and Non-Monetary Factors of Motivation on Employee Productivity, Economic journal of Lesia Ukrainka Eastern European National University 13(1):94-101
2. Pradorn Sureephong, Winai Dahlan, Suepphong Chernbumroong, Yootthapong Tongpaeng (January 2020), The Effect of Non-Monetary Rewards on Employee Performance in Massive Open Online Courses, International Journal of Emerging Technologies in Learning (iJET) 15(01):88
3. Ruth Kanini Bosire , Dr. James Muya (April 2019), NON-MONETARY COMPENSATION PRACTICES AND EMPLOYEE OUTPUT: A CRITICAL REVIEW OF LITERATURE, International Journal of Social Sciences and Information Technology ISSN 2412-0294 Vol V Issue IV,
4. Tavonga Gilson Gudo- dissertation titled An analysis on the impact of non monetary incentives on employee performance.
5. Dr.Shamila Singh , Impact of Employee Engagement on Performance, IOSR Journal of Business and Management (IOSR-JBM) e-ISSN: 2278-487X, p-ISSN: 2319-7668. Volume 20, Issue 6. Ver. VII (June. 2018), PP 66-76
6. Zafar, Marium and Karim, Emadul and Abbas, Omair "Factors of Workplace Environment that Affects Employee Performance in an Organization": A study on Greenwich University of Karachi , 28 April 2017 Online at https://mpra.ub.uni-muenchen.de/78822/ MPRA Paper No. 78822, posted 28 Apr 2017 13:43 UTC
7. Saharuddin1 , Sulaiman (Oct 2016) The Effect Of Promotion And Compensation Toward Working Productivity Through Job Satisfaction And Working Motivation Of Employees In The Department Of Water And Mineral Resources Energy North Aceh District, International Journal of Business and Management Invention ISSN (Online): 2319 – 8028, ISSN (Print): 2319 – 801X www.ijbmi.org || Volume 5 Issue 10 || October. 2016 || PP—33-40
8. Daniel Njoya Ndungu(2017) The Effects of Rewards and Recognition on Employee Performance in Public Educational Institutions: A Case of Kenyatta University, Kenya , Global Journal of Management and Business Research: A Administration and Management Volume 17 Issue 1 Version 1.0 Year 2017

9. Iqbal N , Anwar S and Haider N ( ), Effect of Leadership Style on Employee Performance, Arabian Journal of Business and A Management Review Volume 5 • Issue 5 • ISSN: 2223-5833

10. ASAMU Festus Femi(Aug. 2014), The Impact of Communication on Workers' Performance in Selected Organisations in Lagos State, Nigeria, IOSR Journal Of Humanities And Social Science (IOSR-JHSS), Volume 19, Issue 8, Ver. II (Aug. 2014), PP 75-82, e-ISSN: 2279-0837, p-ISSN: 2279-0845.

11. Parkash Vir Khatri* and Jyoti Behl (June 2013), IMPACT OF WORK-LIFE BALANCE ON PERFORMANCE OF EMPLOYEES IN THE ORGANISATIONS , Global Journal of Business Management, Vol. 7, No. 1, June 2013

12. Miss Somrudee Somsa-ard Mr. Tosaporn Mahamud (May 2016), MOTIVATION FACTORS AFFECTING EMPLOYEES' PERFORMANCE: A CASE STUDY OF TGT CONSTRUCTION PARTNERSHIP LIMITED', Indian Journal of Commerce & Management Studies ISSN: 2249-0310 EISSN: 2229-5674 Volume VII Issue 2(1),

13. Dr. KIRAN KUMAR THOTI, G.N.SRINIVAS CHAKRI and B. PAVANI ( ), A STUDY ON EFFECTIVE TRAINING PROGRAMMES IN AUTO MOBILE INDUSTRY, BIMS International Journal of Social Science Research ISSN 2455-4839

14. R. Anitha and Dr. M. Ashok Kumar (August 2016) , THE IMPACT OF TRAINING ON EMPLOYEE PERFORMANCE IN PRIVATE INSURANCE SECTOR, COIMBATORE DISTRICT , ISSN: 2249-7196 IJMRR/August 2016/ Volume 6/Issue 8/Article No-10/1079-1089 International Journal of Management Research & Review

15. Norida Abdullah, Olurotimi A. Shonubi, Rahman Hashim, and ,Norhidayu Hamid, (Sept 2016), "Recognition and Appreciation and its Psychological Effect on Job Satisfaction and Performance in a Malaysia IT Company: Systematic Review", IOSR Journal Of Humanities And Social Science (IOSR-JHSS) Volume 21, Issue 9, Ver. 6 (Sep. 2016) PP 47-55 e-ISSN: 2279-0837, p-ISSN: 2279-0845.

16. Subha Imtiaz* & Shakil Ahmad(2009)," Impact Of Stress On Employee Productivity, Performance And Turnover; An Important Managerial Issue",

International Review of Business Research Papers,Vol. 5 No. 4 June 2009 Pp. 468-477

17. ALKHALIEL ADEEB ABDULLAH and HOOI LAI WAN (Dec 2013), "Relationships of Non-Monetary Incentives, Job Satisfaction and Employee Job Performance ", International Review of Management and Business Research , ISSN: 2306-9007 ,Vol. 2 Issue.4

18. J., Anitha(Nov 2014) , "Determinants of employee engagement and their impact on employee performance", International Journal of Productivity and Performance Management, Volume 63, Number 3, 2014, pp. 308-323(16)

19. SUDHAMSETTI NAVEEN1 , PRASADARAO YENUGULA(May 2-17), "The Impact of Monetary and Non-Monetary Incentives on Performance of Employees: A Research Study on Beverage Industry, A.P, In India", International Journal of Recent Trends in Engineering & Research (IJRTER) Volume 03, Issue 05; May - 2017 [ISSN: 2455-1457]

20. Himanshu Kushwaha, IMPACT OF FINANCIAL AND NON-FINANCIAL INCENTIVES ON EMPLOYEE PRODUCTIVITY,Review of Business and Technology Research, Vol. 15, No.1, August 2018, ISSN: 1941-9406 (Print), ISSN: 1941-9414 (CD) 20

21. O. C. Olake, A. S. Oni, D. O. Babalola &R. A.Ojelabi, "Incentive Package, Employee's Productivity and Performance of Real Estate Firms in Nigeria",European Scientific Journal, Vol.13,Issue.11, pp.246-260, 2017.

22. N. Khan, H.Waqas& R.Muneer, "Impact of Rewards (Intrinsic and extrinsic) on Employee Performance with Special Reference to Courier Companies of City Faisalabad, Pakistan", International Journal of Management Excellence, Vol.8, Issue.2, pp.937-945, 2017.

23. S. T.Achie&J. T.Kurah, "The Role of Financial Incentives as a Motivator in Employee's Productivity in Nigeria Electricity Distribution Companies", International Journal of Research in Business Studies and Management, Vol.3, Issue.1, pp.1-8,2016.

24. T. S. Ravi,"Impact of Labour Incentives on Productivity in Selected Chennai-Based Manufacturing Companies",Abhinav International Monthly Refereed Journal of Research in Management & Technology, Vol.4, Issue.2, pp.22-32, 2015. +

25. S.Yousaf, M.Latif, S.Aslam& A.Siddiqui, "Impact of Financial and non-Financial Rewards on Employee Motivation",Middle-East Journal of Scientific Research, Vol.21, Issue.10, pp.1776-1786, 2014.
26. A. B.Safiullah,"Impact of Rewards on Employee Motivation of the Telecommunication Industry of Bangladesh: An Empirical Study",Journal of Business and Management,Vol.16, Issue.12, pp.22-30, 2014.
27. G.Ahiabor, "The impact of Incentives on Productivity of Firms in Ghana: A Case Study of Ghana Airport Company Limited",Problems of Management in the 21stCentury,Vol.8, pp.6-1, 2013.
28. A. S. Sajuyigbe, B. O.Olaoye& M. A.Adeyemi, "Impact of Reward on Employees Performance in a Selected Manufacturing Companies in Ibadan, Oyo State, Nigeria',International Journal of Arts and Commerce, Vol.2, Issue.2, pp.27-32, 2013.
29. S. K. Reddy& S. Karim,"Impact of Incentive Schemes on Employee Performance: A Case Study of Singareni Collieries Company Limited, Kothagudem,Andhra Pradesh", India. Science, Technology and Arts Research Journal, Vol.2, Issue.4, pp.122-125, 2013.
30. S. K.Srivastava & K. C.Barmola, "Role of Motivation in Higher Productivity",Management Insight, Vol.7, Issue.1, pp.88-99, 2011.
31. Dr.P.GURUSAMY and J. PRIYADHARSHINI (Jan 2019) , "ENHANCING THE IMPORTANCE OF NON-MONETARY APPRECIATION ON EMPLOYEES PERFORMANCE IN BANKING SECTOR", RESEARCH EXPLORER-A Blind Review & Refereed Quarterly International Journal ISSN: 2250-1940 (P) 2349-1647 (O) Impact Factor: 3.655 (CIF), 2.78 (IRJIF), 2.62 (NAAS) Volume V, Issue 22 January - March 2019
32. Garba Bala.B, Abdu jaafaru. B, M.B. Jakada, K.S. Yakubu (September, 2017) 'Monetary Reward and Teacher Performance in Selected Public Secondary Schools in Kano State, Nigeria', The International Journal of Business and Management, Vol.5, Issue 9, ISSN 2321-8916.
33. Md. Nurun Nabi, Md.Monirul Islam, Tanvir Mahady Dip, and Md.Abdullah Al Hossain (march 2017) 'Impact of Motivation on Employee Performances: A Case Study of Karmasangsthan Bank Limited, Bangladesh', Arabian Journal of Business and Management Review, Vol.7,Issue 1, ISSN 2223-5833.

34. Dr. Jnanes O Samwel (2017), 'Role of Employee Motivation on the Production of Mining Companies in Geita Gold Mine, Tanzania', International Journal of Science and Research, Vol.6, Issue 11, ISSN 2319- 7064.
35. Elumah Lucas O,Ibrahim Olaniyi M and Shobayo Peter B (July, 2016) 'The Impact of Financial and Moral Incentives on Organizational 3 Performance: A Study of Nigerian Universities', Arabian Journal of Business and Management Review, Vol.6,Issue 5, ISSN 2223-5833.
36. Hasan Saliah Suliman Al-Qudah (October, 2016) 'Impact of Moral and Material Incentives on Employee's Performance; An Empirical Study in Private Hospitals at Capital Amman', International Business Research; Vol. 9, No. 11, E-ISSN 1913-9012.
37. Sayeda Ayat-e- Zainab Ali, M. Afridi, M. Shafi, H. Munawar, Sajid M. Alvi (October, 2016), 'Impact of Tangible and Intangible Incentives on Job Satisfaction Among Workers', International Journal of Management Excellence, Vol. 7, No.3, ISSN: 2292-1648.
38. Mary E. Davis, Medford (2016), 'Pay Matters: The Piece Rate and Health in the Developing World', Annals of Global Health, the Author. Published by Elsevier Inc. on behalf of Icahn School of Medical at Mount Sinai. Vol. 82, No.5, ISSN 2214-9996.
39. Er. Prakash Kumar Sen (2016), 'Study on Factor Affecting Motivation of Employees', international journal of advance research in science and engineering, Vol.No.5, Issue No.04. ISSN 2319-8354.

40. Belly Onanda (September 2015), 'The Effects of Motivation on Job Performance: A Case Study of KCB Coast Region', International Journal of Scientific and Research publications, Vol.5, Issue 9, ISSN 2250-3153.
41. Ola Kvaloya and Anja schottnerb (April, 2015), 'Incentives to Motivate', Journal of EconomicBehavior& Organization 116(2015)26-42, http://dx.doi.org/10.1016/j.jebo.2015.03.012. Published by Elsevier.
42. Elizabeth Boye kuranchie-menash and Kwesi Ampnash-Tawaiah (December, 2015), 'Employee motivation and work performance: A comparative study of mining companies in Ghana', Journal of industrial Engineering and Management- http://dx.doi.org/10.3926/jiem.1530, ISSN: 2013-0953.

43. Chukwuma Edwin maduka and Dr. obiefuna okafor (August,2014), 'Effect of Motivation on Employee Productivity: A study of manufacturing companies in Nnewi, International Journal of Management Studies and Research, Vol.2, Issue 7, ISSN 2349-0330.
44. Dr. Ashraf and Dr.Md.shabieb (April, 2014), 'The role of the incentives and reward system in enhancing employee's performance "A case of Jordanian tourism and travel institutions', International Journal of Academic Research in Business and Social Sciences, Vol.4, No.5, ISSN: 2222-6990.
45. Falola H.O, Ibidunni A.S, Olokundun M. (2014), 'Incentive packages and employees' attitude to work: A study of selected government parastatal in Ogun state, south-west, Nigeria', International Journal of Research in Business and Social Science, Vol.3, No.1, ISSN: 2147-4478.
46. Sarah maslen and Andrew Hopkin (July, 2014), 'Do incentives work? A qualitative study of managers' motivations in hazardous industries, School of sociology, college of Arts and Social Sciences, Haydon-Allen Bld (22),The Australian National University,Action,ACT0200.Safety Science, 70, 419-245.
47. kongala Ramprasad (April, 2013), 'Motivation and workforce performance in Indian industries', Research Journal of Management Sciences, Vol. 2(4), 25-29, ISSN 2319-1171.
48. Pankaj Chaudhary (September, 2102), 'Effects of Employees' Motivation on Organizational Performance- A Case Study', International Journal of Research in Economics & Social Sciences, Vol.2, Issue 9, ISSN: 2249-7382.

49. Quratul- Ain Manzoor (2012), 'Impact of Employees Motivation on Organizational Effectiveness', European Journal of Business and Management, Vol.3.No.3. ISSN 2222-1905.
50. Rizwan Qaiser Danish ans Ali Usman (2010), 'impact of reward and recognition on job satisfaction and motivation: an empirical study from Pakistan. International Journal of Business and Management, Vol.5, No.2.
51. Ian Kessler and Stephen Bach (March, 2011), 'The citizen-consumer as industrial relations actor: new ways of working and the end –user in social care', British Journal of Industrial Relations, pp. 80-102, ISSN 0007- 1080. Published by Blackwell Publishing Ltd.

52. K.k. Jain, Fauzia Jabeen, Vinita Mishra and Naveen Gupta (2007), 'Job satisfaction as related to organizational climate and occupational stress: A case study of Indian oil', international review of business research papers, Vol.3 No.5.pp. 193-208

53. Banker,R.D.,Lee,S.,& potter,G.(1996), 'A field study of the impact of a performance-based incentive plan', Journal of Accounting and Economics,21,195-226

54. H. Barum, J. Kutzin and H.Saxenian (1995), 'incentives and provider payment methods', International Journal of Health planning and management, Vol. 10, 23-45, ISSN: 1099-1751.

55. Iqbal N, Anwar S and Haider N(2015) "Effect of Leadership Style on Employee Performance" Arabian J Bus Manag Review ISSN: 2223-5833 AJBMR an open access journal vol. 5 issue 5

56. Marium Zafar and Emadul Karim and Omair Abbas in their research paper "Factors of Workplace Environment that Affects Employee Performance in anrganization": A study on Greenwich"Online at https://mpra.ub.uni-muenchen.de/78822/ MPRA Paper No. 78822, posted 28 April 2017

57. Hassan Hijry a , Asif Haleem b (2017_, "Study the Factors That Influence Employees Performance in the Steel Factory, Saudi Arabia" Proceedings of the 2017International Conference on Industrial Engineering and Operations Management Rabat, Morocco, April 11-13,2017 899

58. Hassan M. E. Aboazoum, Umar Nimran and , Mochammad Al Musadieq(2015), "Analysis Factors Affecting Employees Job Performance in Libya", IOSR Journal of Business and Management (IOSR-JBM) e-ISSN: 2278-487X, p-ISSN: 2319-7668. Volume 17, Issue 7.Ver. I (July 2015), PP 42-49,DOI: 10.9790/487X-17714249 www.iosrjournals.org

59. Le Tran Thach Thao and Chiou-shu J. Hwang ( ) "FACTORS AFFECTING EMPLOYEE PERFORMANCE–EVIDENCE FROM PETROVIETNAM ENGINEERING CONSULTANCY J.S.C"

60. Heydy Jimenez , Toni Didona (2015), "Perceived Job Security and its Effects on Job Performance: Unionized VS. NonUnionized Organizations" The International Journal of Social Sciences and Humanities Invention 4(8): 3761-

3767, 2017 DOI: 10.18535/ijsshi/v4i8.11 ICV 2015: 45.28 ISSN: 2349-2031 © 2017, THEIJSSHI

61. Rashid Saeed, Shireen Mussawar, Rab Nawaz Lodhi, ,Anam Iqbal, Hafiza Hafsa Nayab and Somia Yaseen (2013), "Factors Affecting the Performance of Employees at Work Place in the Banking Sector of Pakistan", Middle-East Journal of Scientific Research 17 (9): 1200-1208, 2013,ISSN 1990-9233© IDOSI Publications, 2013,DOI: 10.5829/idosi.mejsr.2013.17.09.12256

62. Shaju.M and Subhashini.D (2017), "A study on the impact of Job Satisfaction on Job Performance of Employees working in Automobile Industry, Punjab, India",Journal of Management Research ISSN 1941-899X 2017, Vol. 9, No. 1 117 www.macrothink.org/jmr

63. Hamdan Rasheed Al-Jammal and Akif Lutfi Al-Khasawneh and Mohammad Hasan Hamadat(2015), "The impact of the delegation of authority on employees' performance at great Irbid municipality: case study" International Journal of Human Resource Studies ,ISSN 2162-3058 ,2015, Vol. 5, No. 3 48 www.macrothink.org/ijhrs

64. Thevanes, N and Mangaleswaran.T (2018), "Relationship between Work-Life Balance and Job Performance of Employees", IOSR Journal of Business and Management (IOSR-JBM) e-ISSN: 2278-487X, p-ISSN: 2319-7668. Volume 20, Issue 5. Ver. I (May. 2018), PP 11-16 www.iosrjournals.org DOI: 10.9790/487X-2005011116

65. Dr. KIRAN KUMAR THOTI, G.N.SRINIVAS CHAKRI and B. PAVANI, "A STUDY ON EFFECTIVE TRAINING PROGRAMMES IN AUTO MOBILE INDUSTRY", BIMS International Journal of Social Science Research ISSN 2455-4839

Chapter 3

Research Methodology

1. Introduction

Research process forms an integral part of any research work. A systematic plan is not only necessary but also plays the role of a backbone in a research. Research is dynamic in nature. Its significance is justified in various fields like business, management, economics, math etc. Any study requires considerable attention towards the research methods that has to be applied by the researcher. The process includes defining research problem, review of literature, making assumptions or formulating hypotheses, data collection (primary & secondary), and analysis of data & drawing conclusions. The objective of this study is to make systematic usage of the research methods available in order to draw conclusion that is significant for the hospitality Industry in specific.

What is Research?

Definition: Research is characterized as cautious thought of study in regards to a specific concern or issue utilizing logical techniques. As per the American social scientist Earl Robert Babbie, research is a methodical request to depict, clarify, anticipate, and control the noticed peculiarity. It includes inductive and logical techniques.

Inductive examination techniques dissect a noticed occasion, while insightful strategies confirm the noticed occasion. Inductive methodologies are related with subjective examination, and rational strategies are all the more ordinarily connected with quantitative investigation.

Examination is led with a reason to:
- Distinguish potential and new clients
- Comprehend existing clients
- Put out practical objectives
- Foster useful market systems
- Address business challenges
- Set up a business extension plan
- Recognize new business openings
- What are the attributes of exploration?

Great exploration follows a precise way to deal with catch exact information. Analysts need to rehearse morals and an implicit rule while mentioning observable facts or making determinations.

The examination depends on sensible thinking and includes both inductive and insightful strategies. Continuous information and information is gotten from genuine perceptions in normal settings.

There is a top to bottom investigation of all information gathered so that there are no peculiarities related with it.

It makes a way for producing new inquiries. Existing information sets out more examination open doors.

It is scientific and utilizes every one of the accessible information so that there is no vagueness in derivation.

Exactness is one of the most basic parts of examination. The data should be exact and right. For instance, research facilities give a controlled climate to gather information. Precision is estimated in the instruments utilized, the adjustments of instruments or apparatuses, and the trials eventual outcome.

What are the Types & reason for research?

There are three primary purposes:

Exploratory: As the name recommends, analysts lead exploratory examinations to investigate a gathering of inquiries. The appropriate responses and examination may not offer an end to the apparent issue. It is attempted to deal with new pain points that haven't been investigated previously. This exploratory cycle establishes the framework for more definitive information assortment and examination.

Illustrative: It centers around growing information on recent concerns through a course of information assortment. Engaging exploration depict the conduct of an example populace. Just a single variable is needed to direct the review. The three main roles of enlightening investigations are portraying, clarifying, and approving the discoveries. For instance, a review directed to know whether high level administration pioneers in the 21st century have the ethical right to get a significant amount of cash from the organization benefit.

Informative: Causal or logical examination is led to comprehend the effect of explicit changes in existing standard techniques. Running investigations is the most well-known structure. For instance, a review that is directed to comprehend the impact of rebranding on client dependability.

Examination starts by posing the right inquiries and picking a fitting strategy to research the issue. Subsequent to gathering replies to your inquiries, you can investigate the discoveries or perceptions to make sensible determinations.

With regards to clients and market studies, the more intensive your inquiries, the better the examination. You get fundamental bits of knowledge into brand discernment and item needs by completely gathering client information through studies and surveys. You can utilize this information to settle on brilliant choices about your advertising systems to situate your business adequately.

To have the option to sort out your examination and get bits of knowledge quicker, it assists with utilizing an exploration store as a solitary wellspring of truth in your association and to deal with your exploration information in one incorporated archive.

Sorts of examination strategies and model

Examination techniques are extensively delegated Qualitative and Quantitative.
The two techniques have unmistakable properties and information assortment strategies.

Subjective techniques

Subjective examination is a technique that gathers information utilizing conversational strategies, typically open-finished inquiries. The reactions gathered are basically non-mathematical. This technique assists a specialist with getting what members think and why they think with a certain goal in mind.

Kinds of subjective techniques include:

Balanced Interview

Center Groups

Ethnographic examinations

Text Analysis

Contextual analysis

Quantitative techniques

Quantitative techniques manage numbers and quantifiable structures. It utilizes a precise method of researching occasions or information. It addresses inquiries to legitimize associations with quantifiable factors to either clarify, foresee, or control a peculiarity.

Kinds of quantitative strategies include:

Review research

Clear exploration

Correlational examination

Keep in mind, research is just important and valuable when it is legitimate, exact, and dependable. Inaccurate outcomes can prompt client stir and a diminishing in deals.

It is fundamental to guarantee that your information is:

Substantial established, legitimate, thorough, and fair-minded.

Exact liberated from mistakes and including required subtleties.

Solid others who explore similarly can deliver comparative outcomes.

Ideal current and gathered inside a fitting time period.

Complete incorporates every one of the information you want to help your business choices.

When to Use Qualitative Research

When to utilize subjective exploration

Subjective examination can help you

Foster theories for additional testing and for quantitative survey improvement,

Comprehend the sentiments, qualities, and insights that underlie and impact conduct

Distinguish client needs

Catch the language and symbolism clients use to depict and identify with an item, administration, brand, and so forth

Impression of advertising/correspondence messages

Data got in quantitative review and to all the more likely comprehend the specific situation/which means of the information

Create thoughts for upgrades and additionally augmentations of an item, line, or brand

Reveal expected vital headings for marking or interchanges programs

See how individuals see a showcasing message or correspondence piece

Foster boundaries (i.e., important inquiries, scope of reactions) for a quantitative report

Circumstances where subjective exploration is regularly utilized:

New item thought age and advancement

Examining current or possible item/administration/brand situating and advertising methodology

Qualities and shortcomings of items/brands

Understanding elements of procurement choice elements

Concentrating on responses to publicizing and advertising efforts, other showcasing interchanges, realistic character/marking, bundle plan, and so on

Investigating market fragments, for example, segment and client gatherings

Concentrating on feelings and mentalities on cultural and public undertakings issues

Surveying the ease of use of sites or other intelligent items or administrations

Understanding impression of an organization, brand, classification and item

Deciding customer language as a primer advance to foster a quantitative overview

Try not to anticipate that qualitative research should

Count, measure or deal factual approval

Decide the best item idea or value point; or build up the significance of explicit client needs or fulfillment standards

Sub for quantitative exploration due to time and additionally monetary limitations when quantitative assessment is basic.

Quantitative Research

Quantitative strategies accentuate objective estimations and the measurable, numerical, or mathematical investigation of information gathered through surveys, polls, and overviews, or by controlling prior factual information utilizing computational procedures. Quantitative examination centers around social event mathematical information and summing it up across gatherings of individuals or to clarify a specific peculiarity.

Qualities of Quantitative Research

Your objective in directing quantitative exploration study is to decide the connection between one thing [an autonomous variable] and another [a ward or result variable] inside a populace. Quantitative examination plans are either graphic [subjects normally estimated once] or exploratory [subjects estimated prior and then afterward a treatment]. An expressive report sets up just relationship between factors; a trial study builds up causality.

Quantitative exploration bargains in numbers, rationale, and a goal position. Quantitative exploration centers around numeric and constant information and nitty gritty, united thinking rather than unique thinking [i.e., the age of an assortment of thoughts regarding an examination issue in an unconstrained, free-streaming manner].

Its principle attributes are:

The information is typically accumulated utilizing organized examination instruments.

The outcomes depend on bigger example estimates that are illustrative of the populace.

The examination study can generally be recreated or rehashed, given its high dependability.

Scientist has an unmistakably characterized research question to which objective answers are looked for.

All parts of the review are painstakingly planned before information is gathered.

Information is as numbers and insights, frequently organized in tables, graphs, figures, or other non-text based structures.

Task can be utilized to sum up ideas all the more broadly, foresee future outcomes, or examine causal connections.

Specialist utilizes apparatuses, like surveys or PC programming, to gather mathematical information.

The general point of a quantitative exploration review is to arrange highlights, count them, and develop measurable models trying to clarify what is noticed.

Things to remember when revealing the aftereffects of a review utilizing quantitative strategies:

Clarify the information gathered and their measurable treatment just as all significant outcomes corresponding to the examination issue you are exploring. Understanding of results isn't suitable in this part.

Report unexpected occasions that happened during your information assortment. Clarify how the real examination contrasts from the arranged investigation. Clarify your treatment of missing information and why any missing information doesn't subvert the legitimacy of your examination.

Clarify the procedures you used to "clean" your informational index.

Pick an insignificantly adequate measurable system; give a reasoning to its utilization and a reference for it. Determine any PC programs utilized.

Portray the suppositions for every system and the means you took to guarantee that they were not disregarded.

When utilizing inferential insights, give the illustrative measurements, certainty spans, and test sizes for every factor just as the worth of the test measurement, its bearing, the levels of opportunity, and the importance level [report the real p value].

Try not to gather causality, especially in nonrandomized plans or minus any additional experimentation.

Use tables to give accurate qualities; use figures to pass on worldwide impacts. Keep figures little in size; incorporate realistic portrayals of certainty stretches sooner rather than later.

Continuously let the peruser know what to search for in tables and figures.

Essential Research Design for Quantitative Studies

Prior to planning a quantitative exploration study, you should conclude whether it will be illustrative or trial since this will direct how you accumulate, dissect, and decipher the outcomes. An elucidating study is represented by the accompanying standards:

subjects are by and large estimated once; the aim is to just set up relationship among factors; and, the review might incorporate an example populace of hundreds or thousands of subjects to guarantee that a legitimate gauge of a summed up connection between factors has been gotten. An exploratory plan incorporates subjects estimated prior and then afterward a specific treatment, the example populace might be tiny and intentionally picked, and it is expected to build up causality between factors.

Qualities of Using Quantitative Methods

Quantitative specialists attempt to perceive and detach explicit factors held inside the review system, look for connection, connections and causality, and endeavor to control the climate in which the information is gathered to stay away from the danger of factors, other than the one being contemplated, representing the connections distinguished.

Among the particular qualities of utilizing quantitative techniques to concentrate on sociology research issues.

Considers a more extensive review, including a more prominent number of subjects, and improving the speculation of the outcomes.

Takes into account more noteworthy objectivity and exactness of results. By and large, quantitative techniques are intended to give rundowns of information that help speculations about the peculiarity under study. To achieve this, quantitative examination ordinarily includes not many factors and many cases and utilizes endorsed strategies to guarantee legitimacy and dependability.

Applying grounded guidelines implies that the examination can be duplicated, and afterward broke down and contrasted and comparable investigations.

Constraints of Using Quantitative Methods

Quantitative strategies attempt to have a true way to deal with concentrating on research issues, where information is controlled and estimated, to address the amassing of realities, and to decide the reasons for conduct. As an outcome, the aftereffects of quantitative examination might be measurably critical however are frequently humanly irrelevant. Some particular limits related with utilizing quantitative techniques to concentrate on research issues in the sociologies include:

Quantitative information is more productive and ready to test theories, however may miss logical detail; Utilizations a static and unbending methodology thus utilizes a resolute course of revelation;

The advancement of standard inquiries by scientists can prompt "underlying inclination" and bogus portrayal, where the information really mirrors the perspective on the analyst rather than the taking an interest subject. Results give less detail on conduct, mentalities, and inspiration; Analyst might gather a much smaller and now and again shallow dataset.

Results are restricted as they give mathematical depictions rather than definite story and by and large give less intricate records of human insight.

The exploration is regularly done in an unnatural, fake climate with the goal that a degree of control can be applied to the activity. This degree of control may not typically be set up in reality hence yielding "lab results" rather than "true outcomes"; and, Preset answers won't really reflect how individuals truly feel about a subject and, sometimes, may very well be the nearest match to the biased speculation.

Different tools in Research - What is Regression Analysis?

Relapse examination is a bunch of factual techniques utilized for the assessment of connections between a reliant variable and at least one free factor. It very well may be used to survey the strength of the connection among factors and for displaying the future connection between them.

Relapse Analysis

Relapse investigation incorporates a few varieties, for example, straight, different direct, and nonlinear. The most widely recognized models are basic straight and different direct. Nonlinear relapse examination is normally utilized for more convoluted informational indexes in which the reliant and autonomous factors show a nonlinear relationship.

Relapse examination offers various applications in different disciplines, including finance.

Relapse Analysis Linear Model Assumptions

Straight relapse investigation depends on six basic suspicions:

The reliant and free factors show a direct connection between the slant and the catch.

The free factor isn't irregular.

The worth of the leftover (mistake) is zero.

The worth of the leftover (mistake) is steady across all perceptions.

The worth of the leftover (mistake) isn't corresponded across all perceptions.

The leftover (mistake) values follow the ordinary conveyance.

Relapse Analysis Simple Linear Regression

Basic straight relapse is a model that surveys the connection between a reliant variable and an autonomous variable. The straightforward direct model is communicated utilizing the accompanying condition:

$Y = a + bX +$

Where:

Y Dependent variable

X Independent (logical) variable

an Intercept

b Slope

Leftover (mistake)

Relapse Analysis Multiple Linear Regression

Different straight relapse examination is basically like the straightforward direct model, with the exemption that various autonomous factors are utilized in the model. The numerical portrayal of different straight relapse is:

$Y = a + bX_1 + cX_2 + dX_3 +$

Where:

Y Dependent variable

X_1, X_2, X_3 Independent (logical) factors

an Intercept

b, c, d Slopes

Leftover (mistake)

Numerous direct relapse follows similar conditions as the basic straight model. In any case, since there are a few free factors in numerous straight investigation, there is one more compulsory condition for the model:

Non-collinearity: Independent factors should show a base connection with one another. On the off chance that the autonomous factors are exceptionally connected with one another, it will be hard to survey the genuine connections between the reliant and free factors.

What is Analysis of Variance (ANOVA)?

Examination of difference (ANOVA) is an investigation apparatus utilized in measurements that parts a noticed total inconstancy found inside an informational index into two sections: methodical elements and arbitrary elements. The orderly factors impact the given informational collection, while the irregular elements don't. Examiners utilize the ANOVA test to decide the impact that free factors have on the reliant variable in a relapse review.

The t-and z-test strategies created in the twentieth century were utilized for measurable investigation until 1918, when Ronald Fisher made the examination of change method.12 ANOVA is additionally called the Fisher examination of fluctuation, and it is the augmentation of the t-and z-tests. The term turned out to be notable in 1925, in the wake of showing up in Fisher's book, "Measurable Methods for Research Workers."3 It was utilized in exploratory brain science and later extended to subjects that were more perplexing.

KEY TAKEAWAYS

Investigation of difference, or ANOVA, is a measurable strategy that isolates noticed fluctuation information into various parts to use for extra tests.

A single direction ANOVA is utilized for at least three gatherings of information, to acquire data about the connection between the reliant and autonomous factors.

In the event that no obvious fluctuation exists between the gatherings, the ANOVA's F-proportion should approach near 1.

What Is the Analysis of Variance (ANOVA)?

The Formula for ANOVA is:

\begin{aligned} &\text{F} = \frac{ \text{MST} }{ \text{MSE} } \\ &\textbf{where:} \\ &\text{F} = \text{ANOVA coefficient} \\ &\text{MST} = \text{Mean amount of squares due to treatment} \\ &\text{MSE} = \text{Mean amount of squares due to error} \\ \end{aligned}

F= MSE / MST

where:

F=ANOVA coefficient

MST=Mean amount of squares because of treatment

MSE=Mean amount of squares because of mistake

What Does the Analysis of Variance Reveal?

The ANOVA test is the underlying advance in breaking down factors that influence a given informational collection. When the test is done, an expert plays out extra testing on the deliberate elements that quantifiably add to the informational collection's irregularity. The examiner uses the ANOVA test brings about a f-test to create extra information that lines up with the proposed relapse models.

The ANOVA test permits a correlation of multiple gatherings simultaneously to decide if a relationship exists between them. The consequence of the ANOVA recipe, the F measurement (additionally called the F-proportion), takes into consideration the examination of numerous gatherings of information to decide the inconstancy among tests and inside examples.

On the off chance that no genuine contrast exists between the tried gatherings, which is known as the invalid theory, the aftereffect of the ANOVA's F-proportion measurement will be near 1. The conveyance of all potential upsides of the F measurement is the F-circulation. This is really a gathering of appropriation capacities, with two trademark numbers, called the numerator levels of opportunity and the denominator levels of opportunity.

Illustration of How to Use ANOVA

An analyst may, for instance, test understudies from various universities to check whether understudies from one of the schools reliably outflank understudies from different schools. In a business application, a R&D specialist may test two distinct cycles of making an item to check whether one interaction is superior to the next as far as cost proficiency.

The sort of ANOVA test utilized relies upon various variables. It is applied when information should be trial. Investigation of fluctuation is utilized in the event that there is no admittance to factual programming bringing about figuring ANOVA manually. It is easy to utilize and most appropriate for little examples. With numerous trial plans, the example sizes must be something very similar for the different element level mixes.

ANOVA is useful for testing at least three factors. It is like numerous two-example t-tests. Nonetheless, it brings about less kind I mistakes and is suitable for a scope of issues. ANOVA bunches contrasts by looking at the method for each gathering and incorporates fanning out the difference into different sources. It is utilized with subjects, test gatherings, among gatherings and inside gatherings.

Single direction ANOVA Versus Two-Way ANOVA

There are two principle kinds of ANOVA: single direction (or unidirectional) and two-way. There additionally varieties of ANOVA. For instance, MANOVA (multivariate ANOVA) varies from ANOVA as the previous tests for quite some time factors at the same time while the last option evaluates just a single ward variable at a time. Single direction or two-way alludes to the quantity of autonomous factors in your examination of fluctuation test. A single direction ANOVA assesses the effect of a sole component on a sole reaction variable. It decides if every one of the examples are something very similar. The single direction ANOVA is utilized to decide if there are any genuinely huge contrasts between the method for at least three free (irrelevant) gatherings.

A two-way ANOVA is an augmentation of the single direction ANOVA. With a single direction, you have one free factor influencing a reliant variable. With a two-way ANOVA, there are two free movers. For instance, a two-way ANOVA permits an organization to think about specialist usefulness dependent on two free factors, for example, compensation and range of abilities. It is used to notice the association between the two factors and tests the impact of two factors simultaneously.

2. Defining Research

Research in general terms is the search of the unknown. It is actually a movement from known to unknown. A well done research is a contribution by a researcher in the existing stock of knowledge to make it more advance & better. Research according to the Advance Learner's Dictionary of Current English can be defined as "a careful investigation or enquiry especially through search for new facts in any branch of knowledge". Prof. CR Kothari[1] views it as an academic activity & a systematic approach concerning generalization & the formulation of a theory. Research is thus a journey towards discovery. Clifford Woody define the term as "defining & redefining problems, formulating hypothesis or suggested solutions , collecting, organizing & evaluating data, making decisions & reaching conclusions. It is therefore, a systematic process that helps the researcher to pave a way towards improving & enhancing the existing knowledge in the area. Redman & Mory explain research as a systematized effort to gain new knowledge. It requires critical thinking for a researcher to carry out a search on any problem. According to Mr. Kumar[2] "research is one of the ways of collecting accurate, sound & reliable information about the effectiveness of your interventions, thereby providing you with evidence of its effectiveness. It is always important to follow an organized analysis about the subject area based on primary & secondary material with proper acknowledgement in the body of paper. Research is thus, to search again & again with an objective to find new that is unknown in the subject area. The research process includes defining research problem, formulating hypothesis, stating the research design, collecting facts & figures via secondary data, analyzing the data with the help of various statistical tools & reaching towards conclusions. Research is significant in business & management decision making as it helps in reaching a conclusion based on which proper decision can be taken. Research is the systematic process of collecting & analyzing information in order to increase our understanding of the phenomenon about which we are concerned or interested (Dr. S.L Gupta, 2011)[3]. Prof. Hitesh Gupta coined the term as "to re-search from available primary & secondary data into relevant information to form a substantial knowledge.

3. Research Process

The process of research includes a series of steps carried out by a research to reach the ultimate conclusion. The general steps to be followed by a researcher in any research work areas follow

1. Defining the research problem
2. Reviewing literature
3. Formulation of hypothesis
4. Development & implementation of a research plan
5. Data Collection
6. Analyzing data & testing of Hypothesis
7. Interpretation of data & reaching conclusions
8. Preparation of report & reporting the findings
9. The researcher in order to carry out this study had followed the systematic research process plan.

4. Need for the Study

Monetary & Non-Monetary factors both impacting performance of employees in an organization, but over a period as the employees matures, there is shift in impact of both the factors on performance of employee. Generally, it is evident that, for first 4-5 years, monetary factors play important role, but post a certain amount of experience to credit the Non-Monetary factors impact most to performance of an employee. Also, in constantly evolving and disruptive world, were organizations are under tremendous pressures to cut costs and have highly engaged and productive employees, it's very much imperative for them to find ways and means to derive high performance from employees using Non-Monetary Factors. The findings from this study will help organization with deeper insights on relationship between Non-Monetary factors and performance. Further engagement surveys conducted by different renowned consulting firms like Gallup, Mercer and Aon-Hewitt have stress upon evident importance of Non-Monetary factors affecting employee's performance.

5. Statement of the Research Problem

A study of Non-Monetary factors impacting employee's performance in selected automobile manufacturing industry"- Specifically to 4-wheeler manufacturing - Original Equipment manufacturers spreaded across the country predominantly in with the intent to understand impact of each Non-Monetary factor on employee's performance.

6. Objective of the Study

The objectives of the proposed study are:

5. Identify of Non- Monetary of Factors which impact performance in Automobile manufacturing industries.
6. To establish relationship between Non-Monetary factors and performance of employee.
7. To establish or rank non-monetary factors based on their positive impact on employee's performance.
8. Based on the finding of study, Creation of Model/structure to enhance performance of employees.

7. Research Hypothesis

Hypothesis will be drawn in the course of study - Multiple Hypothesis will be tested to establish correlation between various Non-Monetary factors and employee's performance in automobile industry.

H1: There is impact of non-monetary factors on performance of employee.

H2: There is positive impact of Leadership/Managerial factors on performance of employee.

H3: There is positive impact of Institutional factors on performance of employee.

H4: There is positive impact of Job Related factors on performance of employee.

H5: There is positive impact of Organisational Cultural factors on performance of employee.

H6: There is positive impact of Opportunity factors on performance of employee.

H7: There is positive impact of Motivational factors on performance of employee.

8. Research Methodology

A) Sampling Design:

The sample universe for this research will be Auto Manufacturing plant in like FIAT CHRYSLER, TATA Motors, Jeep, Mahindra & Mahindra, Skoda and VW. The sample will be collected using random sampling method. We will target samples (employees) with experience range from 5 years to 15 years, the reason being, in early stage of the careers mostly young professionals are behind monetary factors.

B) Sources and Methods of Collection of Data:

The applied methodology of the study is the use of the questionnaires. The participants are the employees that are employed by auto manufacturing OEMs. We will use online software's like survey monkey to collect the data. The participants are allowed to answer on the basis of their work nature. Participants will be classified on the basis of Experience, Gender, and Levels in Organization, Education and Location.

The researcher seeks to collect the data through primary as well as secondary sources.

i) Primary Data:

- Questionnaire: Online Format.

It will be collected through structured Questionnaire from 600 employees working with different auto manufacturing organizations.

ii) Secondary Data:

It will be gathered through the following sources:-

- Use of library-

Relevant data will be collected through books, journals etc.

- Use of Internet-

Internet will be extensively used to seek data from the websites like SHRM, Gallup, and Employee engagement agency sites.

- Published/ Unpublished data-

Journals regarding Employee performance and Organizational Development and HRM.

- Published and unpublished PhD thesis regarding Factors affecting Employee performance and Organizational Development.

C) Methods of Analysis and Statistical Tools:

Both Qualitative and Quantitative methods of analysis will be used by the researcher. Sophisticated statistical tools like SPSS and AMOS will be used for the analysis purpose.

Firstly, a pilot study will be conducted and then the questionnaire will be finalized.

Sample Size Calculation – Determination of Population size:

I have worked as HR in auto industry for more than 10 Years and during my association I have collected the data related to headcount in different auto OEM'S. the below table summarizes the staff working in different auto OEM's across india. This data has been collected by speaking to different employee working in the auto OEM's and is also validated by checking in against SIAM reference reports.

Table 1:Sample Size Calculation – determination of Population size

Company	Estimated White Collars
FIAT	450
TATA Motors	1400
Honda Cars	550
Mahindra & Mahindra	1400
Skoda	200
VW	500
Force Motors	300

Toyota	500
Mercedes Benz	400
Nissan/Renault	700
Hyundai / Kia	800
Maruti Suzuki	1400
Kohler Engineers	100
Hero Motors	600
Ford Sanand & Chennai	600
Total	**9900**

Population size is approx. 9900 employees working in different auto OEM's.

As per Morgan and Krejcie table the minimum acceptable sample size should be 370 sample

Using the calculations provided by Krejcie & Morgan in their "Determining Sample Size for Research Activities" the sample size for the population mentioned above shall be 384 at a Confidence interval 4.9, Confidence Level of 95% with Margin of Error 5%.

Sample duration: 6 months

Sampling procedure: Random Sample

Sample size determination :

S S using mean

$$\text{Sample size, } n = N * \frac{\frac{Z^2 * p * (1-p)}{e^2}}{[N - 1 + \frac{Z^2 * p * (1-p)}{e^2}]}$$

N = population size

• e = Margin of error (percentage in decimal form)

• z = z-score (from the table it is 1.96)

N= 342
E=0.05
Z=1.96
P=0.5

And considering confidence interval is 4.9

Sample size :

SS = (9900*(1.96^2)*0.5*(1-0.5)/(0.05^2)/(9900-1+((1.96^2)*0.5*(1-0.5)/(0.05^2))))

Sample is : 384

9. Scope of study
1. The research is restricted to selected Auto OEMs.
2. The research would comprise of inputs from employees above 5 years of experience to 15 years of experience.
3. Employees from Different levels of Management pyramid would be considered for this research.

10. Limitation of study
1. Performance is function of both the factors Monetary as well as Non-Monetary, this study is limited to Non-Monetary factors only.
2. Researcher will not consider fresher's or employees with experience less than 4 to 5 years, as for most them primary factors that affect performance are monetary.
3. Study findings may be limited to the data collection period.
4. During this study, data will be collected from respondents, which may be representation of particular time response at that point in time and may be the response from respondent may vary at other point in time.

References:
1. Prof. C. R Kothari, "Research Methodology Tools and Techniques, ISBN (13) : 978-81-224-2488-1, NEW AGE INTERNATIONAL (P) LIMITED, PUBLISHERS
2. Ranjit Kumar, RESEARCH METHODOLOGY a step-by-step guide for beginners, ISBN 978-1-84920-300-5, SAGE Publications Asia-Pacific Pte Ltd
3. Hitesh Gupta, S. L. Gupta , Research Methodology: Text and Cases with CPSS Applications 2nd Edition , Publisher: International Book House, ISBN: 9788191064278, 8191064278,Edition: 2nd Edition, 2011

Chapter 4

Data Analysis

Researcher has considered 6 factors to understand their impact on employee's performance. Below is the list of Factors and their subfactors considered for the study.

Table 2: Factors and sub factors considered for study

F1-Leadership / Managerial	F2 - Institutional	F3 - Job Related
Vision & Mission of Leader	Brand Image	Job Fit
Leadership Style	Reponsiblity	Clear Goals and Expectations
Coaching by Lead	Technology	Tools and Equipment / Resources
Camaradarie with Colleagues	Infrastructure	Work Life Balance
Relationship with Manager	Production Systems	Usage of Technology
Performance Pressure	Structure	Risk associated with Job
Empowement	Indian / MNC	Location of work
	Organisational Stability	Reputation/Status of the Job
	Market Position	Diversity in Job

F4 - Organisational Culture	F5-Opportunity	H-6 Motivation
Culture	Development Opportunities	Motivation
Communication	Career Path	Recognition
social learning	Growth Options	Job Enrichment
Ethics	Job Security	Job Satisfaction
Innovation	Diversity	Passion towards car
Discipline		Ability
Standardisation		Performance Appraisal Process
Reputation in eyes of Customer		

Figure 2: Factors and subfactors considered for study impacting employee's performance.

Normality of the data

Part A] Variables under consideration:

Variable1: Leadership / Managerial Factors

Leadership / Managerial Factors is comprised of the responses of all following questions together.

Leadership / Managerial Factors
I have clarity about my role from my leader and it excites me to give my best
Leadership Style of my manager affects me drastically
My leader makes decision based on my and my team members inputs
My Leader make decision without taking inputs from any of team member
My Leader doesn't take me review and gives me complete ownership of my results
My Leader has strategy in place to deal with uncertainties
My Leader puts me out of my comfort zone and always motivates me to do more
My Leaders give me Clears Roles and Responsibilities along with Timeline and KPIs.
My leader knows my strengths and Weakness and he guides me accordingly
My Leader doesn't not appreciate new and innovative ways of working
My Manager provides me with regular coaching/feedback
I Enjoy my camaraderie with my Colleagues
My Manager is supportive & I like interacting with him
Pressure with respective to performance affects me drastically
There is low pressure with respect to performance
There is Healthy pressure impacting my performance positively
There is Continuous Pressure impacting me drastically
There is empowerment with respect to my role

Variable2: Institutional Factors

Institutional Factors is comprised of the responses of all following questions together.

Institutional Factors
I feel proud to be associated with my organisation
I feel happy when I have entrusted with Responsibility
Technology impacts my performance positively

Infrastructure supports me a lot in my current role
It is my experience that Production systems plays a important role in increasing Productivity
Reporting / Org Structure affects my performance drastically
I prefer to work with MNCs
Organisational Stability Impacts me performance drastically
I feel proud about my organisations market position

Variable3: Job Related Factors

Job Related Factors is comprised of the responses of all following questions together.

Job Related Factors
I like my job if my skills my matching with offered role
Clear Goals & Expectations helps me in achieving my Targets
I feel Training provided helps me grow in the organisation
Tools and Equipment's help me improve my productivity
I take break from work , which rejunuvates me and helps me to improve my focus on work
Technology help me improve my productivity
I feel worried if I perceive risk in the job
Location of Work impacts my performance drastically
I like to work for reputed / Status focused jobs
I like to have diversity in my work

Variable4: Organisational Cultural Factors

Organisational Cultural Factors is comprised of the responses of all following questions together.

Organisational Cultural Factors
Organisational Culture affects me drastically
My Organisation friendly, Innovative, committed and provides me mentoring
My Organisation is Dynamic, Innovative, Transformational and Learning from mistakes
My Organisation is Agile and Flexible to meet customer & market demand
My Organisation is Structured, Stability oriented and Cost oriented

Communication affects my performance drastically
I feel low when I am just communicated to inform
I feel motivated when I am included/involved in the communication
I Learn from my colleagues and also enthusiastically share my learnings with them
I am proud to work with organisation of high ethics and repute
I believe Innovation is key towards organisational growth
My Discipline helps to improve organisations productivity
My Organisation has required level of standardization
I feel proud to work when customer are satisfied with our product

Variable5: Opportunity Factors

Opportunity Factors is comprised of the responses of all following questions together.

Opportunity Factors
I feel passionate to perform when I see development opportunities in my organisation
I feel motivate when my managers discuss career path with me
I feel motivated when in grow in the organisation
I feel worried if job security is a concern
Diversity in my team keeps me excited about my role

Variable6: Motivational Factors

Motivational Factors is comprised of the responses of all following questions together.

Motivational Factors
My Manager motivates me at my job/work
I feel good when my efforts are recognised
I feel motivated when additional responsibilities are entrusted upon me.
I give my best when I am satisfied with my Job
I Love Automobiles (Cars / Bikes / Auto)
My ability impacts my performance drastically
I feel satisfied when I performance appraisal process is fair and transparent

Variable7: Performance of Employee

Performance of Employee is comprised of the responses of all following questions together.

Performance of Employee
I am able to complete my targets
My Organisations management is happy with my work
I am able to complete my targets within the timeline
My manager is Happy with my work
I am recognised by my team mates for quality of my work
I am getting recognition I deserve
My Colleagues approach me for Challenges they face at work
I got the growth that I deserve in the organisation
I feel good to attend work

Part B] Normality Check

To verify the normality of the data set two statistical measures used are

1> **Skewness & Kurtosis**
2> **Histogram**
3> **P-P plots**

1> **Skewness & Kurtosis**

Table 3 : Skewness and Kurtosis of Data

Descriptive Statistics					
	N	Skewness		Kurtosis	
	Statistic	Statistic	Std. Error	Statistic	Std. Error
Leadership / Managerial Factor	416	-.222	.120	-.196	.239
Institutional Factor	416	-.643	.120	.383	.239
Job Related Factor	416	-.366	.120	-.019	.239
Organizational Cultural Factor	416	-.782	.120	.899	.239
Opportunity Factor	416	-.704	.120	.757	.239
Motivational Factor	416	-.738	.120	.537	.239

Performance of Employee	416	-.272	.120	.015	.239
Valid N (listwise)	416				

We can assume normality if skewness is in the range of -0.8 to 0.8 and kurtosis is in the range
of -3.0 to 3.0

Here all skewness & kurtosis values are within the range & hence skewness and kurtosis indicates that the distribution for all factors can be considered as normal.

2> Histogram

Histograms are plotted below for each factor under study

Graph No 1 : The Histogram of Leadership Factors to check outliers

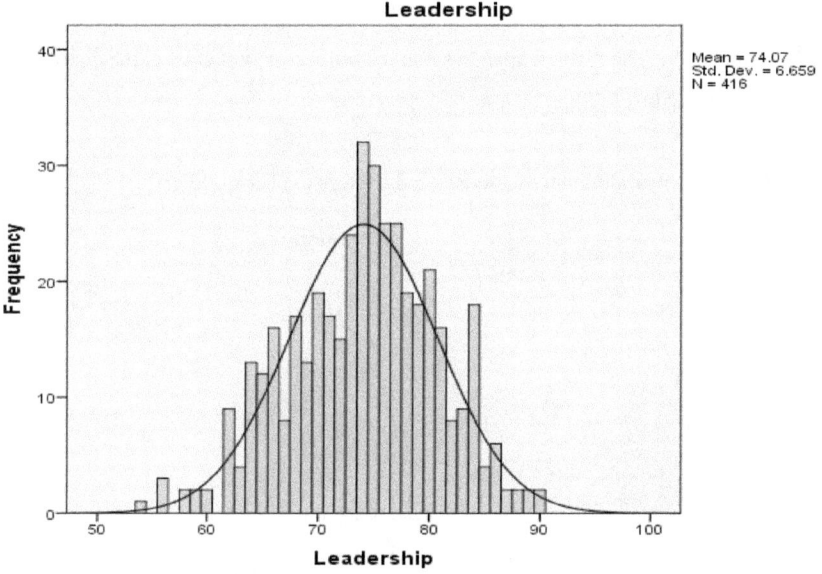

Conclusion: The histogram shows that the outliers do not exist & the distribution is normal for Leadership / Managerial factor.

Graph No 2: The Histogram of Institutional Factors to check outliers

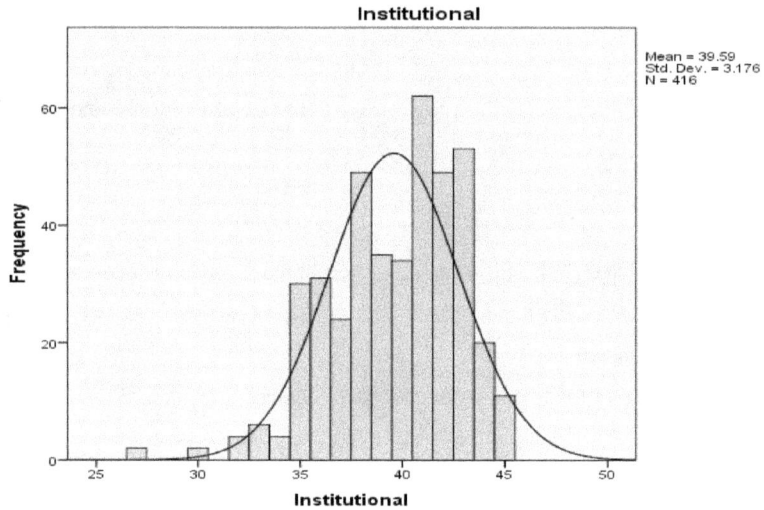

Conclusion: The histogram shows that the outliers do not exist & the distribution is normal for Institutional factor.

Graph No 3: Histogram of Job-Related Factors to check outliers.

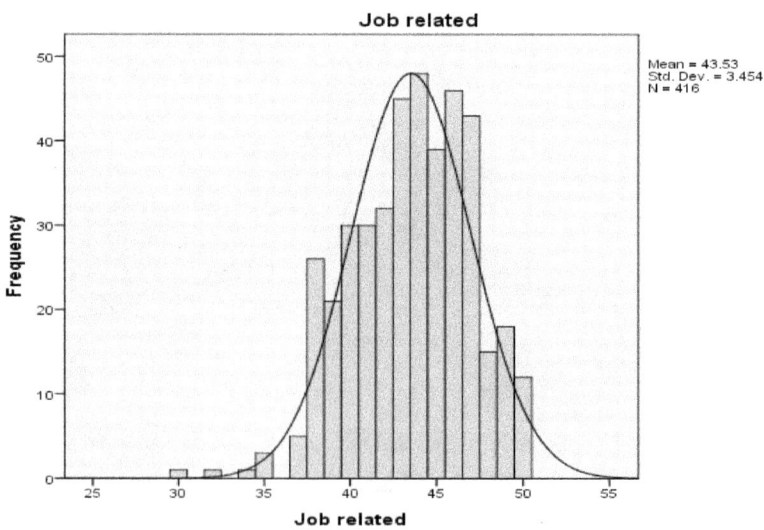

Conclusion: The histogram shows that the outliers do not exist & the distribution is normal for Job related factor.

Graph No 4: The Histogram of Organizational Cultural Factors to check outliers

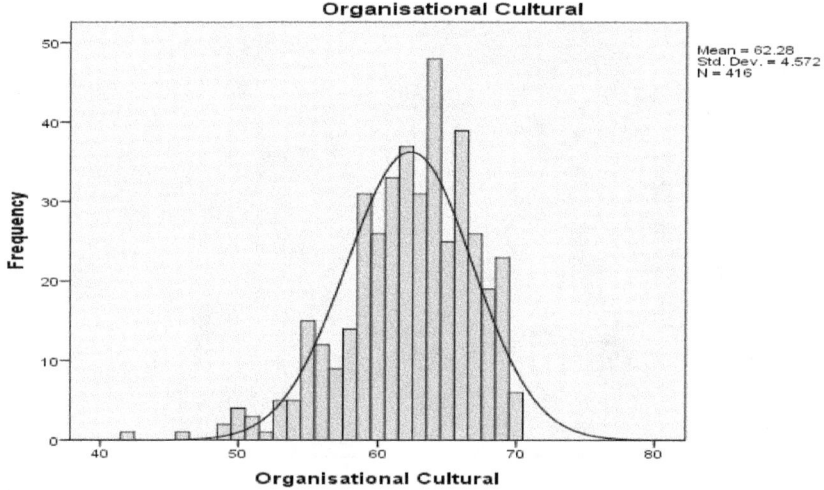

Conclusion: The histogram shows that the outliers do not exist & the distribution is normal for Organizational Cultural factor.

Graph No 5: The Histogram of Opportunity Factor to check outliers

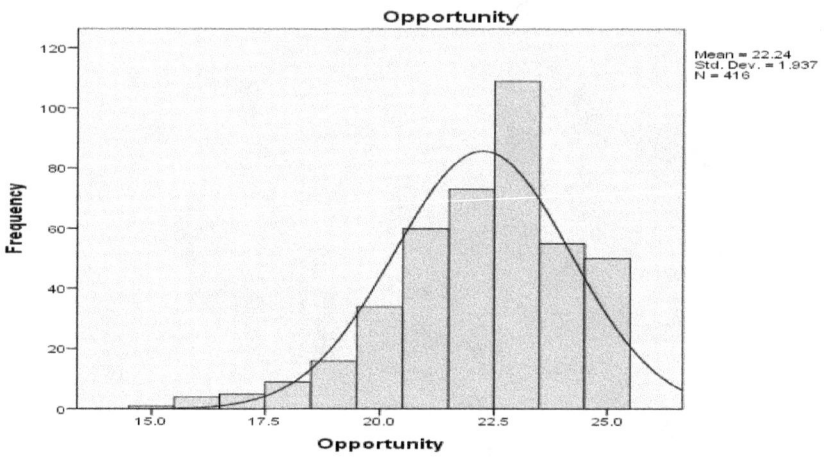

Conclusion: The histogram shows that the outliers do not exist & the distribution is normal for Opportunity factor.

Graph No 6: The Histogram of Motivational Factors to check outliers

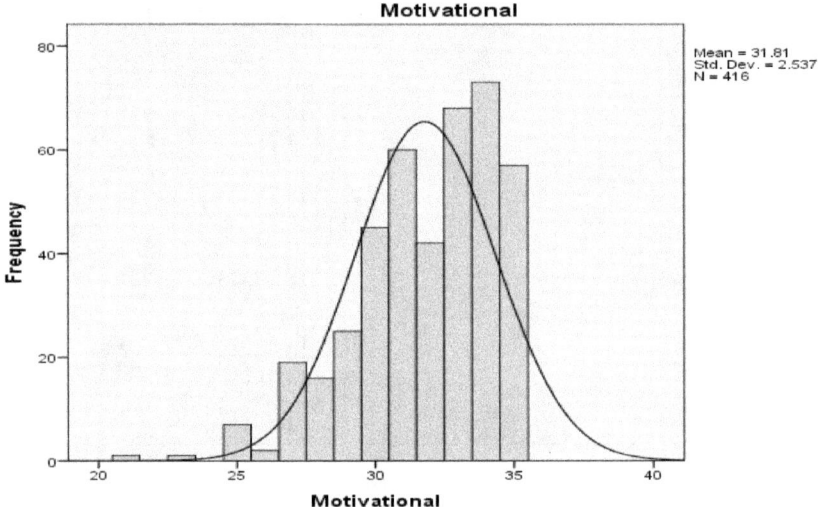

Conclusion: The histogram shows that the outliers do not exist & the distribution is normal for Motivational factor.

Graph No 7: The Histogram of Performance measures to check outliers

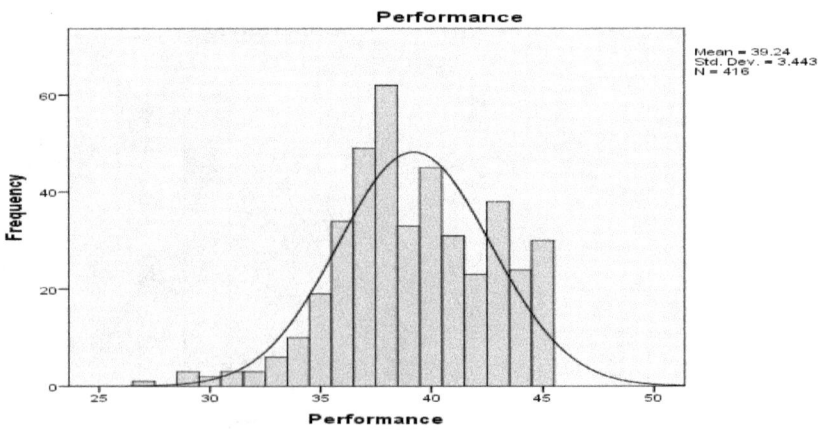

Conclusion: The histogram shows that the outliers do not exist & the distribution is normal for Performance of employee.

3> P-P Plots

Graph No 8: Showing P-P plot deviation and normality of data for Leadership

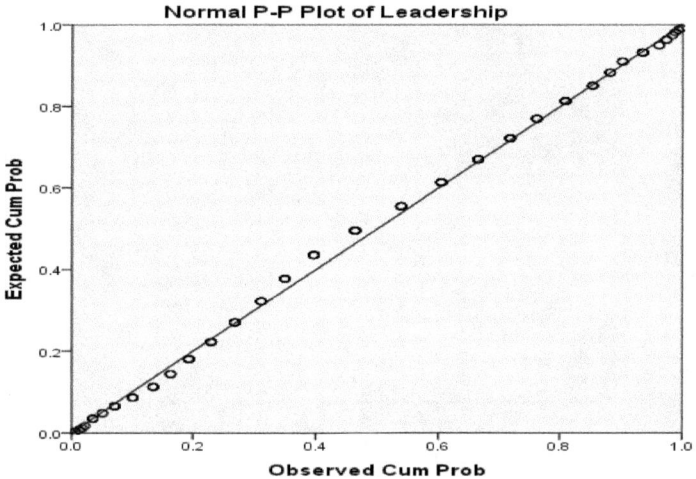

The PP plot shows the minimum deviation of the Leadership / Managerial factor data from normality.

Graph No 9: Showing P-P plot deviation and normality of data for Institutional

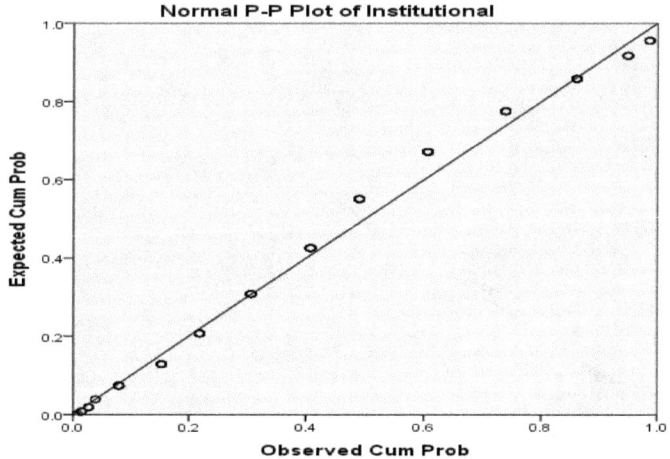

The PP plot shows the minimum deviation of the Institutional factor data from normality.

Graph No 10: Showing P-P plot deviation and normality of data for Job Related

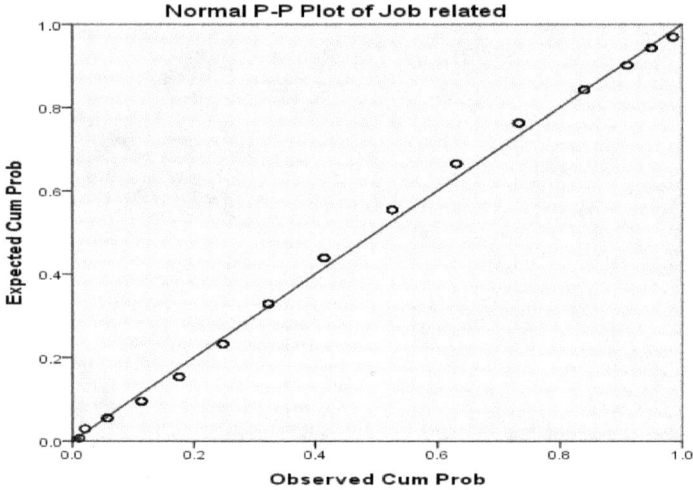

The PP plot shows the minimum deviation of the job-related factor data from normality.

Graph No 11: Showing P-P plot deviation and normality of data for Organisational Cultural

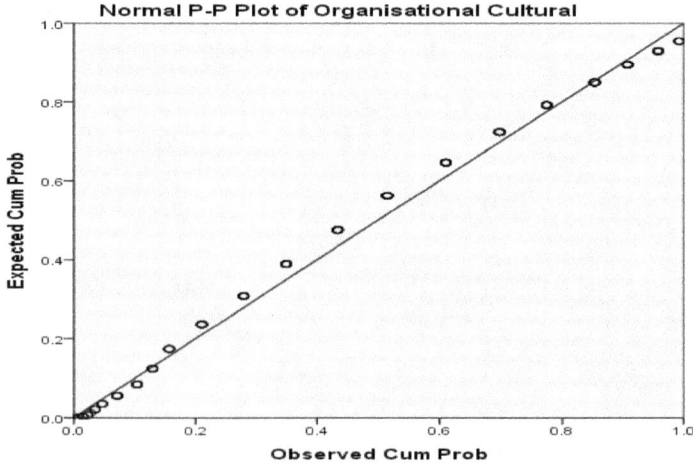

The PP plot shows the minimum deviation of the organizational culture factor data from normality.

Graph No 12: Showing P-P plot deviation and normality of data for Opportunity

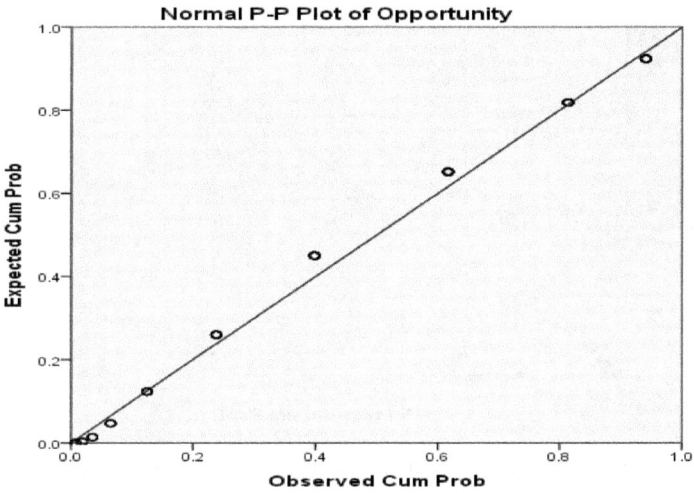

The PP plot shows the minimum deviation of the Opportunity factor data from normality.

Graph No 13: Showing P-P plot deviation and normality of data for Motivational

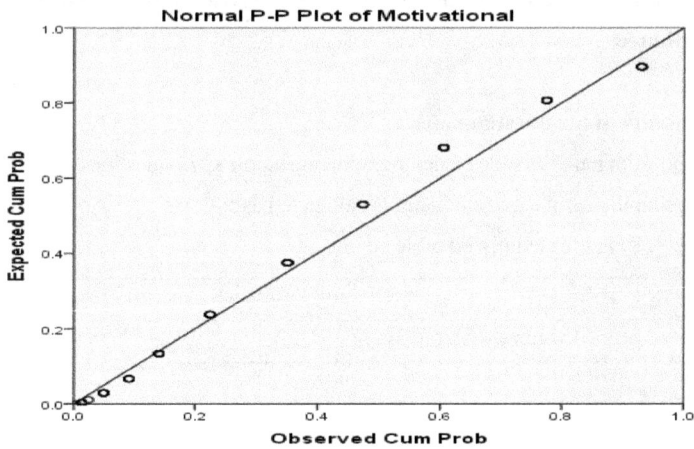

The PP plot shows the minimum deviation of the Motivational factor data from normality.

Graph No 14: Showing P-P plot deviation and normality of data for Performance

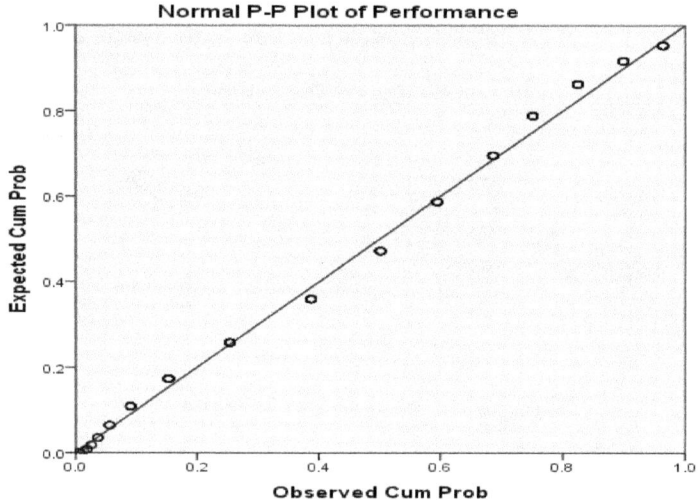

The PP plot shows the minimum deviation of the Performance of employee data from normality.

Conclusion: Histogram, skewness & kurtosis values & P-P plots indicates that the data for factors - Leadership / Managerial Factor, Institutional Factor, Job Related Factor, Organizational Cultural Factor, Opportunity Factor, Motivational Factor and Performance of Employee can be considered as normally distributed.

Reliability of the questionnaire:

The questionnaire includes 5 demographic question & 72 questions related to study. The reliability of the questionnaire is calculated as follows.

Table 4: Reliability Statistics table

Reliability Statistics	
Cronbach's Alpha	N of Items
.941	72

The reliability of the questionnaire i.e. the Cronbach alpha = 0.941

Hence the Cronbach alpha; reliability of the questionnaire is excellent.

Table 5: Cronbach alpha questions wise.

Sr. No.	Factors		Cronbach's Alpha if Question Deleted
	Leadership / Managerial Factors		
1	Vision & Mission of Leader	I have clarity about my role from my leader and it excites me to give my best	.940
2	Leadership Style	Leadership Style of my manager affects me drastically	.941
3	Democratic Leadership	My leader makes decision based on my and my team members inputs	.939
4	Autocratic Leadership	My Leader make decision without taking inputs from any of team member	.941
5	Laissez-Faire Leadership	My Leader doesn't take me review and gives me complete ownership of my results	.941
6	Strategic Leadership	My Leader has strategy in place to deal with uncertainties	.940
7	Transformational Leadership	My Leader puts me out of my comfort zone and always motivates me to do more	.940
8	Transactional Leadership	My Leaders give me Clears Roles and Responsibilities along with Timeline and KPIs.	.940
9	Coach-Style Leadership	My leader knows my strengths and Weakness and he guides me accordingly	.940
10	Bureaucratic Leadership	My Leader doesn't not appreciate new and innovative ways of working	.940
11	Coaching by Manager	My Manager provides me with regular coaching/feedback	.940
12	Camaraderie with Colleagues	I Enjoy my camaraderie with my Colleagues	.940

13	Relationship with Manager	My Manager is supportive & I like interacting with him	.939
14	Performance Pressure	Pressure with respective to performance affects me drastically	.941
15	Low Pressure	There is low pressure with respect to performance	.941
16	Healthy Pressure	There is Healthy pressure impacting my performance positively	.940
17	High Pressure	There is Continuous Pressure impacting me drastically	.942
18	Empowerment	There is empowerment with respect to my role	.939
	Institutional Factors		
19	Brand Image	I feel proud to be associated with my organization	.940
20	Responsibility	I feel happy when I have entrusted with Responsibility	.941
21	Technology	Technology impacts my performance positively	.940
22	Infrastructure	Infrastructure supports me a lot in my current role	.940
23	Production Systems	It is my experience that Production systems plays a important role in increasing Productivity	.940
24	Structure	Reporting / Org Structure affects my performance drastically	.941
25	Indian / MNC	I prefer to work with MNCs	.941
26	Organizational Stability	Organizational Stability Impacts me performance drastically	.940
27	Market Position	I feel proud about my organizations market position	.940
	Job Related Factors		

28	Job Fit	I like my job if my skills my matching with offered role	.940
29	Clear Goals and Expectations	Clear Goals & Expectations helps me in achieving my Targets	.940
30	Training provide	I feel Training provided helps me grow in the organization	.940
31	Tools and Equipment / Resources	Tools and Equipment help me improve my productivity	.940
32	Work Life Balance	I take break from work, which rejunuvates me and helps me to improve my focus on work	.942
33	Usage of Cutting Edge Technology	Technology help me improve my productivity	.940
34	Risk associated with Job	I feel worried if I perceive risk in the job	.941
35	Location of work	Location of Work impacts my performance drastically	.941
36	Reputation/Status of the Job	I like to work for reputed / Status focused jobs	.940
37	Diversity in Job	I like to have diversity in my work	.940
	Organizational Cultural Factors		
38	Culture	Organizational Culture affects me drastically	.941
39	Clan Culture	My Organization friendly, Innovative, committed and provides me mentoring	.940
40	Adhocracy Culture	My Organization is Dynamic, Innovative, Transformational and Learning from mistakes	.940
41	Market Culture	My Organization is Agile and Flexible to meet customer & market demand	.940
42	Hierarchy Culture	My Organization is Structured, Stability oriented and Cost oriented	.940

43	Communication	Communication affects my performance drastically	.941
44	Communication to Inform	I feel low when I am just communicated to inform	.941
45	Communication to Involve	I feel motivated when I am included/involved in the communication	.939
46	social learning	I Learn from my colleagues and also enthusiastically share my learnings with them	.939
47	Ethics	I am proud to work with organization of high ethics and repute	.940
48	Innovation	I believe Innovation is key towards organizational growth	.940
49	Discipline	My Discipline helps to improve organizations productivity	.939
50	Standardization	My Organisation has required level of standardization	.940
51	Reputation in eyes of Customer	I feel proud to work when customer are satisfied with our product	.940
	Opportunity Factors		
52	Development Opportunities	I feel passionate to perform when I see development opportunities in my organisation	.940
53	Career Path	I feel motivate when my managers discuss career path with me	.940
54	Growth Options	I feel motivated when in grow in the organisation	.940
55	Job Security	I feel worried if job security is a concern	.942
56	Diversity	Diversity in my team keeps me excited about my role	.940
	Motivational Factors		
57	Motivation	My Manager motivates me at my job/work	.939

58	Recognition	I feel good when my efforts are recognized	.940
59	Job Enrichment	I feel motivated when additional responsibilities are entrusted upon me.	.940
60	Job Satisfaction	I give my best when I am satisfied with my Job	.940
61	Passion towards car	I Love Automobiles (Cars / Bikes / Auto)	.940
62	Ability	My ability impacts my performance drastically	.940
63	Performance Appraisal Process	I feel satisfied when I performance appraisal process is fair and transparent	.940
	Performance of Employee		
64	Targets	I am able to complete my targets	.940
65	Satisfaction / Motivation	My Organisations management is happy with my work	.940
66	Timeline	I am able to complete my targets within the timeline	.940
67	Satisfaction / Motivation	My manager is Happy with my work	.940
68	Recognition from Colleagues	I am recognized by my team mates for quality of my work	.940
69	Recognition from Management	I am getting recognition I deserve	.940
70	Helping others	My Colleagues approach me for Challenges they face at work	.940
71	Growth	I got the growth that I deserve in the organisation	.941
72	Motivation	I feel good to attend work	.940

If the reliability alpha (if the question deleted) is less than 0.941, then the corresponding question is important (must be kept in questionnaire). If the reliability alpha (if the question deleted) is greater than 0.941, then the corresponding question is unnecessary (must be removed from questionnaire).

Since there is no high variation of the reliability alpha (if the question deleted) from the Cronbach alpha, which is 0.941; all the questions are equally important. Hence the same questionnaire is applied for main study.

Objective2: To establish relationship between Non-Monetary factors and performance of employee.

The Regression Model for Performance of Employee (Y) on Leadership / Managerial Factor (X1); Institutional Factor (X2); Job Related Factor (X3); Organisational Cultural Factor (X4); Opportunity Factor (X5); Motivational Factor (X6)

Independent variables: 1) Leadership / Managerial Factor (X1); 2) Institutional Factor (X2); 3) Job Related Factor (X3); 4) Organisational Cultural Factor (X4); 5) Opportunity Factor (X5); 6) Motivational Factor (X6)

Dependent variable: Performance of Employee (Y)

The Regression Model for Performance of Employee (Y) on Leadership / Managerial Factor (X1); Institutional Factor (X2); Job Related Factor (X3); Organisational Cultural Factor (X4); Opportunity Factor (X5); Motivational Factor (X6):

Table 6: Descriptive Statistics with Dependent Variable as Performance of Employee (Y)

Descriptive Statistics			
	Mean	Std. Deviation	N
Performance of Employee	39.24	3.443	416
Leadership / Managerial Factor	74.07	6.659	416
Institutional Factor	39.59	3.176	416
Job Related Factor	43.53	3.454	416
Organisational Cultural Factor	62.28	4.572	416

Opportunity Factor	22.24	1.937	416
Motivational Factor	31.81	2.537	416

Table 7: Table showing summary of model

Model Summary

Model	R	R Square	Adjusted R Square	Std. Error of the Estimate
1	.666[a]	.444	.442	2.571
2	.712[b]	.507	.505	2.422
3	.727[c]	.528	.525	2.374
a. Predictors: (Constant), Organisational Cultural			
b. Predictors: (Constant), Organisational Cultural, Motivational			
c. Predictors: (Constant), Organisational Cultural, Motivational, Leadership			

Since coefficient of determination i.e. R square = 0.444, 44.4% of the total variation in the dependent variable is explained by independent variables in model 1.

Table 8: Table showing results of ANOVA

ANOVA[a]

Model		Sum of Squares	df	Mean Square	F	Sig.
1	Regression	2182.656	1	2182.656	330.176	.000[b]
	Residual	2736.784	414	6.611		
	Total	4919.440	415			
2	Regression	2495.970	2	1247.985	212.678	.000[c]
	Residual	2423.470	413	5.868		
	Total	4919.440	415			
3	Regression	2598.102	3	866.034	153.707	.000[d]
	Residual	2321.338	412	5.634		
	Total	4919.440	415			
a. Dependent Variable: Performance						
b. Predictors: (Constant), Organisational Cultural						
c. Predictors: (Constant), Organisational Cultural, Motivational						
d. Predictors: (Constant), Organisational Cultural, Motivational, Leadership						

Since F = 330.176 & p value = 0.00 < 0.05, there is strong evidence to conclude that the regression model 1 is significant.

Table 9: Table showing the regression coefficients & T stat

Coefficients[a]							
Model		Unstandardized Coefficients		Standardized Coefficients	t	Sig.
		B	Std. Error	Beta		
1	(Constant)	7.996	1.724		4.638	.000
	Organisational Cultural	.502	.028	.666	18.171	.000
2	(Constant)	4.465	1.695		2.635	.009
	Organisational Cultural	.310	.037	.411	8.381	.000
	Motivational	.487	.067	.359	7.307	.000
3	(Constant)	3.500	1.676		2.089	.037
	Organisational Cultural	.242	.040	.321	6.119	.000
	Motivational	.412	.068	.304	6.101	.000
	Leadership	.102	.024	.197	4.258	.000
a. Dependent Variable: Performance							

The regression model had six independent variables & was reached to one independent variable in three steps.

The regression model for Performance of Employee (Y) on Organisational Cultural Factor (X4) is given as

Y = 7.996 + 0.502*X4

Here the intercept is 7.996 implies that the initial Performance of Employee would be 7.996 when the independent variable value is zero.

The slope of variable Organisational Cultural Factor (X4) is 0.502 implies that the Performance of Employee would be increased by 0.502 per unit increase in variable Organisational Cultural Factor (X4).

Objective3: To Rank non-monetary factors based on their positive impact on employee's performance.

To test the hypotheses,

The null hypothesis, H0: All non-monetary factors are of same occurrence on an average.

Vs.

The alternative hypothesis, Ha: At least one non-monetary factor is different with respect to occurrence on an average.

Averages for factors are drawn for each respondent based on number of statements under each factor.

The test used is one way ANOVA.

Table 10: Calculation Table

					95% Confidence Interval for Mean	
Descriptives Score	N	Mean	Std. Deviation	Std. Error	Lower Bound	Upper Bound
Leadership / Managerial Factor	416	4.12	.3699	.01814	4.08	4.15
Institutional Factor	416	4.40	.3529	.01730	4.37	4.43
Job Related Factor	416	4.35	.3454	.01694	4.32	4.39
Organisational Cultural Factor	416	4.45	.3266	.01601	4.42	4.48
Opportunity Factor	416	4.45	.3873	.01899	4.41	4.49
Motivational Factor	416	4.54	.3624	.01777	4.51	4.58
Total	2496	4.38	.3818	.00764	4.37	4.40

Table 11: Anova Table

ANOVA					
Score					
	Sum of Squares	df	Mean Square	F	p
Between Groups	44.692	5	8.938	69.768	.000
Within Groups	319.006	2490	.128		
Total	363.698	2495			

Since p value < 0.05, the level of significance; there is strong evidence to reject the null hypothesis.

Conclusion:

At least one non-monetary factor is different with respect to occurrence on an average.

Table 12: Post Hoc Tests

Multiple Comparisons						
Dependent Variable:						
LSD						
(I) Factor		Mean Difference (I-J)	Std. Error	Sig.	95% Confidence Interval	
					Lower Bound	Upper Bound
Leadership / Managerial Factor	Institutional Factor	-.28419*	.02482	.000	-.3329	-.2355
	Job Related Factor	-.23777*	.02482	.000	-.2864	-.1891
	Organisational Cultural Factor	-.33354*	.02482	.000	-.3822	-.2849
	Opportunity Factor	-.33344*	.02482	.000	-.3821	-.2848

	Motivational Factor	-.42884*	.02482	.000	-.4775	-.3802
Institutional Factor	Leadership / Managerial Factor	.28419*	.02482	.000	.2355	.3329
	Job Related Factor	.04642	.02482	.062	-.0022	.0951
	Organisational Cultural Factor	-.04936*	.02482	.047	-.0980	-.0007
	Opportunity Factor	-.04925*	.02482	.047	-.0979	-.0006
	Motivational Factor	-.14465*	.02482	.000	-.1933	-.0960
Job Related Factor	Leadership / Managerial Factor	.23777*	.02482	.000	.1891	.2864
	Institutional Factor	-.04642	.02482	.062	-.0951	.0022
	Organisational Cultural Factor	-.09578*	.02482	.000	-.1444	-.0471
	Opportunity Factor	-.09567*	.02482	.000	-.1443	-.0470
	Motivational Factor	-.19107*	.02482	.000	-.2397	-.1424
Organisational Cultural Factor	Leadership / Managerial Factor	.33354*	.02482	.000	.2849	.3822
	Institutional Factor	.04936*	.02482	.047	.0007	.0980
	Job Related Factor	.09578*	.02482	.000	.0471	.1444

		Opportunity Factor	.00010	.02482	.997	-.0486	.0488
		Motivational Factor	-.09530*	.02482	.000	-.1440	-.0466
Opportunity Factor		Leadership / Managerial Factor	.33344*	.02482	.000	.2848	.3821
		Institutional Factor	.04925*	.02482	.047	.0006	.0979
		Job Related Factor	.09567*	.02482	.000	.0470	.1443
		Organisational Cultural Factor	-.00010	.02482	.997	-.0488	.0486
		Motivational Factor	-.09540*	.02482	.000	-.1441	-.0467
Motivational Factor		Leadership / Managerial Factor	.42884*	.02482	.000	.3802	.4775
		Institutional Factor	.14465*	.02482	.000	.0960	.1933
		Job Related Factor	.19107*	.02482	.000	.1424	.2397
		Organisational Cultural Factor	.09530*	.02482	.000	.0466	.1440
		Opportunity Factor	.09540*	.02482	.000	.0467	.1441
*. The mean difference is significant at the 0.05 level.							

Summary:

Looking at the p values it can be concluded that, there is no significant difference between mean scores for Institutional Factor and Job Related Factor (p=0.062) AND

Job Related Factor and Opportunity Factor (p=0.997). The mean score for Leadership / Managerial Factor and Motivational Factor are different from all other non-monetary factors significantly. For all other pairs of non-monetary factors, there is significant difference in the mean scores.

The Means Plot for all non-monetary factors:

Graph No 15: The means plot showing means of all non-monetary factors is as given below.

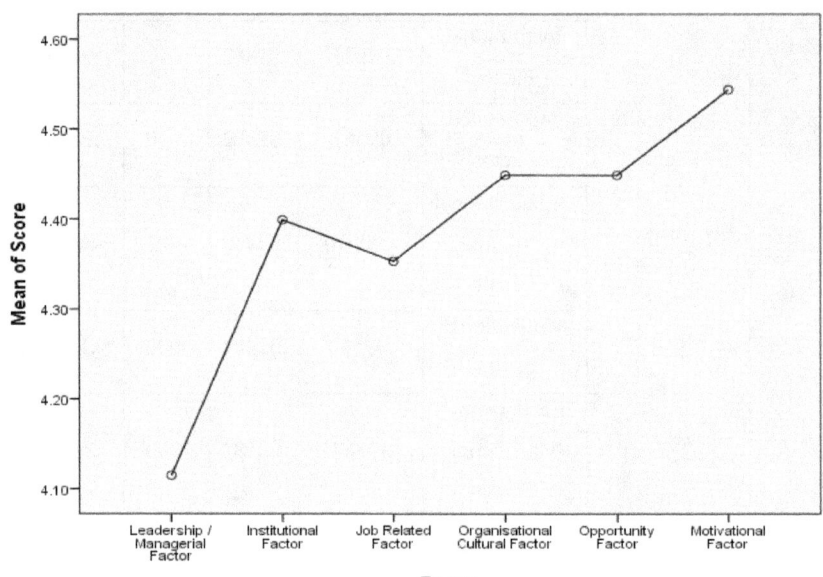

Summary:

The factor of highest importance is Motivational Factor, then Organisational Cultural Factor and Opportunity Factor, then Institutional Factor, then Job Related Factor and lastly Leadership / Managerial Factor.

Objective4: To Create Model/structure to enhance performance of employees based on the findings of study

To achieve this objective following sections are analyzed.

Section A] Leadership / Managerial Factors

Table 13: The ranking & frequencies of respondents with respect to Section A responses are as given below.

Sr. No.	Leadership / Managerial Factors		Percent (Often+ Always)	Rank
1	Vision & Mission of Leader	I have clarity about my role from my leader and it excites me to give my best	87.02	2
2	Leadership Style	Leadership Style of my manager affects me drastically	79.09	9
3	Democratic Leadership	My leader makes decision based on my and my team members inputs	81.25	6
4	Autocratic Leadership	My Leader make decision without taking inputs from any of team member	73.56	11
5	Laissez-Faire Leadership	My Leader doesn't take me review and gives me complete ownership of my results	70.67	13
6	Strategic Leadership	My Leader has strategy in place to deal with uncertainties	80.29	8
7	Transformational Leadership	My Leader puts me out of my comfort zone and always motivates me to do more	80.77	7
8	Transactional Leadership	My Leaders give me Clears Roles and Responsibilities along with Timeline and KPIs.	85.58	3
9	Coach-Style Leadership	My leader knows my strengths and Weakness and he guides me accordingly	81.73	5
10	Bureaucratic Leadership	My Leader doesn't not appreciate new and innovative ways of working	78.85	10
11	Coaching by Manager	My Manager provides me with regular coaching/feedback	71.39	12

12	Camaraderie with Colleagues	I Enjoy my comrade with my Colleagues	88.46	1
13	Relationship with Manager	My Manager is supportive & I like interacting with him	85.10	4
14	Performance Pressure	Pressure with respective to performance affects me drastically	65.63	15
15	Low Pressure	There is low pressure with respect to performance	66.11	14
16	Healthy Pressure	There is Healthy pressure impacting my performance positively	81.25	6
17	High Pressure	There is Continuous Pressure impacting me drastically	60.58	16
18	Empowerment	There is empowerment with respect to my role	78.85	10

Graph No 14: Plot of ranking & frequencies for Leadership / Managerial Factors

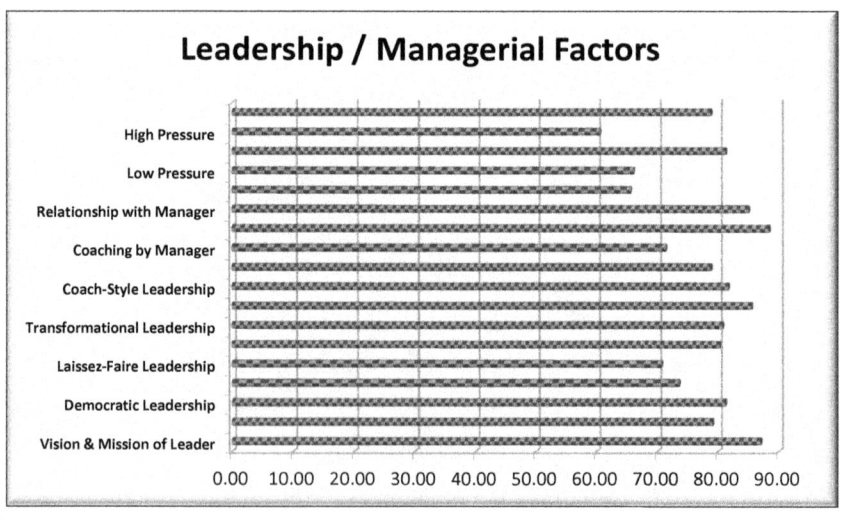

Summary:

The high rated factor is 'Camaraderie with Colleagues'; then 'Vision & Mission of Leader'; then 'Transactional Leadership', then 'Relationship with Manager'; then 'Coach-Style Leadership'; then 'Democratic Leadership' and 'Healthy Pressure'; then 'Transformational Leadership'; then 'Strategic Leadership'; then 'Leadership Style'; then 'Bureaucratic Leadership' and 'Empowerment'; then 'Autocratic Leadership'; then 'Coaching by Manager'; then 'Laissez-Faire Leadership'; then 'Low Pressure'; then 'Performance Pressure'; lastly 'High Pressure'.

Section B] Institutional Factors

Table 14: The ranking & frequencies of respondents with respect to Section B responses are as given below.

Sr. No.	Institutional Factors		Percent (Often+ Always)	Rank
1	Brand Image	I feel proud to be associated with my organization	92.3	1
2	Responsibility	I feel happy when I have entrusted with Responsibility	92.1	2
3	Technology	Technology impacts my performance positively	92.3	1
4	Infrastructure	Infrastructure supports me a lot in my current role	80.5	6
5	Production Systems	It is my experience that Production systems plays a important role in increasing Productivity	90.9	3
6	Structure	Reporting / Org Structure affects my performance drastically	69.5	8
7	Indian / MNC	I prefer to work with MNCs	88.9	4
8	Organizational Stability	Organizational Stability Impacts me performance drastically	80.3	7

| 9 | Market Position | I feel proud about my organizations market position | 85.1 | 5 |

Graph No 16: Plot of ranking & frequencies for Institutional Factors

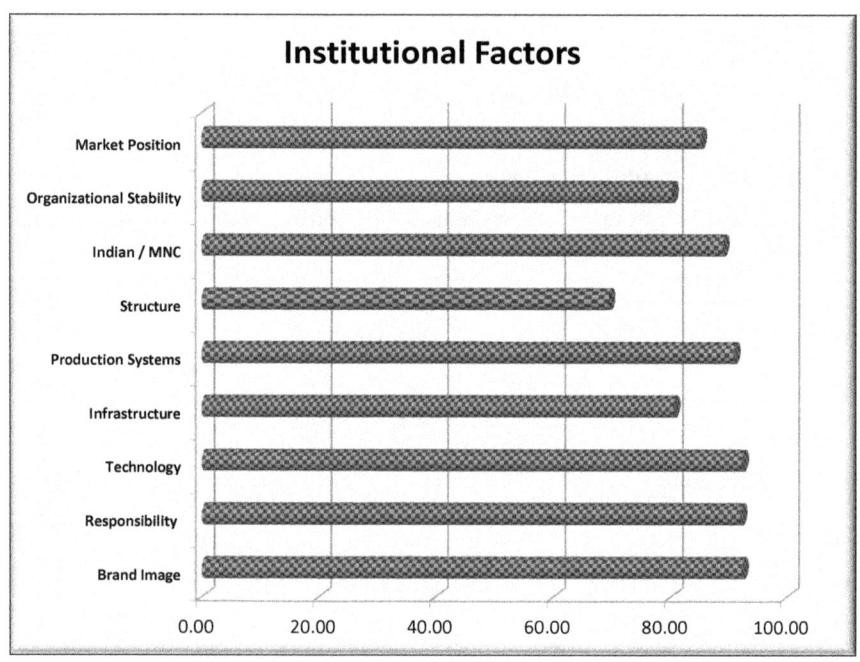

Summary:

The high rated factor is 'Brand Image' and 'Technology'; then 'Responsibility'; then 'Production Systems'; then 'Indian / MNC'; then 'Market Position'; then 'Infrastructure'; then 'Organizational Stability'; lastly 'Structure'.

Section C] Job Related Factors

Table 15:The ranking & frequencies of respondents with respect to Section C responses are as given below

Sr. No.	Job Related Factors		Percent	Rank
1	Job Fit	I like my job if my skills my matching with offered role	94.0	2

2	Clear Goals and Expectations	Clear Goals & Expectations helps me in achieving my Targets	96.2	1
3	Training provide	I feel Training provided helps me grow in the organization	85.8	7
4	Tools and Equipment / Resources	Tools and Equipment's help me improve my productivity	93.3	4
5	Work Life Balance	I take break from work, which rejunuvates me and helps me to improve my focus on work	67.1	9
6	Usage of Cutting Edge Technology	Technology help me improve my productivity	93.8	3
7	Risk associated with Job	I feel worried if I perceive risk in the job	59.6	10
8	Location of work	Location of Work impacts my performance drastically	76.2	8
9	Reputation/Status of the Job	I like to work for reputed / Status focused jobs	88.0	6
10	Diversity in Job	I like to have diversity in my work	91.1	5

Graph No 17 :Plot of ranking & frequencies for Job Related Factors

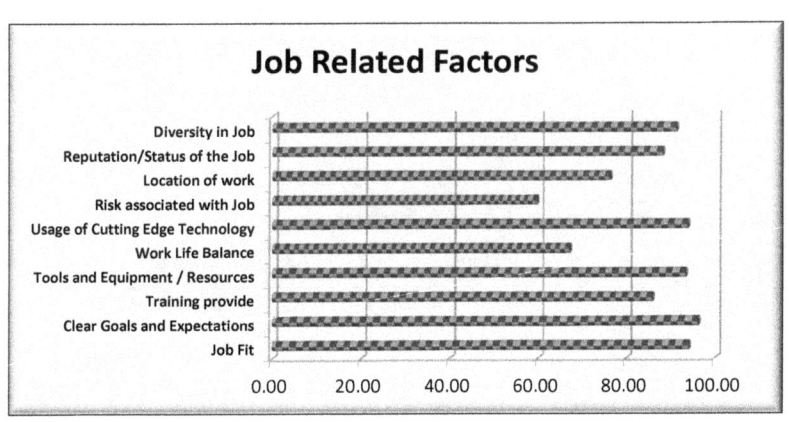

Summary:

The high rated factor is 'Clear Goals and Expectations'; then 'Job Fit'; then 'Usage of Cutting Edge Technology'; then 'Tools and Equipment / Resources'; then 'Diversity in Job'; then 'Reputation/Status of the Job'; then 'Training provide'; then 'Location of work'; then 'Work Life Balance'; lastly 'Risk associated with Job'.

Section D] Organizational Cultural Factors

Table 16 : The ranking & frequencies of respondents with respect to Section D responses are as given below.

Sr. No.	Organizational Cultural Factors		Percent (Often+ Always)	Rank
1	Culture	Organizational Culture affects me drastically	88.7	9
2	Clan Culture	My Organization friendly, Innovative, committed and provides me mentoring	82.2	13
3	Adhocracy Culture	My Organization is Dynamic, Innovative, Transformational and Learning from mistakes	82.9	12
4	Market Culture	My Organization is Agile and Flexible to meet customer & market demand	89.7	8
5	Hierarchy Culture	My Organization is Structured, Stability oriented and Cost oriented	91.6	7
6	Communication	Communication affects my performance drastically	83.4	11
7	Communication to Inform	I feel low when I am just communicated to inform	65.4	14
8	Communication to Involve	I feel motivated when I am included/involved in the communication	95.2	4
9	social learning	I Learn from my colleagues and also enthusiastically share my learning with them	92.1	6
10	Ethics	I am proud to work with organization of high ethics and repute	97.6	2

11	Innovation	I believe Innovation is key towards organizational growth	92.8	5
12	Discipline	My Discipline helps to improve organizations productivity	96.6	3
13	Standardization	My Organization has required level of standardization	85.1	10
14	Reputation in eyes of Customer	I feel proud to work when customer are satisfied with our product	98.1	1

Graph No 18: Plot of ranking & frequencies for Organisational Cultural Factors

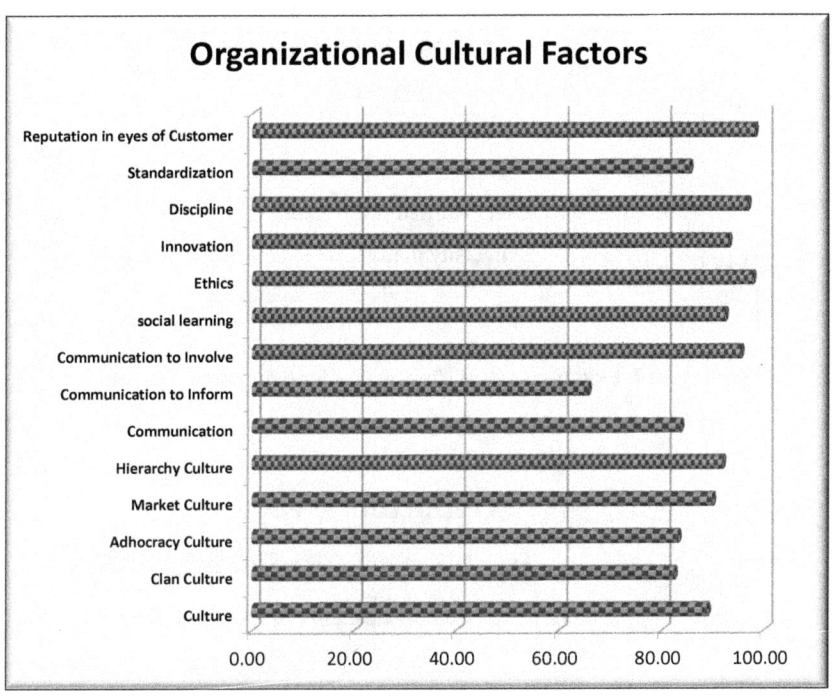

Summary:

The high rated factor is 'Reputation in eyes of Customer'; then 'Ethics'; then 'Discipline'; then 'Communication to Involve'; then 'Innovation'; then 'social learning'; then 'Hierarchy Culture'; then 'Market Culture'; then 'Culture'; then

'Standardization'; then 'Communication'; then 'Adhocracy Culture'; then 'Clan Culture'; then; lastly 'Communication to Inform'.

Section E] Opportunity Factors

Table 17: The ranking & frequencies of respondents with respect to Section E responses are as given below.

Sr. No.	Opportunity Factors		Percent (Often+ Always)	Rank
1	Development Opportunities	I feel passionate to perform when I see development opportunities in my organization	97.1	1
2	Career Path	I feel motivate when my managers discuss career path with me	87.0	3
3	Growth Options	I feel motivated when in grow in the organization	92.1	2
4	Job Security	I feel worried if job security is a concern	69.7	5
5	Diversity	Diversity in my team keeps me excited about my role	86.3	4

Graph No 19: Plot of ranking & frequencies for Opportunity Factors

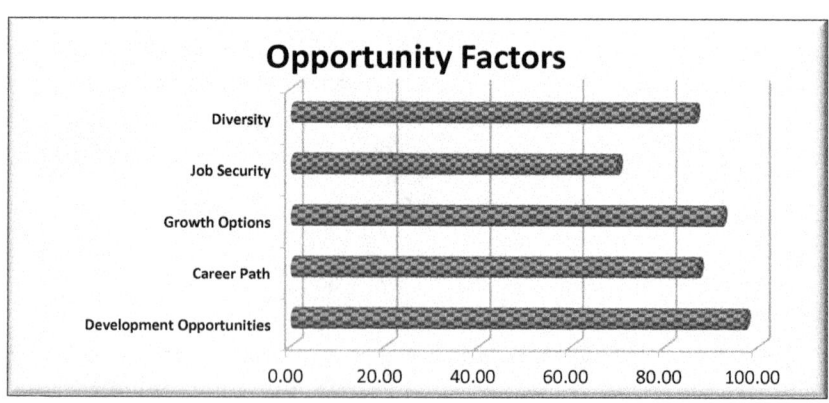

Summary:

The high rated factor is 'Development Opportunities'; then 'Growth Options'; then 'Career Path'; then 'Diversity'; then Job Security'.

Section F] Motivational Factors

Table 18: The ranking & frequencies of respondents with respect to Section F responses are as given below.

Sr. No.	Motivational Factors		Percent (Often+ Always)	Rank
1	Motivation	My Manager motivates me at my job/work	81.7	7
2	Recognition	I feel good when my efforts are recognized	97.6	2
3	Job Enrichment	I feel motivated when additional responsibilities are entrusted upon me.	89.4	5
4	Job Satisfaction	I give my best when I am satisfied with my Job	99.0	1
5	Passion towards car	I Love Automobiles (Cars / Bikes / Auto)	96.2	3
6	Ability	My ability impacts my performance drastically	88.5	6
7	Performance Appraisal Process	I feel satisfied when I performance appraisal process is fair and transparent	90.4	4

Graph No 20: Plot of ranking & frequencies for Motivational Factors

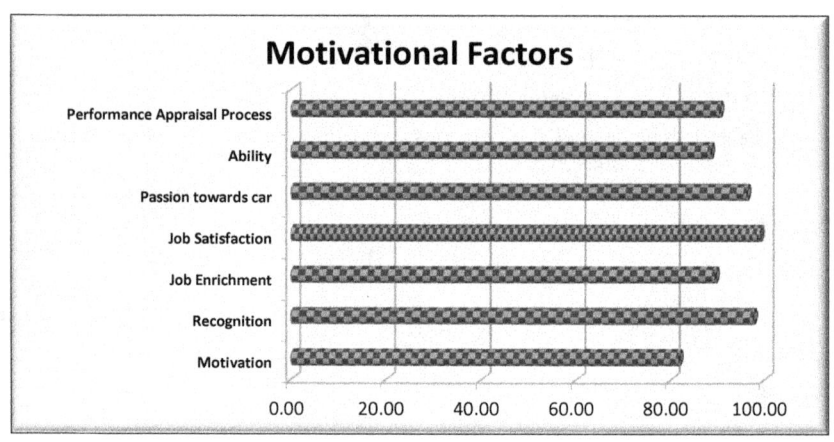

Summary:

The high rated factor is 'Job Satisfaction'; then 'Recognition'; then 'Passion towards car'; then 'Performance Appraisal Process'; then 'Job Enrichment'; then 'Ability'; then 'Motivation'.

Section G] Performance of Employee

Table 19: The ranking & frequencies of respondents with respect to Section G responses are as given below.

Sr. No.	Performance of Employee		Frequency (Often+ Always)	Rank
1	Targets	I am able to complete my targets	95.7	3
2	Satisfaction / Motivation Organization	My Organization management is happy with my work	93.3	5
3	Timeline	I am able to complete my targets within the timeline	95.9	2
4	Satisfaction / Motivation Manager	My manager is Happy with my work	93.8	4

5	Recognition from Colleagues	I am recognized by my team mates for quality of my work	93.3	5
6	Recognition from Management	I am getting recognition I deserve	76.9	8
7	Helping others	My Colleagues approach me for Challenges they face at work	84.1	6
8	Growth	I got the growth that I deserve in the organisation	81.0	7
9	Motivation	I feel good to attend work	96.4	1

Graph No 21: Plot of ranking & frequencies for Performance of Employee

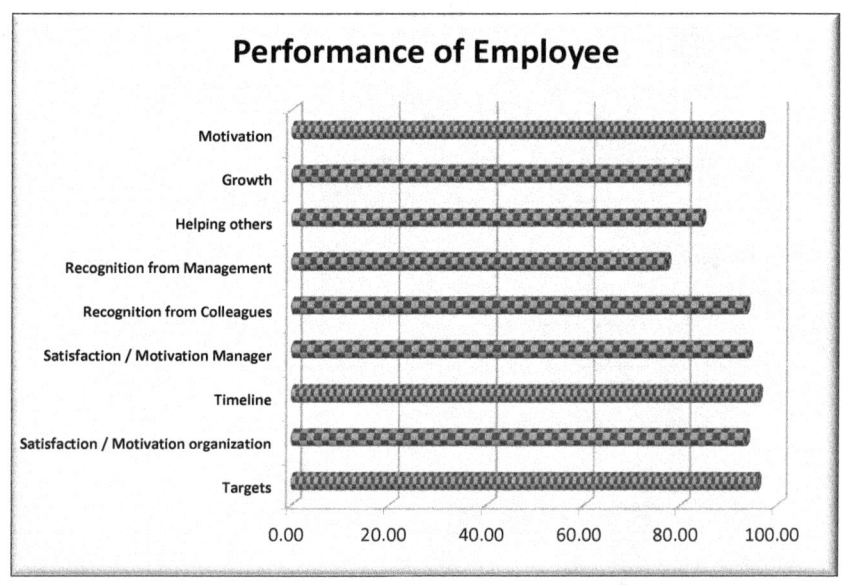

Summary:

The high rated factor is 'Motivation'; then 'Timeline'; then 'Targets'; then 'Satisfaction / Motivation Manager'; then 'Satisfaction / Motivation Organization' and 'Recognition from Colleagues'; then 'Satisfaction / Motivation'; then 'Helping others'; then 'Growth'; lastly 'Recognition from Management'.

Tables & Graphs

Table 20: Leadership / Managerial Factors

The frequency distribution of respondents according to Leadership / Managerial Factors along with its bar graph is as given below.

Leadership / Managerial Factors	Never	Rarely	Sometimes	Often	Always	Total
I have clarity about my role from my leader and it excites me to give my best	0	0	54	142	220	416
%	0.0	0.0	13.0	34.1	52.9	100
Leadership Style of my manager affects me drastically	0	0	87	162	167	416
%	0.0	0.0	20.9	38.9	40.1	100
My leader makes decision based on my and my team members inputs	0	0	78	208	130	416
%	0.0	0.0	18.8	50.0	31.3	100
My Leader make decision without taking inputs from any of team member	0	0	110	217	89	416
%	0.0	0.0	26.4	52.2	21.4	100
My Leader doesn't take me review and gives me complete ownership of my results	0	0	122	201	93	416
%	0.0	0.0	29.3	48.3	22.4	100
My Leader has strategy in place to deal with uncertainties	0	0	82	175	159	416

%	0.0	0.0	19.7	42.1	38.2	100
My Leader puts me out of my comfort zone and motivates me to do more	0	0	80	184	152	416
%	0.0	0.0	19.2	44.2	36.5	100
My Leaders give me Clears Roles and Responsibilities along with Timeline and KPIs.	0	0	60	174	182	416
%	0.0	0.0	14.4	41.8	43.8	100
My leader knows my strengths and Weakness and he guides me accordingly	0	0	76	193	147	416
%	0.0	0.0	18.3	46.4	35.3	100
My Leader doesn't appreciate new and innovative ways of working	0	0	88	182	146	416
%	0.0	0.0	21.2	43.8	35.1	100
My Manager provides me with regular coaching/feedback	0	0	119	187	110	416
%	0.0	0.0	28.6	45.0	26.4	100
I Enjoy my camaraderie with my Colleagues	0	0	48	198	170	416
%	0.0	0.0	11.5	47.6	40.9	100
My Manager is supportive & I like interacting with him	0	0	62	154	200	416
%	0.0	0.0	14.9	37.0	48.1	100

	Never	Rarely	Sometimes	Often	Always	Total
Pressure with respective to performance affects me drastically	0	0	143	189	84	416
%	0.0	0.0	34.4	45.4	20.2	100
There is low pressure with respect to performance	0	0	141	189	86	416
%	0.0	0.0	33.9	45.4	20.7	100
There is Healthy pressure impacting my performance positively	0	0	78	198	140	416
%	0.0	0.0	18.8	47.6	33.7	100
There is Continuous Pressure impacting me drastically	0	0	164	172	80	416
%	0.0	0.0	39.4	41.3	19.2	100
There is empowerment with respect to my role	0	0	88	141	187	416
%	0.0	0.0	21.2	33.9	45.0	100

Table 21: Institutional factors

Institutional Factors	Never	Rarely	Sometimes	Often	Always	Total
I feel proud to be associated with my organisation	0	0	32	107	277	416
%	0.0	0.0	7.7	25.7	66.6	100
I feel happy when I am entrusted with Responsibility	0	0	33	119	264	416
%	0.0	0.0	7.9	28.6	63.5	100

Technology impacts my performance positively	0	0	32	116	268	416
%	0.0	0.0	7.7	27.9	64.4	100
Infrastructure supports me a lot in my current role	0	0	81	161	174	416
%	0.0	0.0	19.5	38.7	41.8	100
It is my experience that Production systems plays a important role in increasing Productivity	0	0	38	112	266	416
%	0.0	0.0	9.1	26.9	63.9	100
Reporting / Org Structure affects my performance drastically	0	0	127	153	136	416
%	0.0	0.0	30.5	36.8	32.7	100
I prefer to work with MNCs	0	0	46	138	232	416
%	0.0	0.0	11.1	33.2	55.8	100
Organisational Stability Impacts me performance drastically	0	0	82	156	178	416
%	0.0	0.0	19.7	37.5	42.8	100
I feel proud about my organisations market position	0	0	62	121	233	416
%	0.0	0.0	14.9	29.1	56.0	100

Graph No 22:Plot of Frequency Distributions of Leadership / Managerial Factors

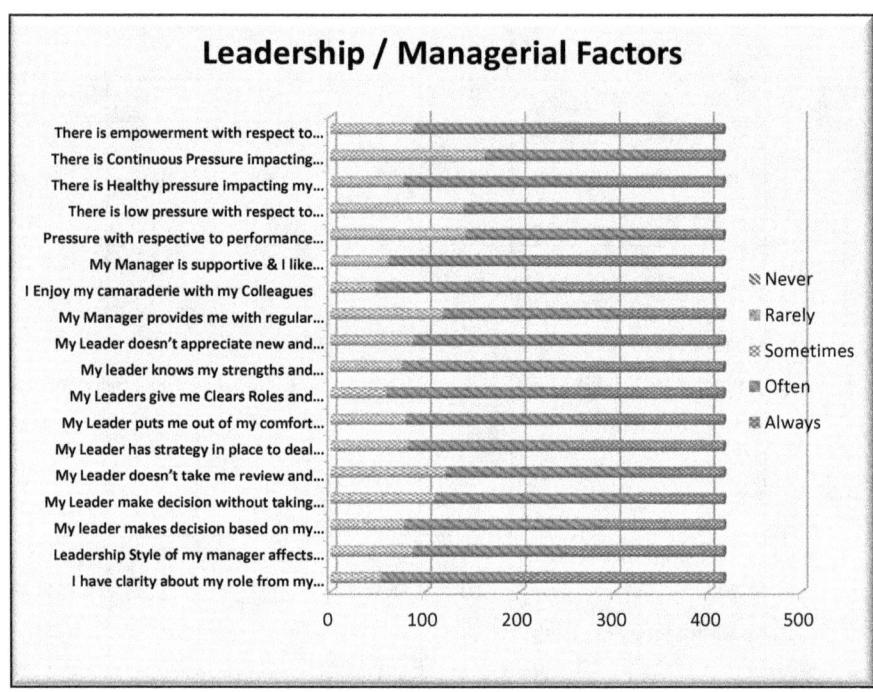

The frequency distribution of respondents according to Institutional Factors along with its bar graph is as given below.

Graph No 23: Plot of Frequency Distributions of Institutional Factors

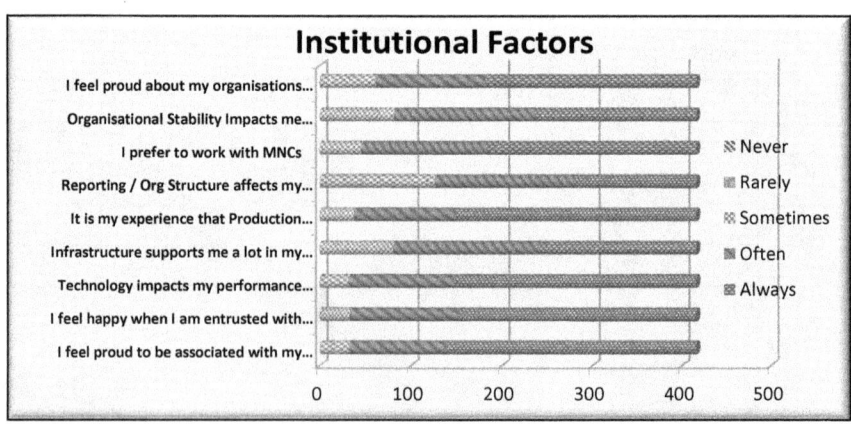

Table 22 : Job Related Factors

The frequency distribution of respondents according to Job Related Factors along with its bar graph is as given below.

Job Related Factors	Never	Rarely	Sometimes	Often	Always	Total
I like my job if my skills my matching with offered role	0	0	25	114	277	416
%	0.0	0.0	6.0	27.4	66.6	100
Clear Goals & Expectations helps me in achieving my Targets	0	0	16	107	293	416
%	0.0	0.0	3.8	25.7	70.4	100
I feel Training provided helps me grow in the organisation	0	0	59	166	191	416
%	0.0	0.0	14.2	39.9	45.9	100
Tools and Equipment's help me improve my productivity	0	0	28	125	263	416
%	0.0	0.0	6.7	30.0	63.2	100
I take break from work, which rejuvenates me and helps me to improve my focus on work	0	0	137	166	113	416
%	0.0	0.0	32.9	39.9	27.2	100
Technology help me improve my productivity	0	0	26	116	274	416
%	0.0	0.0	6.3	27.9	65.9	100
I feel worried if I perceive risk in the job	0	0	168	164	84	416
%	0.0	0.0	40.4	39.4	20.2	100

Location of Work impacts my performance drastically	0	0	99	156	161	416
%	0.0	0.0	23.8	37.5	38.7	100
I like to work for reputed / Status focused jobs	0	0	50	123	243	416
%	0.0	0.0	12.0	29.6	58.4	100
I like to have diversity in my work	0	0	37	165	214	416
%	0.0	0.0	8.9	39.7	51.4	100

Graph No 24: Plot of Frequency Distributions of Job Related Factors

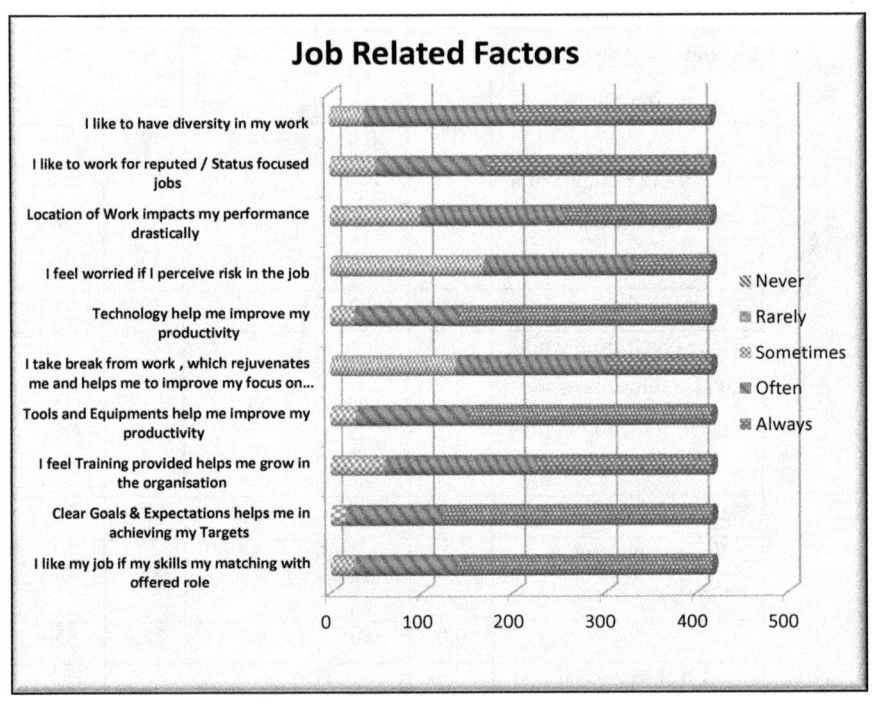

Table 23: Organisational Cultural Factors

The frequency distribution of respondents according to Organizational Cultural Factors along with its bar graph is as given below.

Organisational Cultural Factors	Never	Rarely	Sometimes	Often	Always	Total
Organisational Culture affects me drastically	0	0	47	169	200	416
%	0.0	0.0	11.3	40.6	48.1	100
My Organisation friendly, Innovative, committed and provides me mentoring	0	0	74	160	182	416
%	0.0	0.0	17.8	38.5	43.8	100
My Organisation is Dynamic, Innovative, Transformational and Learning from mistakes	0	0	71	145	200	416
%	0.0	0.0	17.1	34.9	48.1	100
My Organisation is Agile and Flexible to meet customer & market demand	0	0	43	152	221	416
%	0.0	0.0	10.3	36.5	53.1	100
My Organisation is Structured, Stability oriented and Cost oriented	0	0	35	152	229	416
%	0.0	0.0	8.4	36.5	55.0	100
Communication affects my performance drastically	0	0	69	165	182	416
%	0.0	0.0	16.6	39.7	43.8	100
I feel low when I am just communicated to inform	0	0	144	190	82	416
%	0.0	0.0	34.6	45.7	19.7	100

I feel motivated when I am included/involved in the communication	0	0	20	132	264	416
%	0.0	0.0	4.8	31.7	63.5	100
I Learn from my colleagues and also enthusiastically share my learnings with them	0	0	33	149	234	416
%	0.0	0.0	7.9	35.8	56.3	100
I am proud to work with organisation of high ethics and repute	0	0	10	59	347	416
%	0.0	0.0	2.4	14.2	83.4	100
I believe Innovation is key towards organisational growth	0	0	30	75	311	416
%	0.0	0.0	7.2	18.0	74.8	100
My Discipline helps to improve organisations productivity	0	0	14	129	273	416
%	0.0	0.0	3.4	31.0	65.6	100
My Organisation has required level of standardization	0	0	62	175	179	416
%	0.0	0.0	14.9	42.1	43.0	100
I feel proud to work when customer are satisfied with our product	0	0	8	39	369	416
%	0.0	0.0	1.9	9.4	88.7	100

Graph No 25:Plot of Frequency Distributions of Organisational Cultural Factors

Table 24:Opportunity Factors

The frequency distribution of respondents according to Opportunity Factors along with its bar graph is as given below.

Opportunity Factors	Never	Rarely	Sometimes	Often	Always	Total
I feel passionate to perform when I see development opportunities in my organisation	0	0	12	68	336	416
%	0.0	0.0	2.9	16.3	80.8	100

I feel motivate when my managers discuss career path with me	0	0	54	119	243	416
%	0.0	0.0	13.0	28.6	58.4	100
I feel motivated when in grow in the organisation	0	0	33	103	280	416
%	0.0	0.0	7.9	24.8	67.3	100
I feel worried if job security is a concern	0	0	126	148	142	416
%	0.0	0.0	30.3	35.6	34.1	100
Diversity in my team keeps me exited about my role	0	0	57	145	214	416
%	0.0	0.0	13.7	34.9	51.4	100

Graph No 26: Plot of Frequency Distributions of Opportunity Factors

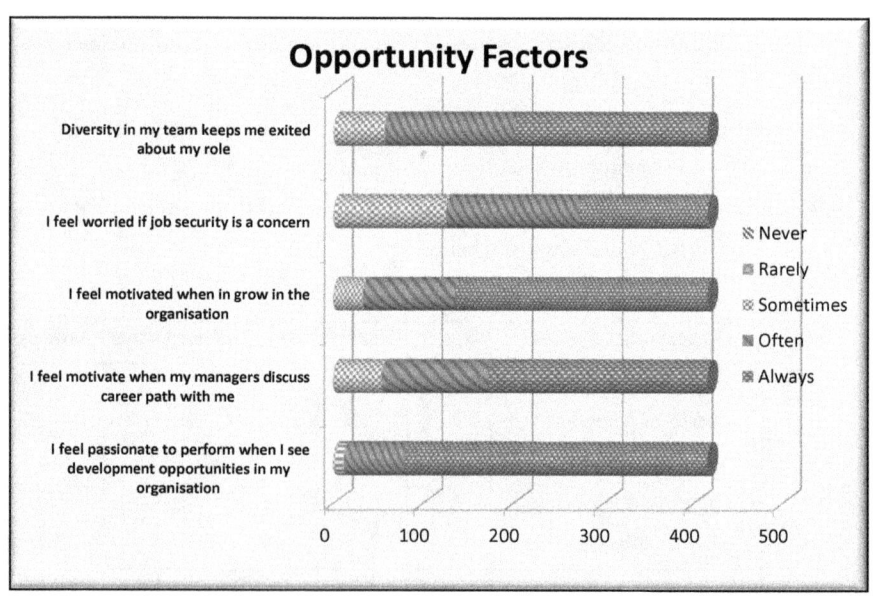

197

Table 25: Motivational Factors

The frequency distribution of respondents according to Motivational Factors along with its bar graph is as given below.

Motivational Factors	Never	Rarely	Sometimes	Often	Always	Total
My Manager motivates me at my job/work	0	0	76	170	170	416
%	0.0	0.0	18.3	40.9	40.9	100
I feel good when my efforts are recognised	0	0	10	113	293	416
%	0.0	0.0	2.4	27.2	70.4	100
I feel motivated when additional responsibilities are entrusted upon me.	0	0	44	102	270	416
%	0.0	0.0	10.6	24.5	64.9	100
I give my best when I am satisfied with my Job	0	0	4	80	332	416
%	0.0	0.0	1.0	19.2	79.8	100
I Love Automobiles (Cars / Bikes / Auto)	0	0	16	100	300	416
%	0.0	0.0	3.8	24.0	72.1	100
My ability impacts my performance drastically	0	0	48	152	216	416
%	0.0	0.0	11.5	36.5	51.9	100
I feel satisfied when I performance appraisal process is fair and transparent	0	0	40	135	241	416
%	0.0	0.0	9.6	32.5	57.9	100

Graph No 27: Plot of Frequency Distributions of Motivational Factors

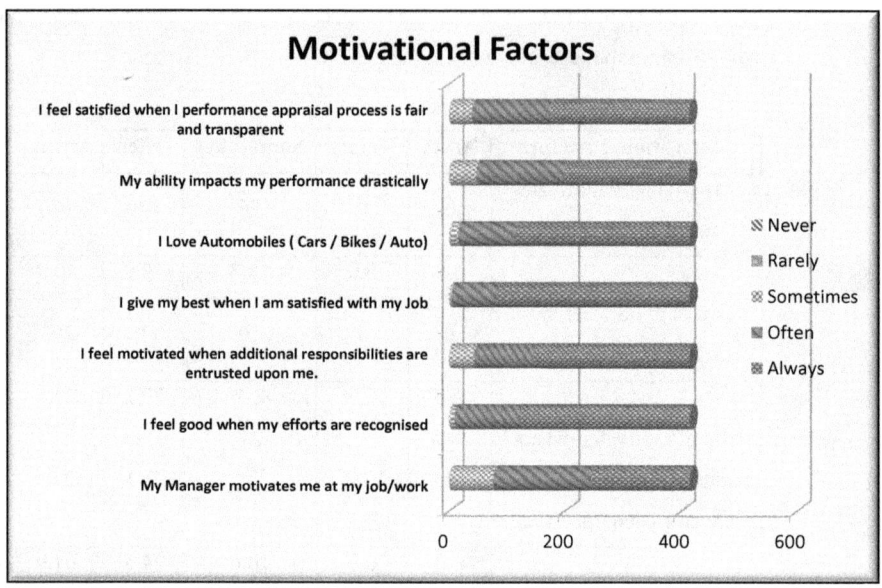

Table 26 : Performance of Employee

The frequency distribution of respondents according to Performance of Employee along with its bar graph is as given below.

Performance of Employee	Never	Rarely	Sometimes	Often	Always	Total
I am able to complete my targets	0	0	18	206	192	416
%	0.0	0.0	4.3	49.5	46.2	100
My Organisations management is happy with my work	0	0	28	200	188	416
%	0.0	0.0	6.7	48.1	45.2	100
I am able to complete my targets within the timeline	0	0	17	207	192	416
%	0.0	0.0	4.1	49.8	46.2	100

My manager is Happy with my work	0	0	26	188	202	416
%	0.0	0.0	6.3	45.2	48.6	100
I am recognised by my team mates for quality of my work	0	0	28	153	235	416
%	0.0	0.0	6.7	36.8	56.5	100
I am getting recognition I deserve	0	0	96	211	109	416
%	0.0	0.0	23.1	50.7	26.2	100
My Colleagues approach me for Challenges they face at work	0	0	66	147	203	416
%	0.0	0.0	15.9	35.3	48.8	100
I got the growth that I deserve in the organisation	0	0	79	211	126	416
%	0.0	0.0	19.0	50.7	30.3	100
I feel good to attend work	0	0	15	128	273	416
%	0.0	0.0	3.6	30.8	65.6	100

Graph No 28: Plot of Frequency Distributions of Performance of Employee

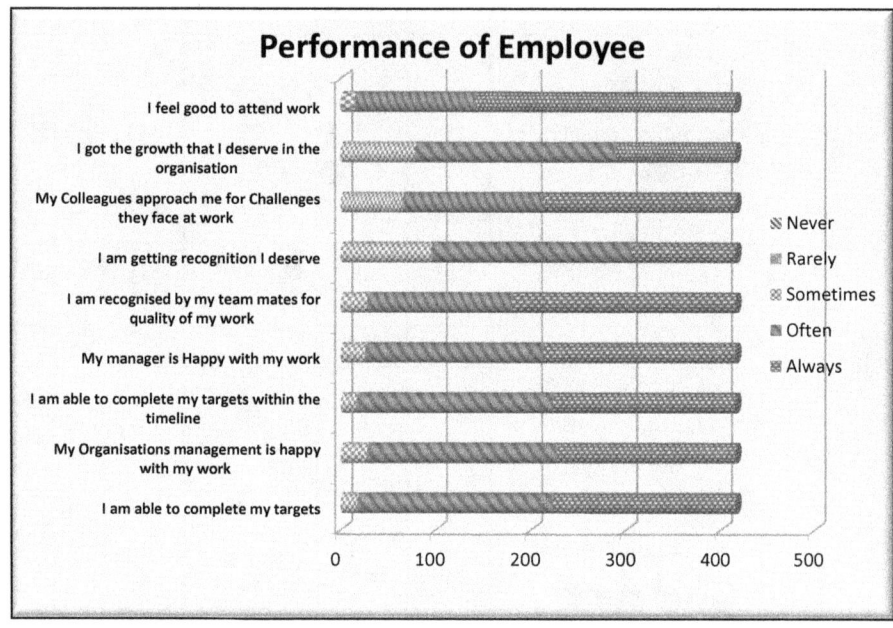

Hypothesis1: There is impact of non-monetary factors on performance of employee.

To test the hypotheses, I

The null hypothesis, H_0:

There is no impact of non-monetary factors on performance of employee.

Vs.

The alternative hypothesis, Ha:

There is impact of non-monetary factors on performance of employee.

The test used is z test for proportions.

Test statistics:

$$Z = \frac{\hat{p} - p_0}{\sqrt{\frac{p_0(1-p_0)}{n}}}$$

Here $\hat{p}$ = sample proportion, p_0 = hypothetical value = 75% = 0.75, n = sample size

Table 27: Calculation table

Sr. No.	Question	Frequency (Often + Always)	Proportion	Z Statistics	P value	Significance
1	Leadership Style of my manager affects me drastically	329	0.79	1.92	0.0271	Significant
2	My leader knows my strengths and Weakness and he guides me accordingly	340	0.82	3.17	0.0008	Significant
3	My Manager is supportive & I like interacting with him	354	0.85	4.76	0.0000	Significant
4	It is my experience that Production systems plays a important role in increasing Productivity	378	0.91	7.47	0.0000	Significant
5	Reporting / Org Structure affects my performance drastically	289	0.69	-2.60	0.9954	Not Significant
6	I like my job if my skills my matching with offered role	391	0.94	8.94	0.0000	Significant

7	Clear Goals & Expectations helps me in achieving my Targets	400	0.96	9.96	0.0000	Significant
8	I feel Training provided helps me grow in the organisation	357	0.86	5.10	0.0000	Significant
9	My Organisation is Agile and Flexible to meet customer & market demand	373	0.90	6.91	0.0000	Significant
10	I feel motivated when I am included/involved in the communication	396	0.95	9.51	0.0000	Significant
11	My Organisation has required level of standardization	354	0.85	4.76	0.0000	Significant
12	I feel passionate to perform when I see development opportunities in my organisation	404	0.97	10.42	0.0000	Significant
13	I feel motivated when in grow in the organisation	383	0.92	8.04	0.0000	Significant

14	I feel good when my efforts are recognised	406	0.98	10.64	0.0000	Significant
15	I feel motivated when additional responsibilities are entrusted upon me.	372	0.89	6.79	0.0000	Significant
16	I give my best when I am satisfied with my Job	412	0.99	11.32	0.0000	Significant
17	I am able to complete my targets	398	0.96	9.74	0.0000	Significant
18	My Organisations management is happy with my work	388	0.93	8.61	0.0000	Significant
19	I am getting recognition I deserve	320	0.77	0.91	0.1825	Not Significant
20	I got the growth that I deserve in the organisation	337	0.81	2.83	0.0023	Significant

If p value < 0.05, the level of significance; the null hypothesis is rejected.

Since p value is less than 0.05 for 18 factors out of 20 factors; the null hypothesis can be rejected for 18 factors out of 20 factors.

Conclusion:

For the majority of parameters, the null hypothesis is being rejected.

Hence there is impact of non-monetary factors on performance of employee.

Hypothesis1 is accepted. Null Hypothesis is Rejected, and Alternate Hypothesis is Accepted.

Hypothesis2: There is positive impact of Leadership/Managerial factors on performance of employee.

This hypothesis is assessed by two distinct tools of statistics; first is Pearson's correlation coefficient & second is Regression model.

To test the hypotheses,

The Null Hypothesis, H_0: There is no impact of Leadership/Managerial factors on performance of employee.

Vs.

The Alternative Hypothesis, H_a: There is positive impact of Leadership/Managerial factors on performance of employee.

Part 1] Pearson's Correlation coefficient

Table 28:The Pearson's correlation coefficient between Leadership/Managerial factors & performance of employee is given as below.

Correlations		Performance of Employee	Leadership / Managerial Factor
Pearson Correlation	Performance of Employee	1.000	.590
	Leadership / Managerial Factor	.590	1.000
P Value	Performance of Employee	-	.000
	Leadership / Managerial Factor	.000	-
N	Performance of Employee	416	416
	Leadership / Managerial Factor	416	416

Since P value is less than 0.05, level of significance; the correlation is significant.

Conclusion:

The correlation between Leadership/Managerial factors & Performance of employee is significant. The positive value of correlation coefficient suggests that one variable increases with the other.

Part 2] Regression Model

The regression model for Performance of employee (Y) on Leadership/Managerial factors (X) is as given below.

Table 29: Descriptive for Hypothesis2

Descriptive Statistics			
	Mean	Std. Deviation	N
Performance of Employee	39.24	3.443	416
Leadership / Managerial Factor	74.07	6.659	416

Table 30: Model Summary for Hypothesis2

Model Summary				
Model	R	R Square	Adjusted R Square	Std. Error of the Estimate
1	.590[a]	.348	.347	2.783
a. Predictors: (Constant), Leadership / Managerial Factor				

Since coefficient of determination i.e. R square = 0.348, 34.8% of the total variation in the dependent variable is explained by independent variables in model 1.

Table 31: ANOVA for Hypothesis2

ANOVA[a]						
Model		Sum of Squares	df	Mean Square	F	Sig.
1	Regression	1714.031	1	1714.031	221.379	.000[b]
	Residual	3205.409	414	7.743		
	Total	4919.440	415			
a. Dependent Variable: Performance of Employee						
b. Predictors: (Constant), Leadership / Managerial Factor						

Since F = 221.379 & p value = 0.00 < 0.05, there is strong evidence to conclude that the regression model is significant.

Table 32 : Regression coefficients & T stat for Hypothesis2

Model		Unstandardized Coefficients		Standardized Coefficients	t	Sig.
		B	Std. Error	Beta		
1	(Constant)	16.630	1.526		10.901	.000
	Leadership / Managerial Factor	.305	.021	.590	14.879	.000
a. Dependent Variable: Performance of Employee						

The regression model for Performance of Employee (Y) on Leadership / Managerial Factor (X) is given as

Y = 16.630 + 0.305*X

Here the intercept is 16.630 implies that the initial Performance of Employee would be 16.630 when the independent variable value is zero.

The slope of variable Leadership / Managerial Factor (X) is 0.305 implies that the Performance of Employee would be increased by 0.305 per unit increase in variable Leadership / Managerial Factor (X).

The positive correlation coefficient (R = 0.590) & positive slope (0.305) indicate that there is positive impact of Leadership/Managerial factors on performance of employee.

Hypothesis2 is accepted. Null Hypothesis is Rejected, and Alternate Hypothesis is Accepted.

Hypothesis3: There is positive impact of Institutional factors on performance of employee.

This hypothesis is assessed by two distinct tools of statistics; first is Pearson's correlation coefficient & second is Regression model.

To test the hypotheses,

The Null Hypothesis, H_0: There is no impact of Institutional factors on performance of employee.

Vs.

The Alternative Hypothesis, H_a: There is positive impact of Institutional factors on performance of employee.

Part 1] Pearson's Correlation coefficient

Table No. 4.29 - The Pearson's correlation coefficient between Institutional factors & performance of employee is given as below.

Correlations			
		Performance of Employee	Institutional Factor
Pearson Correlation	Performance of Employee	1.000	.587
	Institutional Factor	.587	1.000
P value	Performance of Employee	-	.000
	Institutional Factor	.000	-
N	Performance of Employee	416	416
	Institutional Factor	416	416

Since P value is less than 0.05, level of significance; the correlation is significant.

Conclusion:

The correlation between Institutional factors & Performance of employee is significant. The positive value of correlation coefficient suggests that one variable increases with the other.

Part 2] Regression Model

The regression model for Performance of employee (Y) on Institutional factors (X) is as given below.

Table 33 : Descriptive for Hypothesis 3

Descriptive Statistics			
	Mean	Std. Deviation	N
Performance of Employee	39.24	3.443	416
Institutional Factor	39.59	3.176	416

Table 34 : Model Summary for Hypothesis 3

Model Summary				
Model	R	R Square	Adjusted R Square	Std. Error of the Estimate
1	.587[a]	.344	.343	2.791
a. Predictors: (Constant), Institutional Factor				

Since coefficient of determination i.e. R square = 0.344, 34.4% of the total variation in the dependent variable is explained by independent variables in model 1.

Table 35: ANOVA for Hypothesis 3

ANOVA[a]						
Model		Sum of Squares	df	Mean Square	F	Sig.
1	Regression	1694.255	1	1694.255	217.483	.000[b]
	Residual	3225.185	414	7.790		
	Total	4919.440	415			
a. Dependent Variable: Performance of Employee						
b. Predictors: (Constant), Institutional Factor						

Since F = 217.483 & p value = 0.00 < 0.05, there is strong evidence to conclude that the regression model is significant.

Table 36 : Regression coefficients & T stat for Hypothesis 3

Model		Unstandardized Coefficients		Standardized Coefficients	t	Sig.
		B	Std. Error	Beta		
1	(Constant)	14.050	1.713		8.200	.000
	Institutional Factor	.636	.043	.587	14.747	.000
a. Dependent Variable: Performance of Employee						

The regression model for Performance of Employee (Y) on Institutional factors (X) is given as

Y = 14.050 + 0.636*X

Here the intercept is 14.050 implies that the initial Performance of Employee would be 14.050 when the independent variable value is zero.

The slope of variable Institutional factors (X) is 0.636 implies that the Performance of Employee would be increased by 0.636 per unit increase in variable Institutional factors (X).

The positive correlation coefficient (R = 0.587) & positive slope (0.636) indicate that there is positive impact of Institutional factors on performance of employee.

Hypothesis3 is accepted. Null Hypothesis is Rejected, and Alternate Hypothesis is Accepted.

Hypothesis4: There is positive impact of Job Related factors on performance of employee.

This hypothesis is assessed by two distinct tools of statistics; first is Pearson's correlation coefficient & second is Regression model.

To test the hypotheses,

The Null Hypothesis, H_0: There is no impact of Job Related factors on performance of employee.

Vs.

The Alternative Hypothesis, H_a: There is positive impact of Job Related factors on performance of employee.

Part 1] Pearson's Correlation coefficient

Table 37: The Pearson's correlation coefficient between Job Related factors & performance of employee is given as below.

		Performance of Employee	Job Related Factor
Pearson Correlation	Performance of Employee	1.000	.513
	Job Related Factor	.513	1.000
P value	Performance of Employee	-	.000
	Job Related Factor	.000	-
N	Performance of Employee	416	416
	Job Related Factor	416	416

Since P value is less than 0.05, level of significance; the correlation is significant.

Conclusion:

The correlation between Job Related factors & Performance of employee is significant. The positive value of correlation coefficient suggests that one variable increases with the other.

Part 2] Regression Model

The regression model for Performance of employee (Y) on Job Related factors (X) is as given below.

Table 38: Descriptive for Hypothesis 4

Descriptive Statistics			
	Mean	Std. Deviation	N

Performance of Employee	39.24	3.443	416
Job Related Factor	43.53	3.454	416

Table 39 : Model Summary for Hypothesis 4

Model Summary				
Model	R	R Square	Adjusted R Square	Std. Error of the Estimate
1	.513[a]	.264	.262	2.958
a. Predictors: (Constant), Job Related Factor				

Since coefficient of determination i.e. R square = 0.264, 26.4.0% of the total variation in the dependent variable is explained by independent variables in model 1.

Table 40: ANOVA for Hypothesis 4

ANOVA[a]						
Model		Sum of Squares	df	Mean Square	F	Sig.
1	Regression	1296.406	1	1296.406	148.139	.000[b]
	Residual	3623.034	414	8.751		
	Total	4919.440	415			
a. Dependent Variable: Performance of Employee						
b. Predictors: (Constant), Job Related Factor						

Since F = 148.139 & p value = 0.00 < 0.05, there is strong evidence to conclude that the regression model is significant.

Table 41 :Regression coefficients & T stat for Hypothesis 4

Coefficients[a]						
Model		Unstandardized Coefficients		Standardized Coefficients	t	Sig.
		B	Std. Error	Beta		
1	(Constant)	16.965	1.836		9.242	.000

	Job Related Factor	.512	.042	.513	12.171	.000
a. Dependent Variable: Performance of Employee						

The regression model for Performance of Employee (Y) on Job Related factors (X) is given as

Y = 16.965 + 0.512*X

Here the intercept is 16.965 implies that the initial Performance of Employee would be 16.965 when the independent variable value is zero.

The slope of variable Job Related factors (X) is 0.512 implies that the Performance of Employee would be increased by 0.512 per unit increase in variable Job Related factors (X).

The positive correlation coefficient (R = 0.513) & positive slope (0.512) indicate that there is positive impact of Job Related factors on performance of employee.

Hypothesis4 is accepted. Null Hypothesis is Rejected, and Alternate Hypothesis is Accepted.

Hypothesis5: There is positive impact of Organisational Cultural factors on performance of employee.

This hypothesis is assessed by two distinct tools of statistics; first is Pearson's correlation coefficient & second is Regression model.

To test the hypotheses,

The Null Hypothesis, H_0: There is no impact of Organisational Cultural factors on performance of employee.

Vs.

The Alternative Hypothesis, H_a: There is positive impact of Organisational Cultural factors on performance of employee.

Part 1] Pearson's Correlation coefficient

Table 42: The Pearson's correlation coefficient between Organisational Cultural factors & performance of employee is given as below

		Correlations	
		Performance of Employee	Organisational Cultural Factor
Pearson Correlation	Performance of Employee	1.000	.666
	Organisational Cultural Factor	.666	1.000
P Value	Performance of Employee	-	.000
	Organisational Cultural Factor	.000	-
N	Performance of Employee	416	416
	Organisational Cultural Factor	416	416

Since P value is less than 0.05, level of significance; the correlation is significant.

Conclusion:

The correlation between Organisational Cultural factors & Performance of employee is significant. The positive value of correlation coefficient suggests that one variable increases with the other.

Part 2] Regression Model

The regression model for Performance of employee (Y) on Organisational Cultural factors (X) is as given below.

Table 43 : Descriptive for Hypothesis 5

Descriptive Statistics			
	Mean	Std. Deviation	N
Performance of Employee	39.24	3.443	416
Organisational Cultural Factor	62.28	4.572	416

Table 44: Model Summary for Hypothesis 5

Model Summary				
Model	R	R Square	Adjusted R Square	Std. Error of the Estimate
1	.666[a]	.444	.442	2.571
a. Predictors: (Constant), Organisational Cultural Factor				

Since coefficient of determination i.e. R square = 0.444, 44.4% of the total variation in the dependent variable is explained by independent variables in model 1.

Table 45 : ANOVA for Hypothesis 5

ANOVA[a]						
Model		Sum of Squares	df	Mean Square	F	Sig.
1	Regression	2182.656	1	2182.656	330.176	.000[b]
	Residual	2736.784	414	6.611		
	Total	4919.440	415			
a. Dependent Variable: Performance of Employee						
b. Predictors: (Constant), Organisational Cultural Factor						

Since F = 330.176 & p value = 0.00 < 0.05, there is strong evidence to conclude that the regression model is significant.

Table 46: Regression coefficients & T stat for Hypothesis 5

Coefficients[a]						
Model		Unstandardized Coefficients		Standardized Coefficients	t	Sig.
		B	Std. Error	Beta		
1	(Constant)	7.996	1.724		4.638	.000

| | Organisational Cultural Factor | .502 | .028 | .666 | 18.171 | .000 |

a. Dependent Variable: Performance of Employee

The regression model for Performance of Employee (Y) on Organisational Cultural factors (X) is given as

$Y = 7.996 + 0.502*X$

Here the intercept is 7.996 implies that the initial Performance of Employee would be 7.996 when the independent variable value is zero.
The slope of variable Organisational Cultural factors (X) is 0.502 implies that the Performance of Employee would be increased by 0.502 per unit increase in variable Organisational Cultural factors (X).
The positive correlation coefficient (R = 0.666) & positive slope (0.502) indicate that there is positive impact of Organisational Cultural factors on performance of employee.

Hypothesis5 is accepted. Null Hypothesis is Rejected, and Alternate Hypothesis is Accepted.

Hypothesis6: There is positive impact of Opportunity factors on performance of employee.
This hypothesis is assessed by two distinct tools of statistics; first is Pearson's correlation coefficient & second is Regression model.
To test the hypotheses,
The Null Hypothesis, H_0: There is no impact of Opportunity factors on performance of employee.
Vs.
The Alternative Hypothesis, H_a: There is positive impact of Opportunity factors on performance of employee.
Part 1] Pearson's Correlation coefficient

Table 47: The Pearson's correlation coefficient between Opportunity factors & performance of employee is given as below.

Correlations				
		Performance of Employee	Opportunity Factors
Pearson Correlation	Performance of Employee	1.000	.472
	Opportunity Factors	.472	1.000
P value	Performance of Employee	-	.000
	Opportunity Factors	.000	-
N	Performance of Employee	416	416
	Opportunity Factors	416	416

Since P value is less than 0.05, level of significance; the correlation is significant.

Conclusion:

The correlation between Opportunity factors & Performance of employee is significant. The positive value of correlation coefficient suggests that one variable increases with the other.

Part 2] Regression Model

The regression model for Performance of employee (Y) on Opportunity factors (X) is as given below.

Table 48 : Descriptive for Hypothesis 6

Descriptive Statistics			
	Mean	Std. Deviation	N
Performance of Employee	39.24	3.443	416
Opportunity Factors	22.24	1.937	416

Table 49: Model Summary for Hypothesis 6

Model Summary

Model	R	R Square	Adjusted R Square	Std. Error of the Estimate
1	.472[a]	.223	.221	3.039
a. Predictors: (Constant), Opportunity Factors				

Since coefficient of determination i.e. R square = 0.223, 22.3% of the total variation in the dependent variable is explained by independent variables in model 1.

Table 50: ANOVA for Hypothesis 6

ANOVA[a]						
Model		Sum of Squares	df	Mean Square	F	Sig.
1	Regression	1095.770	1	1095.770	118.642	.000[b]
	Residual	3823.670	414	9.236		
	Total	4919.440	415			
a. Dependent Variable: Performance of Employee						
b. Predictors: (Constant), Opportunity Factors						

Since F = 118.642 & p value = 0.00 < 0.05, there is strong evidence to conclude that the regression model is significant.

Table 51: Regression coefficients & T stat for Hypothesis 6

Coefficients[a]						
Model		Unstandardized Coefficients		Standardized Coefficients	t	Sig.
		B	Std. Error	Beta		
1	(Constant)	20.575	1.720		11.963	.000
	Opportunity Factors	.839	.077	.472	10.892	.000
a. Dependent Variable: Performance of Employee						

The regression model for Performance of Employee (Y) on Opportunity factors (X) is given as

Y = 20.575 + 0. 839*X

Here the intercept is 20.575 implies that the initial Performance of Employee would be 20.575 when the independent variable value is zero.

The slope of variable Opportunity factors (X) is 0. 839 implies that the Performance of Employee would be increased by 0. 839 per unit increase in variable Opportunity factors (X).

The positive correlation coefficient (R = 0.472) & positive slope (0. 839) indicate that there is positive impact of Opportunity factors on performance of employee.

Hypothesis6 is accepted. Null Hypothesis is Rejected, and Alternate Hypothesis is Accepted.

Hypothesis7: There is positive impact of Motivational factors on performance of employee.

This hypothesis is assessed by two distinct tools of statistics; first is Pearson's correlation coefficient & second is Regression model.

To test the hypotheses,

The Null Hypothesis, H_0: There is no impact of Motivational factors on performance of employee.

Vs.

The Alternative Hypothesis, H_a: There is positive impact of Motivational factors on performance of employee.

Part 1] Pearson's Correlation coefficient

Table 52: The Pearson's correlation coefficient between Motivational factors & performance of employee is given as below.

Correlations			
		Performance of Employee	Motivational Factor
Pearson Correlation	Performance of Employee	1.000	.651

		Motivational Factor	.651	1.000
P value	Performance of Employee	-	.000
	Motivational Factor	.000	-
N	Performance of Employee	416	416
	Motivational Factor	416	416

Since P value is less than 0.05, level of significance; the correlation is significant.

Conclusion:

The correlation between Motivational factors & Performance of employee is significant. The positive value of correlation coefficient suggests that one variable increases with the other.

Part 2] Regression Model

Table No. 4.49 - The regression model for Performance of employee (Y) on Motivational factors (X) is as given below.

Table 53: Descriptive for Hypothesis 7

Descriptive Statistics			
	Mean	Std. Deviation	N
Performance of Employee	39.24	3.443	416
Motivational Factor	31.81	2.537	416

Table 54: Model Summary for Hypothesis 7

Model Summary				
Model	R	R Square	Adjusted R Square	Std. Error of the Estimate
1	.651[a]	.424	.422	2.617
a. Predictors: (Constant), Motivational Factor				

Since coefficient of determination i.e. R square = 0.424, 42.4% of the total variation in the dependent variable is explained by independent variables in model 1.

Table 55: ANOVA for Hypothesis 7

Model		Sum of Squares	df	Mean Square	F	Sig.
1	Regression	2083.813	1	2083.813	304.236	.000[b]
	Residual	2835.627	414	6.849		
	Total	4919.440	415			
a. Dependent Variable: Performance of Employee						
b. Predictors: (Constant), Motivational Factor						

Since F = 304.236 & p value = 0.00 < 0.05, there is strong evidence to conclude that the regression model is significant.

Table 56: Regression coefficients & T stat for Hypothesis 7

Model		Unstandardized Coefficients		Standardized Coefficients	t	Sig.
		B	Std. Error	Beta		
1	(Constant)	11.141	1.616		6.895	.000
	Motivational Factor	.883	.051	.651	17.442	.000
a. Dependent Variable: Performance of Employee						

The regression model for Performance of Employee (Y) on Motivational factors (X) is given as

Y = 11.141 + 0.883*X

Here the intercept is 11.141 implies that the initial Performance of Employee would be 11.141 when the independent variable value is zero.

The slope of variable Motivational factors (X) is 0.883 implies that the Performance of Employee would be increased by 0.883 per unit increase in variable Motivational factors (X).

The positive correlation coefficient (R = 0.651) & positive slope (0.883) indicate that there is positive impact of Motivational factors on performance of employee.

Hypothesis7 is accepted. Null Hypothesis is Rejected, and Alternate Hypothesis is Accepted.

Summary of Data Analysis:

Sr No	Hypothesis (H0)	Hypothesis (H1)	Test Applied	Result
1	There is no impact of non-monetary factors on performance of employee.	There is impact of non-monetary factors on performance of employee.	Z test for proportion	There is Impact of non-monetary factors on performance of employees. Alternative Hypothesis1 is accepted
2	There is no impact of Leadership/Managerial factors on performance of employee.	There is positive impact of Leadership/Managerial factors on performance of employee.	ANOVA & Regression Coefficient	The positive correlation coefficient (R = 0.590) & positive slope (0.305) indicate that there is positive impact of Leadership/Managerial factors on performance of employee. Alternate Hypothesis2 is accepted
3	There is no impact of Institutional factors on	There is positive impact of Institutional	ANOVA &	The positive correlation coefficient (R = 0.587) & positive

	performance of employee.	factors on performance of employee.	Regression Coefficient	slope (0.636) indicate that there is positive impact of Institutional factors on performance of employee. Alternate Hypothesis3 is accepted.
4	There is no impact of Job Related factors on performance of employee.	There is positive impact of Job Related factors on performance of employee.	ANOVA & Regression Coefficient	The positive correlation coefficient (R = 0.513) & positive slope (0.512) indicate that there is positive impact of Job Related factors on performance of employee. Alternate Hypothesis4 is accepted.
5	There is no impact of Organisational Cultural factors on performance of employee.	There is positive impact of Organisational Cultural factors on performance of employee.	ANOVA & Regression Coefficient	The positive correlation coefficient (R = 0.666) & positive slope (0.502) indicate that there is positive impact of Organisational Cultural factors on performance of employee. Alternate Hypothesis5 is accepted.
6	There is no impact of Opportunity factors on performance of employee.	There is positive impact of Opportunity factors on performance of employee.	ANOVA & Regression Coefficient	The positive correlation coefficient (R = 0.472) & positive slope (0. 839) indicate

				that there is positive impact of Opportunity factors on performance of employee. Alternate Hypothesis6 is accepted
7	There is no impact of Motivational factors on performance of employee.	There is positive impact of Motivational factors on performance of employee.	ANOVA & Regression Coefficient	The positive correlation coefficient (R = 0.651) & positive slope (0.883) indicate that there is positive impact of Motivational factors on performance of employee. Alternate Hypothesis7 is accepted

CHAPTER 5

Findings

Below are the findings under the 6 Factors which we focused for study

1. **Leadership / Managerial Factors**

Among the total number of respondents, 52.9% of respondents were always agreed for I have clarity about my role from my leader and it excites me to give my best

Among the total number of respondents, 40.1% of respondents were always agreed for Leadership Style of my manager affects me drastically

Among the total number of respondents, 31.3% of respondents were always agreed for My leader makes decision based on my and my team members inputs

Among the total number of respondents, 52.2% of respondents were often agreed for My Leader make decision without taking inputs from any of team member

Among the total number of respondents, 48.3% of respondents were always agreed for My Leader doesn't take me review and gives me complete ownership of my results

Among the total number of respondents, 42.1% of respondents were always agreed for My Leader has strategy in place to deal with uncertainties

Among the total number of respondents, 44.2% of respondents were always agreed for My Leader puts me out of my comfort zone and motivates me to do more

Among the total number of respondents, 43.8% of respondents were always agreed for My Leaders give me Clears Roles and Responsibilities along with Timeline and KPIs.

Among the total number of respondents, 46.4% of respondents were often agreed for My leader knows my strengths and Weakness and he guides me accordingly

Among the total number of respondents, 43.8% of respondents were often agreed for My Leader doesn't appreciate new and innovative ways of working

Among the total number of respondents, 45% of respondents were often agreed for My Manager provides me with regular coaching/feedback

Among the total number of respondents, 47% of respondents were often agreed for I Enjoy my camaraderie with my Colleagues

Among the total number of respondents, 48.1% of respondents were always agreed for My Manager is supportive & I like interacting with him

Among the total number of respondents, 45.4% of respondents were often agreed for Pressure with respective to performance affects me drastically

Among the total number of respondents, 45.4% of respondents were often agreed There is low pressure with respect to performance

Among the total number of respondents, 47.6% of respondents were often agreed There is Healthy pressure impacting my performance positively

Among the total number of respondents, 41.3% of respondents were often agreed There is Continuous Pressure impacting me drastically

Among the total number of respondents, 45% of respondents were always agreed for There is empowerment with respect to my role

2. **Institutional Factors**

Among the total number of respondents, 66.6% of respondents were always agreed for I feel proud to be associated with my organisation

Among the total number of respondents, 63.5% of respondents were always agreed for I feel happy when I am entrusted with Responsibility

Among the total number of respondents, 64.4 % of respondents were always agreed for Technology impacts my performance positively

Among the total number of respondents, 41.8% of respondents were always agreed for Infrastructure supports me a lot in my current role

Among the total number of respondents, 64.9% of respondents were always agreed for It is my experience that Production systems plays a important role in increasing Productivity

Among the total number of respondents, 36.8% of respondents were often agreed for Reporting / Org Structure affects my performance drastically

Among the total number of respondents, 55.8% of respondents were always agreed for I prefer to work with MNCs

Among the total number of respondents, 42.8% of respondents were always agreed for Organisational Stability Impacts me performance drastically

Among the total number of respondents, 56% of respondents were always agreed for I feel proud about my organisations market position.

3. **Job Related Factors**

Among the total number of respondents, 66.6 % of respondents were always agreed for I like my job if my skills my matching with offered role

Among the total number of respondents, 70.4% of respondents were always agreed for Clear Goals & Expectations helps me in achieving my Targets

Among the total number of respondents, 45.9% of respondents were always agreed for I feel Training provided helps me grow in the organisation

Among the total number of respondents, 63.2% of respondents were always agreed for Tools and Equipment's help me improve my productivity

Among the total number of respondents, 39.9% of respondents were often agreed for I take break from work, which rejuvenates me and helps me to improve my focus on work

Among the total number of respondents, 65.9% of respondents were always agreed for Technology help me improve my productivity

Among the total number of respondents, 40.4% of respondents were sometimes agreed for I feel worried if I perceive risk in the job

Among the total number of respondents, 38.7% of respondents were always agreed for Location of Work impacts my performance drastically

Among the total number of respondents, 58.4% of respondents were always agreed for I like to work for reputed / Status focused jobs

Among the total number of respondents, 51.4% of respondents were always agreed for I like to have diversity in my work.

4. **Organisational Cultural Factors**

Among the total number of respondents, 48.1% of respondents were always agreed for Organisational Culture affects me drastically

Among the total number of respondents, 43.8% of respondents were always agreed for My Organisation friendly, Innovative, committed and provides me mentoring

Among the total number of respondents, 48.1% of respondents were always agreed for My Organisation is Dynamic, Innovative, Transformational and Learning from mistakes

Among the total number of respondents, 53.1% of respondents were always agreed for My Organisation is Agile and Flexible to meet customer & market demand

Among the total number of respondents, 55% of respondents were always agreed for My Organisation is Structured, Stability oriented and Cost oriented

Among the total number of respondents, 43.8% of respondents were always agreed for Communication affects my performance drastically

Among the total number of respondents, 45.7% of respondents were often agreed for I feel low when I am just communicated to inform

Among the total number of respondents, 65.3% of respondents were always agreed for I feel motivated when I am included/involved in the communication

Among the total number of respondents, 56.3% of respondents were always agreed for I Learn from my colleagues and also enthusiastically share my learnings with them

Among the total number of respondents, 74.8% of respondents were always agreed for I am proud to work with organisation of high ethics and repute

Among the total number of respondents, 83.4% of respondents were always agreed for I believe Innovation is key towards organisational growth

Among the total number of respondents, 65.6% of respondents were always agreed for My Discipline helps to improve organisations productivity

Among the total number of respondents, 43% of respondents were always agreed for My Organisation has required level of standardization

Among the total number of respondents, 88.7% of respondents were always agreed for I feel proud to work when customer are satisfied with our product.

5. Opportunity Factors

Among the total number of respondents, 80.8% of respondents were always agreed for I feel passionate to perform when I see development opportunities in my organisation

Among the total number of respondents, 58.4% of respondents were always agreed for I feel motivate when my managers discuss career path with me

Among the total number of respondents, 67.3% of respondents were always agreed for I feel motivated when in grow in the organisation

Among the total number of respondents, 35.6% of respondents were often agreed for I feel worried if job security is a concern

Among the total number of respondents, 51.4% of respondents were always agreed for Diversity in my team keeps me excited about my role.

6. Motivational Factors

Among the total number of respondents, 40.9% of respondents were always agreed for My Manager motivates me at my job/work

Among the total number of respondents, 70.4% of respondents were always agreed for I feel good when my efforts are recognized

Among the total number of respondents, 64.9% of respondents were always agreed for I feel motivated when additional responsibilities are entrusted upon me.

Among the total number of respondents, 79.8% of respondents were always agreed for I give my best when I am satisfied with my Job

Among the total number of respondents, 72.1% of respondents were always agreed for I Love Automobiles (Cars / Bikes / Auto)

Among the total number of respondents, 51.9% of respondents were always agreed for My ability impacts my performance drastically

Among the total number of respondents, 45.9% of respondents were always agreed for I feel satisfied when I performance appraisal process is fair and transparent

7. Performance factors

Among the total number of respondents, 49.5% of respondents were often agreed for I am able to complete my targets

Among the total number of respondents, 48.1% of respondents were often agreed for My Organizations management is happy with my work

Among the total number of respondents, 49.8% of respondents were often agreed for I am able to complete my targets within the timeline

Among the total number of respondents, 48.6% of respondents were always agreed for My manager is Happy with my work

Among the total number of respondents, 56.5% of respondents were always agreed for I am recognized by my team mates for quality of my work

Among the total number of respondents, 50.7% of respondents were often agreed for I am getting recognition I deserve

Among the total number of respondents, 48.8% of respondents were always agreed for My Colleagues approach me for Challenges they face at work

Among the total number of respondents, 50.7% of respondents were often agreed for I got the growth that I deserve in the organisation

Among the total number of respondents, 65.6% of respondents were always agreed for I feel good to attend work.

All the Factors are positively impacting employee's performance.

Table 57: Summary of Regression Model for all the factors.

Factors	R-Square	Anova	Regression	Correlation Coefficient (R) and +slope
1. Leadership/Managerial factors	R square = 0.348, 34.8% Variations Explained	F = 221.379 & p value = 0.00 < 0.05	Y = 16.630 + 0.305*X	+ correlation coefficient (R = 0.590) & + slope (0.305)
2. Institutional factors	R square = 0.344, 34.4% variation explained	F = 217.483 & p value = 0.00 < 0.05	Y = 14.050 + 0.636*X	+ correlation coefficient (R = 0.587) & + slope (0.636)
3. Job Related factors	R square = 0.264, 26.4.0% variation Explained	F = 148.139 & p value = 0.00 < 0.05	Y = 16.965 + 0.512*X	+ correlation coefficient (R = 0.513) & + slope (0.512)
4. Organizational Cultural factors.	R square = 0.444, 44.4% of variation explained	F = 330.176 & p value = 0.00 < 0.05	Y = 7.996 + 0.502*X	+correlation coefficient (R = 0.666) & + slope (0.502)
5. Opportunity factors	R square = 0.223, 22.3% Variation Explained	F = 118.642 & p value = 0.00 < 0.05	Y = 20.575 + 0.839*X	+ correlation coefficient (R = 0.472) & + slope (0.839)
6. Motivational factors	R square = 0.424, 42.4% Explained	F = 304.236 & p value = 0.00 < 0.05	Y = 11.141 + 0.883*X	positive correlation coefficient (R = 0.651) & positive slope (0.883)

With reference to above table researcher has observed following findings.

1. Motivation Factors are having highest impact on employee's performance considering the slope of variable Motivational factors (X) is 0.883 implies that the Performance of Employee would be increased by 0.883 per unit increase in variable Motivational factors (X).

2. Opportunity Factors are having second highest impact on employee's performance considering the slope of variable Opportunity factors (X) is 0. 839 implies that the Performance of Employee would be increased by 0. 839 per unit increase in variable Opportunity factors (X).

3. Institutional factors are having Third highest impact on employee's performance considering the slope of variable Institutional factors (X) is 0.636 implies that the Performance of Employee would be increased by 0.636 per unit increase in variable Institutional factors (X

4. Job Related Factors are having fourth highest impact on employee's performance considering slope of variable Job-Related factors (X) is 0.512 implies that the Performance of Employee would be increased by 0.512 per unit increase in variable Job-Related factors (X).

5. Organisational Cultural Factors are having fifth highest impact on employee's performance considering slope of variable Organisational Cultural factors (X) is 0.502 implies that the Performance of Employee would be increased by 0.502 per unit increase in variable Organisational Cultural factors (X).

6. Leadership/Managerial Factors are having fifth highest impact on employee's performance considering slope of variable Leadership / Managerial Factor (X) is 0.305 implies that the Performance of Employee would be increased by 0.305 per unit increase in variable Leadership / Managerial Factor (X).

Based on the above study researcher is proposing below model to ensure highest performance of employees in Auto industry.

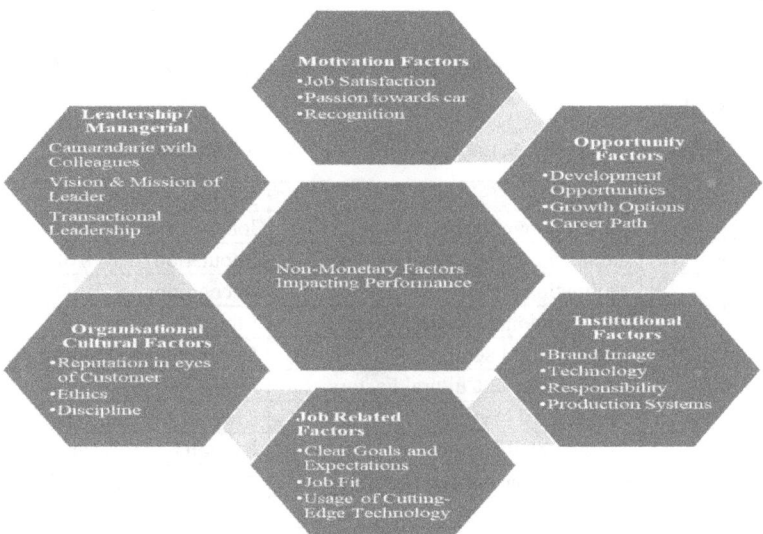

Figure 3: Conceptual Model

Elaboration on Conceptual Model Based on the analysis and findings of study

1. Motivation factor has highest impact on the performance of employee, in which motivation Job satisfaction, Passion towards car and Recognition plays a crucial role in improving the performance of employee.

2. Opportunity Factor has second highest impact on the performance of employee, in which Development opportunities, Growth Options and Clarity of Career path excites employee to deliver high performance

3. Institutional Factors has third highest impact on the performance of employee, in which subfactors like Brand Image, Technology used, Responsibility and Production system used play significant role in supporting employee performance.

4. Job Related Factors has fourth highest impact on the performance of employee, Clear goal setting, Correct Job Fit and Usage of cutting age technology highly positively impacts employee performance.

5. Organisational culture factors has fifth highest impact on performance of employee, sub-factors like Reputation in eyes of Customer, Organisational Ethics and Discipline are important.

6. Leadership / Managerial factor has lowest impact in all the factors, but Camaraderie with Colleagues, Vision & Mission of Leader and Transactional Leadership Subfactors impact most on the employee performance.

Top 10 Factors impacting employee's performance in Auto Industry in Rank Order.

Table 58: – Top 10 Factors Impacting Employee's Performance

Sr No	Factor	Sub-Factor
1	Motivational Factors	Job Satisfaction
2	Organizational Cultural Factors	Reputation in eyes of Customer
3	Motivational Factors	Recognition
4	Organizational Cultural Factors	Ethics
5	Opportunity Factors	Development Opportunities
6	Organizational Cultural Factors	Discipline
7	Job Related Factors	Clear Goals and Expectations
8	Motivational Factors	Passion towards car
9	Organizational Cultural Factors	Communication to Involve
10	Job Related Factors	Job Fit

Communication

Communication plays an important role in success and failure of organization at the same time it also plays a very crucial role in the impacting employee performance. In general, & broadly there are 2 types of communication styles, Communication to Involve and Communication to Inform. It has been found that Communication 83.4% respondents agree that communication impacts performance drastically and in communication, if Style of communication used is "Communication to Involve" then employee will feel motivated and included and will highly impact performance. 95.2% employees prefer "Communication to Involve" Style of motivation.

Organisational Culture

91.6% respondents agreed that the auto OEM's has a "Hierarchy Culture" – which is more towards, Structured, Stability Oriented and Cost Oriented. A mixed or "hierarchy" culture and "Market Culture" would be a good combination to have high performing employees in the organization. 98.1% respondent feel proud when they see customer satisfying with their product.

Leadership

87.02% respondents agree that "Vision & Mission of Leader" impact employee's performance. If the leader provides clear and exciting Vision and Mission which is compelling in nature employees will be excited to give good performance. Vision Literacy, Loftier Vision and Missions should be percolated within the employees.

81.73% respondents believe that if their managers knowns their strengths and weakness and guides / coaches them accordingly the employee can achieve better performance

Passion for Cars / Autos

96.2% respondents agree that if they have passion for cars/auto segment their performance will be better.

Production Support Systems

92.3% respondents agreed that technology used in production of Auto impacts their performance followed by Production systems to which 90.09% respondents agree followed by Infrastructure to which 80.5% respondents agree.

Job Related Factors

Location and Work and Risk associated with the Job are the least impaction factors to employee's performance.

Opportunity Factors

97.1% respondent agreed that the performance passionately when they see development opportunities in the organization, this should be complemented by also provided growth – promotion, Special projects, short term projects to make employee feel that they are growing.

Proud Feeling in Respondents

98.1% respondents feel proud to work when customer is satisfied with their products.
97.6% respondents feel proud to work with organization of high ethics and repute.
92.3% respondents feel proud to be associated with my organization.
85.1% respondents feel proud about my organizations market position.

Based on the above findings we can observe that Customer Satisfaction, Ethics/Reputation & Market positions makes respondent feel proud about their association with their employer in turn impacting their performance.

CHAPTER 6

Conclusion

The study examined the effect of monetary and non-monetary reward factors on employee performance. The organizational challenge is to determine the optimal balance between monetary and non-monetary factors that will improve employee performance supporting in achieving the organization's objectives. Both monetary and Non-Monetary play a crucial role in supporting employee performance.

The study's first purpose was to catalogue the non-monetary factors employed by the automobile industry. According to the study, non-monetary factors considerations such as motivation, recognition, communication, leadership, vision & mission are frequently used the automobile industry. In the automobile industry, non-monetary benefits broadly are categories int 6 categories Motivational, Cultural, Opportunity, Job Related, Institutional and Leadership/Managerial.

A questionnaire containing questions was developed and distributed to the Auto OEM company employees based on the non-monetary aspects in place. The questionnaire included 72 questions on five-point Likert scale about non-monetary factors, in order to explore the research objectives.

Objective 1 - Identify of Non- Monetary of Factors which impact performance in Automobile manufacturing industries.

The study's first purpose was to catalogue the non-monetary factors employed by the automobile industry. According to the study, non-monetary factors considerations such as motivation, recognition, communication, leadership, vision & mission are frequently used the automobile industry. In the automobile industry, non-monetary benefits broadly are categories int 6 categories Motivational, Cultural, Opportunity, Job Related, Institutional and Leadership/Managerial. After exhaustive Literature Review overall we identified 45 factors which were later combined in 6 umbrella factors to carry out the study.

F1-Leadership / Managerial	F2 - Institutional	F3 - Job Related
Vision & Mission of Leader	Brand Image	Job Fit
Leadership Style	Reponsiblity	Clear Goals and Expectations
Coaching by Lead	Technology	Tools and Equipment / Resources
Camaradarie with Colleagues	Infrastructure	Work Life Balance
Relationship with Manager	Production Systems	Usage of Technology
Performance Pressure	Structure	Risk associated with Job
Empowement	Indian / MNC	Location of work
	Organisational Stability	Reputation/Status of the Job
	Market Position	Diversity in Job

F4 - Organisational Culture	F5-Opportunity	H-6 Motivation
Culture	Development Opportunities	Motivation
Communication	Career Path	Recognition
social learning	Growth Options	Job Enrichment
Ethics	Job Security	Job Satisfaction
Innovation	Diversity	Passion towards car
Discipline		Ability
Standardisation		Performance Appraisal Process
Reputation in eyes of Customer		

Figure 4: Factors and subfactors Identified for study impacting employee's performance.

Further for the studies we also considered various dements of Sub-Factors like Communication types, Leadership Styles, Pressure/Stress etc. The identification of these monetary factors impacting performance have given all together a new perspective to factors impacting performance.

Objective 2 - To establish relationship between Non-Monetary factors and performance of employee.

The second purpose of this study was to ascertain the relative importance of monetary and nonmonetary rewards in the case study. As a result, the study establishes a favorable correlation between monetary factors and employee performance. Job Satisfaction and Recognition are the most influential variables. so, the business should develop policies that effectively handle these two factors, which will result in increased motivation and retention rates in the long run. Additionally, automobile industry includes non-monetary incentives, which will result in increased employee motivation in turn resulting into employee performance. Thus, the author can assert that non-monetary benefits have an effect on the organization's employees' performance.

Table 59: Regression Summary

Factors	R-Square	Anova	Regression	Correlation Coefficient (R) and +slope
1. Leadership/Managerial factors	R square = 0.348, 34.8% Variations Explained	F = 221.379 & p value = 0.00 < 0.05	Y = 16.630 + 0.305*X	+ correlation coefficient (R = 0.590) & + slope (0.305)
2. Institutional factors	R square = 0.344, 34.4% variation explained	F = 217.483 & p value = 0.00 < 0.05	Y = 14.050 + 0.636*X	+ correlation coefficient (R = 0.587) & + slope (0.636)
3. Job Related factors	R square = 0.264, 26.4.0% variation Explained	F = 148.139 & p value = 0.00 < 0.05	Y = 16.965 + 0.512*X	+ correlation coefficient (R = 0.513) & + slope (0.512)
4. Organizational Cultural factors.	R square = 0.444, 44.4% of variation explained	F = 330.176 & p value = 0.00 < 0.05	Y = 7.996 + 0.502*X	+correlation coefficient (R = 0.666) & + slope (0.502)
5. Opportunity factors	R square = 0.223, 22.3% Variation Explained	F = 118.642 & p value = 0.00 < 0.05	Y = 20.575 + 0.839*X	+ correlation coefficient (R = 0.472) & + slope (0.839)
6. Motivational factors	R square = 0.424, 42.4% Explained	F = 304.236 & p value = 0.00 < 0.05	Y = 11.141 + 0.883*X	positive correlation coefficient (R = 0.651) & positive slope (0.883)

With the help of statistical tools like Annova and Regression we have established relationship between different factors like Motivational, Cultural, Opportunity, Job Related, Institutional and Leadership/Managerial whose summary is mentioned in above table.

Further it can be concluded that there is positive correlation / impact of all the six factors identified on the impact of employee's performance. This was also tested with **Hypothesis 1** of the study.

Its evident from the study that the employers have put calibrated & balanced efforts to ensure these factors in a right mix to have optimum levels of performance from employees.

Objective 3 - To establish or rank non-monetary factors based on their positive impact on employee's performance.
Table No. -

The third purpose of this study was to establish or rank non-monetary factors based on their positive impact on employee's performance. According to respondents, all the 6 factors positively impact employees' performance. Employees are more likely to stay with a company if they are Satisfied, Recognized, Values and Coached. Employees wish to enhance their professional qualifications through exposure to cutting-edge technology and exposure to latest Auto Production systems.

Table 60: Regression Summary

Factors	R-Square	Anova	Regression	Correlation Coefficient (R) and +slope
1. Leadership/Managerial factors	R square = 0.348, 34.8% Variations Explained	F = 221.379 & p value = 0.00 < 0.05	Y = 16.630 + 0.305*X	+ correlation coefficient (R = 0.590) & + slope (0.305)
2. Institutional factors	R square = 0.344, 34.4% variation explained	F = 217.483 & p value = 0.00 < 0.05	Y = 14.050 + 0.636*X	+ correlation coefficient (R = 0.587) & + slope (0.636)
3. Job Related factors	R square = 0.264, 26.4.0% variation Explained	F = 148.139 & p value = 0.00 < 0.05	Y = 16.965 + 0.512*X	+ correlation coefficient (R = 0.513) & + slope (0.512)
4. Organizational Cultural factors.	R square = 0.444, 44.4% of variation explained	F = 330.176 & p value = 0.00 < 0.05	Y = 7.996 + 0.502*X	+correlation coefficient (R = 0.666) & + slope (0.502)
5. Opportunity factors	R square = 0.223, 22.3% Variation Explained	F = 118.642 & p value = 0.00 < 0.05	Y = 20.575 + 0.839*X	+ correlation coefficient (R = 0.472) & + slope (0.839)
6. Motivational factors	R square = 0.424, 42.4% Explained	F = 304.236 & p value = 0.00 < 0.05	Y = 11.141 + 0.883*X	positive correlation coefficient (R = 0.651) & positive slope (0.883)

Study concluded that the all the non-monetary factors are positively impacting employee's performance. Further based on the data following is the rank of factors impacting employee's performance.

Rank 1 - Motivational Factors

Rank 2 - Opportunity Factors

Rank 3 - Institutional Factors

Rank 4 - Job Related Factors

Rank 5 - Organisational Culture Factors

Rank 6 – Leadership/Managerial

Based on the above ranking employers can calibrate the Employee life cycle management process, focus of factors and make sure that we have optimum level of performance.

Objective 4 - Based on the finding of study, Creation of Model/structure to enhance performance of employees.

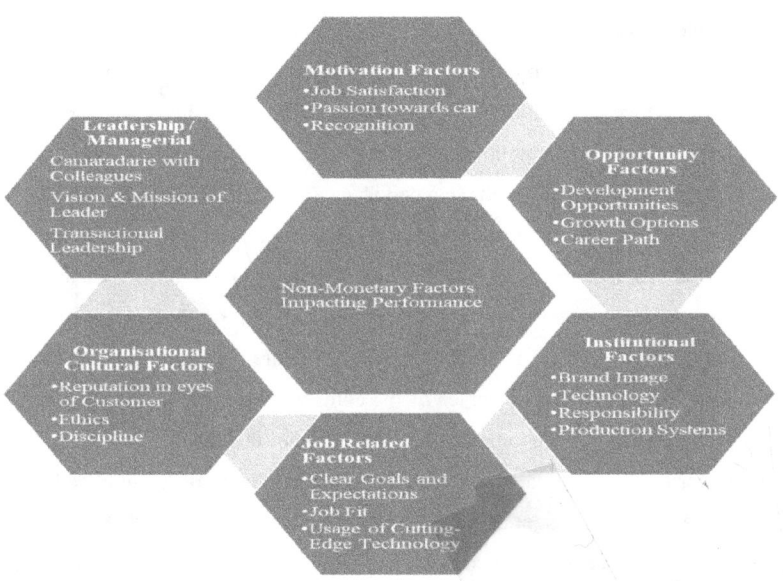

Figure 5: Creation of Model/structure to enhance performance of employees.

Based on the study the author is proposing to have well balanced and synergized combinations of the 6 factors and their Subfactors which will impact employee's performance. Figuring out the right mix is itself a challenge as we are dealing with human beings and not machines, person the person the factors may vary as well.

Finally, it can be demonstrated that "there is in the automobile business, non-monetary factors have a strong and considerable beneficial link with employee performance. The ability and motivation, declarative knowledge, procedural knowledge, motivation to work, attainment of specified goals, staff competence, and established standards all contributed to these performances.

Employment security, decent working circumstances, participation in goal planning and achievement, staff recognition, job expansion, incentives that address social needs, improved working conditions, and fringe benefits were revealed as non-monetary motivations.

Employees have requirements that should be met by their employer to minimize demotivation or distraction from work. As a result, the automobile industry must place a premium on non-monetary motivators in order to maintain, attract, and improve employee performance, satisfaction, and commitment.

Other future research may wish to investigate additional elements affecting employee performance that were not examined or focused on in this study, including employee loyalty, employee emotions, work time flexibility, business culture and values, and employee retention. Another conceivable expansion of this study is to include complete coverage of both companies' other geographical areas. Given that this study did not include enough managers, it would be interesting for future research to include a representative sample of managers and conduct interviews to augment the data collection procedure. If possible, inputs for future publications could come from other sources, such as the outcomes of the companies' performance rating procedures; this would assist assure a more accurate depiction of the data.

Other independent variables, such as the work environment, could be further dissected and analysed in greater detail by focusing on their various facets. For instance, the work environment encompasses office lighting, workstation spacing, office design, and noise levels. Future research may examine the effect of various factors on employee performance by comparing the "before" and "after" effects of these factors. For example, employee performance might be measured before to and following training in order to compare and assign a value to the training received. Additional studies could also look at other demographic aspects and regional trends. Finally, future research may

Chapter 7

Further Scope of Research

Future studies should examine the influence of non-monetary rewards on employee performance in industries other than the automobile sector. Again, additional research should be conducted to determine the effect of non-monetary rewards on employee job satisfaction, security, work environment, job match, and participative management.
Study is focusing on OEM which further can be expanded to Auto Suppliers as well. Blue Collars are not part of the study as they are governed by law of the land and the benefits are as per the Settlement signed between union and company management. Further Going ahead blue collars can also be included in the scope of study.

A study on Monetary factors can be carried out and merged with findings of current study to create a Holistic and robust model understand impact of both the factors on the employee's performance. Geographical Scale be increased and study and be further expanded to the two-wheeler, three-wheeler and truck and Tractor manufacturing plant across the geography of India, also it Can be expanded to manufacturing & IT industries as well to understand the impact of Non-Monetary factors on performance.

Depending on the financial need factor of employees, both monetary and non-monetary play different role in impacting employee performance. A study can be carried out to understand linkage in Financial need factor of employee and his performance.

The conceptual model proposed herein can be implemented in few Auto Industries and its results can be validated by observing actual impact on performance of employee, the study on implementation of model based on the observation can help to calibrate the model and make is more scalable, robust and precise.

As a part of this journey researcher proposes to provide excerpts of this study to auto industry body for their consumptions.

Bibliography

1. A. B.Safiullah,"Impact of Rewards on Employee Motivation of the Telecommunication Industry of Bangladesh: An Empirical Study",Journal of Business and Management,Vol.16, Issue.12, pp.22-30, 2014.
2. A. S. Sajuyigbe, B. O.Olaoye& M. A.Adeyemi, "Impact of Reward on Employees Performance in a Selected Manufacturing Companies in Ibadan, Oyo State, Nigeria',International Journal of Arts and Commerce, Vol.2, Issue.2, pp.27-32, 2013.
3. Aguinis, & Kraiger, 2009). Aguinis, H., & Kraiger, K. (2009). Benefits of training and development for individuals and teams, organizations, and society. Annual review of psychology, 60, 451-459.
4. ALKHALIEL ADEEB ABDULLAH and HOOI LAI WAN (Dec 2013), "Relationships of Non-Monetary Incentives, Job Satisfaction and Employee Job Performance ", International Review of Management and Business Research , ISSN: 2306-9007 ,Vol. 2 Issue.4
5. Amanda and Jonathan (2006), Amanda, G., & Jonathan, H. (2006). Defining a case of work-related stress. Health & Safety Executive Report (449). HSE Books.
6. Ampofo-Boateng, Merican, & Wiegan, 1997). Ampofo-Boateng, K., Merican, W.R.A., Jamil, A., & Wiegand, B. (1997), Employees adaptation to technological changes in a multinational corporation in Malaysia, innovation in technology management – the key to global leadership. PICMET'97- Portland. International Conference on Management and Technology
7. Amponsah-Tawiah, & Darteh-Baah, 2010). Boshoff, C., & Arnolds, C. (1995). Some antecedents of employee commitment and their influence on job performance. South African Journal of Business Management, 26 (4), 125-135.
8. Anna MokhniukLarysa Yushchyshyna (April 2018), The Impact of Monetary and Non-Monetary Factors of Motivation on Employee Productivity, Economic journal of Lesia Ukrainka Eastern European National University 13(1):94-101
9. Armstrong, & Murlis, 2004) Armstrong, & Murlis, H. (2004). Reward management: A handbook of remuneration strategy and practice. 5th Ed. Kogan Page: London.
10. Armstrong, 2010). Boshoff, C., & Arnolds, C. (1995). Some antecedents of employee commitment and their influence on job performance. South African Journal of Business Management, 26 (4), 125-135.

11. Armstrong, 2010). Maslow, A.H. (1987). Motivation and Personality, 3rd Ed. New York, NY: Harper & Row.
12. ASAMU Festus Femi(Aug. 2014), The Impact of Communication on Workers' Performance in Selected Organisations in Lagos State, Nigeria, IOSR Journal Of Humanities And Social Science (IOSR-JHSS), Volume 19, Issue 8, Ver. II (Aug. 2014), PP 75-82, e-ISSN: 2279-0837, p-ISSN: 2279-0845.
13. Banker,R.D.,Lee,S.,& potter,G.(1996), 'A field study of the impact of a performance-based incentive plan', Journal of Accounting and Economics,21,195-226
14. Bartram and Casimir (2007) Ampofo-Boateng, K., Merican, W.R.A., Jamil, A., & Wiegand, B. (1997), Employees adaptation to technological changes in a multinational corporation in Malaysia, innovation in technology management – the key to global leadership. PICMET'97- Portland. International Conference on Management and Technology
15. Baumruk, & Gorman et al., 2006): Baumruk, R., & Gorman, B. (2006). Why managers are crucial to increasing engagement. Melcrum Publishing.
16. Belly Onanda (September 2015), 'The Effects of Motivation on Job Performance: A Case Study of KCB Coast Region', International Journal of Scientific and Research publications, Vol.5, Issue 9, ISSN 2250-3153.
17. Bhattacharyya, 2007). Bhattacharyya, D.K. (2007). Human Resource Research Methods. New Delhi: Oxford University Press.
18. Borman, White, Pulkos, and Oppler (1991) and Hough et al. (1990) Borman, W.C., White, L.A., Pulkos, E.D., & Oppler, S.H. (1991). Models of supervisor job performance ratings. Journal of Applied Psychology, 76, 863-872.
19. Boshoff, & Arnolds, 1995). Boshoff, C., & Arnolds, C. (1995). Some antecedents of employee commitment and their influence on job performance. South African Journal of Business Management, 26 (4), 125-135.
20. Brill, Margulis, Konar, and Bosti (1984) Harrison, L. L., & Novak, D. (2006). Evaluation of a gerontological nursing continuing education programme: Effect on nurses' knowledge and attitudes and on patients' perceptions and satisfaction. Journal of Advanced Nursing, 13(6), 684-692.
21. Carless (2004) Sarah, Y., Nik, K., Pranav, K., (2012) Factors Affecting Employee Satisfaction among Nonteaching Staff in Higher Educational Institutions in Malaysia. American Journal of Economics, Special issue, 93-96.

22. Carrell, Kuzmits, and Elbert (1989) Armstrong, & Murlis, H. (2004). Reward management: A handbook of remuneration strategy and practice. 5th Ed. Kogan Page: London.
23. Caruth and Handlogten (2002), Caruth, D.L., & Handlogten, G.D. (2002). Compensating Sales Personnel. The American Salesman, 47(4), 6-15.
24. Chen and Tjosvold (2006) Ampofo-Boateng, K., Merican, W.R.A., Jamil, A., & Wiegand, B. (1997), Employees adaptation to technological changes in a multinational corporation in Malaysia, innovation in technology management – the key to global leadership. PICMET'97- Portland. International Conference on Management and Technology
25. Cheryl (1999), Sarah, Y., Nik, K., Pranav, K., (2012) Factors Affecting Employee Satisfaction among Nonteaching Staff in Higher Educational Institutions in Malaysia. American Journal of Economics, Special issue, 93-96.
26. Chukwuma Edwin maduka and Dr. obiefuna okafor (August,2014), 'Effect of Motivation on Employee Productivity: A study of manufacturing companies in Nnewi, International Journal of Management Studies and Research, Vol.2, Issue 7, ISSN 2349-0330.
27. Clark, & Watson, 1991). Clark, L.A., & Watson, D. (1991). General affective dispositions in physical and psychological health. In C.R. Snyder & D.R. Forsyth (Eds.) Handbook of social and clinical psychology: The health perspective. New York: Pergamon
28. Cole (2002) Cole, G.A. (2002). Personnel and human resource management, 5th Ed. Continuum London: York Publishers.
29. Costa and McCrae's (1992) Costa, P.T. & McCrae, R.R. (1992). Revised NEO Personality Inventory (NEO-PI-R) and NEO Five Factor Model (NEO-FFI) professional manual. Odessa, FL: Psychological Assessment Resources.
30. Daniel Njoya Ndungu(2017) The Effects of Rewards and Recognition on Employee Performance in Public Educational Institutions: A Case of Kenyatta University, Kenya , Global Journal of Management and Business Research: A Administration and Management Volume 17 Issue 1 Version 0 Year 2017
31. DeCenzo and Robbins (1996) DeCenzo, D. A., & Robbins, S. P. (1996). Human resources management. New York: John Wiley & Sons, Inc.

32. Dernovsek (2008), Ampofo-Boateng, K., Merican, W.R.A., Jamil, A., & Wiegand, B. (1997), Employees adaptation to technological changes in a multinational corporation in Malaysia, innovation in technology management – the key to global leadership. PICMET'97- Portland. International Conference on Management and Technology
33. Dr. Ashraf and Dr.Md.shabieb (April, 2014), 'The role of the incentives and reward system in enhancing employee's performance "A case of Jordanian tourism and travel institutions', International Journal of Academic Research in Business and Social Sciences, Vol.4, No.5, ISSN: 2222-6990.
34. Dr. Jnanes O Samwel (2017), 'Role of Employee Motivation on the Production of Mining Companies in Geita Gold Mine, Tanzania', International Journal of Science and Research, Vol.6, Issue 11, ISSN 2319- 7064.
35. Dr. KIRAN KUMAR THOTI, G.N.SRINIVAS CHAKRI and B. PAVANI ( ), A STUDY ON EFFECTIVE TRAINING PROGRAMMES IN AUTO MOBILE INDUSTRY, BIMS International Journal of Social Science Research ISSN 2455-4839
36. Dr. KIRAN KUMAR THOTI, G.N.SRINIVAS CHAKRI and B. PAVANI, "A STUDY ON EFFECTIVE TRAINING PROGRAMMES IN AUTO MOBILE INDUSTRY", BIMS International Journal of Social Science Research ISSN 2455-4839
37. Dr.P.GURUSAMY and J. PRIYADHARSHINI (Jan 2019) , "ENHANCING THE IMPORTANCE OF NON-MONETARY APPRECIATION ON EMPLOYEES PERFORMANCE IN BANKING SECTOR", RESEARCH EXPLORER-A Blind Review & Refereed Quarterly International Journal ISSN: 2250-1940 (P) 2349-1647 (O) Impact Factor: 3.655 (CIF), 2.78 (IRJIF), 2.62 (NAAS) Volume V, Issue 22 January - March 2019
38. Dr.Shamila Singh , Impact of Employee Engagement on Performance, IOSR Journal of Business and Management (IOSR-JBM) e-ISSN: 2278-487X, p-ISSN: 2319-7668. Volume 20, Issue 6. Ver. VII (June. 2018), PP 66-76
39. Dunlop, P.D. and Lee, K. (2004), Workplace Deviance, Organizational Citizenship Behavior and Business Unit Performance: the Bad Apples do spoil the whole Barrel, Journal of Organizational Behavior, 25, 67-80
40. Ecker, Randal, and Riegel (1995) Becker, T.E., Randal, D.M., & Riegel, C.D. (1995). The multidimensional view of commitment and theory of reasoned action: a comparative evaluation. Journal of Management, 21(4), 617-638.

41. Ekerman, 2006). Baumruk, R., & Gorman, B. (2006). Why managers are crucial to increasing engagement. Melcrum Publishing.
42. Elizabeth Boye kuranchie-menash and Kwesi Ampnash-Tawaiah (December, 2015), 'Employee motivation and work performance: A comparative study of mining companies in Ghana', Journal of industrial Engineering and Management- http://dx.doi.org/10.3926/jiem.1530, ISSN: 2013-0953.
43. Elumah Lucas O, Ibrahim Olaniyi M and Shobayo Peter B (July, 2016) 'The Impact of Financial and Moral Incentives on Organizational 3 Performance: A Study of Nigerian Universities', Arabian Journal of Business and Management Review, Vol.6, Issue 5, ISSN 2223-5833.
44. Er. Prakash Kumar Sen (2016), 'Study on Factor Affecting Motivation of Employees', international journal of advance research in science and engineering, Vol.No.5, Issue No.04. ISSN 2319-8354.
45. Falola H.O, Ibidunni A.S, Olokundun M. (2014), 'Incentive packages and employees' attitude to work: A study of selected government parastatal in Ogun state, south-west, Nigeria', International Journal of Research in Business and Social Science, Vol.3, No.1, ISSN: 2147-4478.
46. Felson, R.B. (1984), The Effect of Self-Appraisals of Ability, on Academic Performance, Journal of Personality and Social Psychology, 47, 944-952
47. Fisher, 1980). Fisher, B. A. (1980). Small group decision making: Communication and the group process 2nd Ed. New York, NY: McGraw-Hill.
48. Fletcher, & Williams, 1996). Fletcher, C., & Williams, R. (1996). Performance management, job satisfaction and organizational commitment. British Journal of Management, 7(2), 169-179.
49. French (1975), French, J. R. (1975). A comparative look at stress and strain in policemen. New York: Elsevier.
50. G.Ahiabor, "The impact of Incentives on Productivity of Firms in Ghana: A Case Study of Ghana Airport Company Limited",Problems of Management in the 21stCentury,Vol.8, pp.6-1, 2013.
51. Garba Bala.B, Abdu jaafaru. B, M.B. Jakada, K.S. Yakubu (September, 2017) 'Monetary Reward and Teacher Performance in Selected Public Secondary Schools in Kano State, Nigeria', The International Journal of Business and Management, Vol.5, Issue 9, ISSN 2321-8916.

52. Greenwald, A.G. (1980), The Totalitarian Ego: Fabrication and Revision of Personal History, American Psychologist, 35, 603-618
53. H. Barum, J. Kutzin and H.Saxenian (1995), 'incentives and provider payment methods', International Journal of Health planning and management, Vol. 10, 23-45, ISSN: 1099-175
54. Hackman and Oldham (1980), Hackman, J.R., & Oldham, G.R. (1980). Work redesign. Readings, MA: Addison-Wesley
55. Hamdan Rasheed Al-Jammal and Akif Lutfi Al-Khasawneh and Mohammad Hasan Hamadat(2015), "The impact of the delegation of authority on employees' performance at great Irbid municipality: case study" International Journal of Human Resource Studies ,ISSN 2162-3058 ,2015, Vol. 5, No. 3 48 www.macrothink.org/ijhrs
56. Harrison and Novak (2006) Harrison, L. L., & Novak, D. (2006). Evaluation of a gerontological nursing continuing education programme: Effect on nurses' knowledge and attitudes and on patients' perceptions and satisfaction. Journal of Advanced Nursing, 13(6), 684-692.
57. Hasan Saliah Suliman Al-Qudah (October, 2016) 'Impact of Moral and Material Incentives on Employee's Performance; An Empirical Study in Private Hospitals at Capital Amman', International Business Research; Vol. 9, No. 11, E-ISSN 1913-9012.
58. Hassan Hijry a , Asif Haleem b (2017_, "Study the Factors That Influence Employees Performance in the Steel Factory, Saudi Arabia" Proceedings of the 2017International Conference on Industrial Engineering and Operations Management Rabat, Morocco, April 11-13,2017 899
59. Hassan M. E. Aboazoum, Umar Nimran and , Mochammad Al Musadieq(2015), "Analysis Factors Affecting Employees Job Performance in Libya", IOSR Journal of Business and Management (IOSR-JBM) e-ISSN: 2278-487X, p-ISSN: 2319-7668. Volume 17, Issue 7.Ver. I (July 2015), PP 42-49,DOI: 10.9790/487X-17714249 www.iosrjournals.org
60. Herzberg (1986) Herzberg, F. (1986). One more time: How do you motivate employees? Harvard Business Review, 65(5), 433-448.
61. Herzberg (1986), Herzberg, F. (1986). One more time: How do you motivate employees? Harvard Business Review, 65(5), 433-448.
62. Heydy Jimenez , Toni Didona (2015), "Perceived Job Security and its Effects on Job Performance: Unionized VS. NonUnionized Organizations" The International Journal

of Social Sciences and Humanities Invention 4(8): 3761-3767, 2017 DOI: 10.18535/ijsshi/v4i8.11 ICV 2015: 45.28 ISSN: 2349-2031 © 2017, THEIJSSHI

63. Himanshu Kushwaha, IMPACT OF FINANCIAL AND NON-FINANCIAL INCENTIVES ON EMPLOYEE PRODUCTIVITY,Review of Business and Technology Research, Vol. 15, No.1, August 2018, ISSN: 1941-9406 (Print), ISSN: 1941-9414 (CD) 20

64. Hitesh Gupta, S. L. Gupta , Research Methodology: Text and Cases with CPSS Applications 2nd Edition , Publisher: International Book House, ISBN: 9788191064278, 8191064278,Edition: 2nd Edition, 2011

65. Hough, Eaton, Dunnette, Kamp, & McCloy, 1990) Hough, L.M., Eaton, N.K., Dunnette, M.D., Kamp, J.D., & McCloy, R.A. (1990). Criterion-related validities of personality constructs and the effect of response distortion on those validities. Journal of Applied Psychology, 75, 581-595.

66. http://studylecturenotes.com/employee-performance-management-system-and-process/

67. https://www.digital-adoption.com/employee-performance/

68. Ian Kessler and Stephen Bach (March, 2011), 'The citizen-consumer as industrial relations actor: new ways of working and the end –user in social care', British Journal of Industrial Relations, pp. 80-102, ISSN 0007- 1080. Published by Blackwell Publishing Ltd.

69. Ichniowski, Shaw, & Prennushi, 1997). Ichniowski, C., Shaw, K., & Prennushi, G. (1997). The effects of human resource management practices on productivity: a study of steel finishing lines. American Economic Review, 87(3), 291-313.

70. Iqbal N , Anwar S and Haider N ( ), Effect of Leadership Style on Employee Performance, Arabian Journal of Business and A Management Review Volume 5 • Issue 5 • ISSN: 2223-5833

71. Iqbal N, Anwar S and Haider N(2015) "Effect of Leadership Style on Employee Performance" Arabian J Bus Manag Review ISSN: 2223-5833 AJBMR an open access journal vol. 5 issue 5

72. J., Anitha(Nov 2014) , "Determinants of employee engagement and their impact on employee performance", International Journal of Productivity and Performance Management, Volume 63, Number 3, 2014, pp. 308-323(16)

73. Jona Tarlengco is a content writer for SafetyCulture, a software company that enables businesses to perform inspections using digital checklists.
74. Judge, Higgins, Thoresen, and Barrick (1999) Judge. T.A., Higgins, C.A., Thoresen, C.J., & Barrick, M.R. (1999). The big five personality traits, general mental ability, and career success across the life span. Personnel Psychology, 52, 621-652.
75. K.k. Jain, Fauzia Jabeen, Vinita Mishra and Naveen Gupta (2007), 'Job satisfaction as related to organizational climate and occupational stress: A case study of Indian oil', international review of business research papers, Vol.3 No.5.pp. 193-208
76. Kongala Ramprasad (April, 2013), 'Motivation and workforce performance in Indian industries', Research Journal of Management Sciences, Vol. 2(4), 25-29, ISSN 2319-117
77. Kotrba, Gillespie, Schmidt, Smerek, Ritchie, & Denison, 2012). Kotrba, L. M., Gillespie, M. A., Schmidt, A. M., Smerek, R. E., Ritchie, S. A., & Denison, D. R. (2012). Do consistent corporate cultures have better business performance? Exploring the interaction effects. Human Relations, 65(2), 241-262.
78. Kress, Norris, Schoenholz, Elias, and Seigle (2004) Kress, J. S., Norris, J. A., Schoenholz, D. A., Elias, M. J., & Seigle, P. (2004). Bringing together educational standards and social and emotional learning: Making the case for educators. American Journal of Education, 111(1), 68-89.
79. Le Tran Thach Thao and Chiou-shu J. Hwang ( ) "FACTORS AFFECTING EMPLOYEE PERFORMANCE–EVIDENCE FROM PETROVIETNAM ENGINEERING CONSULTANCY J.S.C"
80. Leaman (1995) Leaman, A. (1995). Dissatisfaction and office productivity. Journal of Facilities Management, 13(2), 3-19.
81. Marium Zafar and Emadul Karim and Omair Abbas in their research paper "Factors of Workplace Environment that Affects Employee Performance in anrganization": A study on Greenwich"Online at https://mpra.ub.uni-muenchen.de/78822/ MPRA Paper No. 78822, posted 28 April 2017
82. Martensen and Gronholdt (2001). Fletcher, C., & Williams, R. (1996). Performance management, job satisfaction and organizational commitment. British Journal of Management, 7(2), 169-179.

83. Mary E. Davis, Medford (2016), 'Pay Matters: The Piece Rate and Health in the Developing World', Annals of Global Health, the Author. Published by Elsevier Inc. on behalf of Icahn School of Medical at Mount Sinai. Vol. 82, No.5, ISSN 2214-9996.
84. Maslow, 1987). Maslow, A.H. (1987). Motivation and Personality, 3rd Ed. New York, NY: Harper & Row.
85. McCourt, & Derek, 2003). Kotrba, L. M., Gillespie, M. A., Schmidt, A. M., Smerek, R. E., Ritchie, S. A., & Denison, D. R. (2012). Do consistent corporate cultures have better business performance? Exploring the interaction effects. Human Relations, 65(2), 241-262.
86. McFarlin, D.B. and Blascovich, J. (1981), Effects of Self-Esteem and Performance Feedback on Future Affective Preferences and Cognitive Expectations, Journal of Personality and Social Psychology, 40, 521-531
87. Md. Nurun Nabi, Md.Monirul Islam, Tanvir Mahady Dip, and Md.Abdullah Al Hossain (march 2017) 'Impact of Motivation on Employee Performances: A Case Study of Karmasangsthan Bank Limited, Bangladesh', Arabian Journal of Business and Management Review, Vol.7,Issue 1, ISSN 2223-5833.
88. Michailova, 2002) Sarah, Y., Nik, K., Pranav, K., (2012) Factors Affecting Employee Satisfaction among Nonteaching Staff in Higher Educational Institutions in Malaysia. American Journal of Economics, Special issue, 93-96.
89. Miller, Erickson, & Yust, 2001) Miller, N. G., Erickson, A., & Yust, B. L. (2001). Sense of place in the workplace: The relationship between personal objects and job satisfaction and motivation. Journal of Interior Design, 27(1), 35-44.
90. Miss Somrudee Somsa-ard Mr. Tosaporn Mahamud (May 2016), MOTIVATION FACTORS AFFECTING EMPLOYEES' PERFORMANCE: A CASE STUDY OF TGT CONSTRUCTION PARTNERSHIP LIMITED', Indian Journal of Commerce & Management Studies ISSN: 2249-0310 EISSN: 2229-5674 Volume VII Issue 2(1),
91. N. Khan, H.Waqas& R.Muneer, "Impact of Rewards (Intrinsic and extrinsic) on Employee Performance with Special Reference to Courier Companies of City Faisalabad, Pakistan", International Journal of Management Excellence, Vol.8, Issue.2, pp.937-945, 2017.
92. Norida Abdullah, Olurotimi A. Shonubi, Rahman Hashim, and ,Norhidayu Hamid, (Sept 2016), "Recognition and Appreciation and its Psychological Effect on Job Satisfaction and Performance in a Malaysia IT Company: Systematic Review", IOSR

Journal Of Humanities And Social Science (IOSR-JHSS) Volume 21, Issue 9, Ver. 6 (Sep. 2016) PP 47-55 e-ISSN: 2279-0837, p-ISSN: 2279-0845.

93. Northouse (2007), Northouse, P. G. (2007). Leadership Theory and Practice, 7th Ed. London: Sage Publications.

94. O. C. Olake, A. S. Oni, D. O. Babalola &R. A.Ojelabi, "Incentive Package, Employee's Productivity and Performance of Real Estate Firms in Nigeria",European Scientific Journal, Vol.13,Issue.11, pp.246-260, 2017.

95. Ola Kvaloya and Anja schottnerb (April, 2015), 'Incentives to Motivate', Journal of EconomicBehavior& Organization 116(2015)26-42, http://dx.doi.org/10.1016/j.jebo.2015.03.012. Published by Elsevier.

96. Page, 2008). Page, L. (2008). Do not show me the money? The growing popularity of non-monetary incentives in the workplace. American Journal of Economics, 93-96.

97. Palmer (2005) Palmer, B. (2005). Practical Advice for HR Professionals: Create individualized Motivation Strategies. Melcrum Publishing Ltd.

98. Pankaj Chaudhary (September, 2102), 'Effects of Employees' Motivation on Organizational Performance- A Case Study', International Journal of Research in Economics & Social Sciences, Vol.2, Issue 9, ISSN: 2249-7382.

99. Parkash Vir Khatri* and Jyoti Behl (June 2013), IMPACT OF WORK-LIFE BALANCE ON PERFORMANCE OF EMPLOYEES IN THE ORGANISATIONS, Global Journal of Business Management, Vol. 7, No. 1, June 2013

100. Patterson, M.G. et al (1998), Impact of People Management Practices on Business Performance, Institute of Personnel and Development, London, 1-27

101. Pradorn Sureephong, Winai Dahlan, Suepphong Chernbumroong, Yootthapong Tongpaeng (January 2020), The Effect of Non-Monetary Rewards on Employee Performance in Massive Open Online Courses, International Journal of Emerging Technologies in Learning (iJET) 15(01):88

102. Prof. C. R Kothari, "Research Methodology Tools and Techniques, ISBN (13) : 978-81-224-2488-1, NEW AGE INTERNATIONAL (P) LIMITED, PUBLISHERS

103. Quratul- Ain Manzoor (2012), 'Impact of Employees Motivation on Organizational Effectiveness', European Journal of Business and Management, Vol.3.No.3. ISSN 2222-1905.

104. R. Anitha and Dr. M. Ashok Kumar (August 2016), THE IMPACT OF TRAINING ON EMPLOYEE PERFORMANCE IN PRIVATE INSURANCE SECTOR,

COIMBATORE DISTRICT , ISSN: 2249-7196 IJMRR/August 2016/ Volume 6/Issue 8/Article No-10/1079-1089 International Journal of Management Research & Review

105. Ranjit Kumar, RESEARCH METHODOLOGY a step-by-step guide for beginners, ISBN 978-1-84920-300-5, SAGE Publications Asia-Pacific Pte Ltd

106. Rashid Saeed, Shireen Mussawar, Rab Nawaz Lodhi, ,Anam Iqbal, Hafiza Hafsa Nayab and Somia Yaseen (2013), "Factors Affecting the Performance of Employees at Work Place in the Banking Sector of Pakistan", Middle-East Journal of Scientific Research 17 (9): 1200-1208, 2013,ISSN 1990-9233© IDOSI Publications, 2013,DOI: 10.5829/idosi.mejsr.2013.17.09.12256

107. Raudsepp, 1990 Raudsepp, E. (1990). Are you flexible enough to succeed? Manage, 42(90), 6-10.

108. Ricardo, Amy, & Rohit, 2007). French, J. R. (1975). A comparative look at stress and strain in policemen. New York: Elsevier.

109. Rizwan Qaiser Danish ans Ali Usman (2010), 'impact of reward and recognition on job satisfaction and motivation: an empirical study from Pakistan. International Journal of Business and Management, Vol.5, No.2.

110. Robinson et al., 2004) Robinson, D., Perryman, S., & Hayday, S. (2004). The Drivers of Employee Engagement Report 408, Institute for Employment Studies, UK.

111. Robinson, Perryman, and Hayday (2004) Robinson, D., Perryman, S., & Hayday, S. (2004). The Drivers of Employee Engagement Report 408, Institute for Employment Studies, UK.

112. Roca, Chiu, and Martinez (2006) Roca, J. C., Chiu, C. M., & Martínez, F. J. (2006). Understanding e-learning continuance intention: An extension of the Technology Acceptance Model. International Journal of Human-Computer Studies, 64(8), 683-696.

113. Ruth Kanini Bosire , Dr. James Muya (April 2019), NON-MONETARY COMPENSATION PRACTICES AND EMPLOYEE OUTPUT: A CRITICAL REVIEW OF LITERATURE, International Journal of Social Sciences and Information Technology ISSN 2412-0294 Vol V Issue IV,

114. S. K. Reddy& S. Karim,"Impact of Incentive Schemes on Employee Performance: A Case Study of Singareni Collieries Company Limited, Kothagudem,Andhra Pradesh", India. Science, Technology and Arts Research Journal, Vol.2, Issue.4, pp.122-125, 2013.

115. S. K.Srivastava & K. C.Barmola, "Role of Motivation in Higher Productivity",Management Insight, Vol.7, Issue.1, pp.88-99, 201

116. S. T.Achie&J. T.Kurah, "The Role of Financial Incentives as a Motivator in Employee's Productivity in Nigeria Electricity Distribution Companies", International Journal of Research in Business Studies and Management, Vol.3, Issue.1, pp.1-8,2016.

117. S.Yousaf, M.Latif, S.Aslam& A.Siddiqui, "Impact of Financial and non-Financial Rewards on Employee Motivation",Middle-East Journal of Scientific Research, Vol.21, Issue.10, pp.1776-1786, 2014.

118. Saharuddin1 , Sulaiman (Oct 2016) The Effect Of Promotion And Compensation Toward Working Productivity Through Job Satisfaction And Working Motivation Of Employees In The Department Of Water And Mineral Resources Energy North Aceh District, International Journal of Business and Management Invention ISSN (Online): 2319 – 8028, ISSN (Print): 2319 – 801X www.ijbmi.org || Volume 5 Issue 10 || October. 2016 || PP—33-40

119. Sarah maslen and Andrew Hopkin (July, 2014), 'Do incentives work? A qualitative study of managers' motivations in hazardous industries, School of sociology, college of Arts and Social Sciences, Haydon-Allen Bld (22),The Australian National University,Action,ACT0200.Safety Science, 70, 419-245.

120. Sarah, Nik, & Pranav, 2012). Sarah, Y., Nik, K., Pranav, K., (2012) Factors Affecting Employee Satisfaction among Nonteaching Staff in Higher Educational Institutions in Malaysia. American Journal of Economics, Special issue, 93-96.

121. Sayeda Ayat-e- Zainab Ali, M. Afridi, M. Shafi, H. Munawar, Sajid M. Alvi (October, 2016), 'Impact of Tangible and Intangible Incentives on Job Satisfaction Among Workers', International Journal of Management Excellence, Vol. 7, No.3, ISSN: 2292-1648.

122. Shah and Shah (2010) Bhattacharyya, D.K. (2007). Human Resource Research Methods. New Delhi: Oxford University Press.

123. Shaju.M and Subhashini.D (2017), "A study on the impact of Job Satisfaction on Job Performance of Employees working in Automobile Industry, Punjab, India",Journal of Management Research ISSN 1941-899X 2017, Vol. 9, No. 1 117 www.macrothink.org/jmr

124. Spector, 2000) Boshoff, C., & Arnolds, C. (1995). Some antecedents of employee commitment and their influence on job performance. South African Journal of Business Management, 26 (4), 125-135.
125. Strümpfer, Danana, Gouws, & Viviers, 1998). Boshoff, C., & Arnolds, C. (1995). Some antecedents of employee commitment and their influence on job performance. South African Journal of Business Management, 26 (4), 125-135.
126. Subha Imtiaz* & Shakil Ahmad(2009)," Impact Of Stress On Employee Productivity, Performance And Turnover; An Important Managerial Issue", International Review of Business Research Papers,Vol. 5 No. 4 June 2009 Pp. 468-477
127. SUDHAMSETTI NAVEEN1 , PRASADARAO YENUGULA(May 2-17), "The Impact of Monetary and Non-Monetary Incentives on Performance of Employees: A Research Study on Beverage Industry, A.P, In India", International Journal of Recent Trends in Engineering & Research (IJRTER) Volume 03, Issue 05; May - 2017 [ISSN: 2455-1457]
128. Sutermeister, 1976). Sutermeister, R.A. (1976) People and Productivity, 3rd Ed, New York McGraw-Hill.
129. T. S. Ravi,"Impact of Labour Incentives on Productivity in Selected Chennai-Based Manufacturing Companies",Abhinav International Monthly Refereed Journal of Research in Management & Technology, Vol.4, Issue.2, pp.22-32, 2015. +
130. Tavonga Gilson Gudo- dissertation titled An analysis on the impact of non monetary incentives on employee performance.
131. Thevanes, N and Mangaleswaran.T (2018), "Relationship between Work-Life Balance and Job Performance of Employees", IOSR Journal of Business and Management (IOSR-JBM) e-ISSN: 2278-487X, p-ISSN: 2319-7668. Volume 20, Issue 5. Ver. I (May. 2018), PP 11-16 www.iosrjournals.org DOI: 10.9790/487X-2005011116
132. Tosi, Mero, & Rizzo, 2000). Tosi, H.L., Mero, N.P., & Rizzo, J.R. (2000). Managing Organizational Behavior. Cambridge, Massachusetts: Blackwell.
133. Viswesvaran, C. and Ones, D.S. (2000), Perspectives on Models of Job Performance, International Journal of Selection and Assesment, 8, 216-226
134. Vredenburgh, & Brender, 1998). Vredenburgh, D., & Brender, Y. (1998). The Hierarchical Abuse of Power in Work Organizations. Journal of Business Ethics, 17(12), 1337-1347.

135. Weil, & Woodall, 2005). Harrison, L. L., & Novak, D. (2006). Evaluation of a gerontological nursing continuing education programme: Effect on nurses' knowledge and attitudes and on patients' perceptions and satisfaction. Journal of Advanced Nursing, 13(6), 684-692.
136. Wheelan (2010) Wheelan, S.A. (2010). Creating effective teams - A guide for members and leaders. Thousand Oaks, USA: Sage Publications.
137. Wilson (2010) Wilson, G. (2010). The effects of external rewards on intrinsic motivation. Available at: http://www.abcbodybuilding.com/rewards.pdf
138. Wright, & Geroy, 2001). Wright, P. C., & Geroy, G. D. (2001). Human competency engineering and world class performance: a cross-cultural approach, Cross Cultural Management. An International Journal, 8(2), 25-46.
139. Wu, & Norman, 2006) Wu, L., & Norman, I.J. (2006). An investigation of job satisfaction, organizational commitment and role conflict and ambiguity in a sample of Chinese undergraduate nursing students. Nurse Education Today, 26, 304-314.
140. Zafar, Marium and Karim, Emadul and Abbas, Omair "Factors of Workplace Environment that Affects Employee Performance in an Organization": A study on Greenwich University of Karachi , 28 April 2017 Online at https://mpra.ub.uni-muenchen.de/78822/ MPRA Paper No. 78822, posted 28 Apr 2017 13:43 UTC
141. Zeynep, 2013). Zeynep, O. (2013). Managing emotions in the workplace: It's mediating effect on the relationship between organizational trust and occupational stress. International Business Research, 6, 81- 88.
142. https://ncert.nic.in/textbook/pdf/legy208.pdf- Chapter 8
143. https://bizfluent.com/how-6885971-measure-employee-performance-production-metrics.html
144. https://www.managementstudyguide.com/managing-employee-performance.htm

ANNEXURE

Questionnaire used for the Research.

Introduction Part

	Enter Complete Name	
	Enter your Highest Educational Qualification	Diploma, Bachelor, Masters
	Enter total Years of Experience	
	Enter Automobile Company Name	
	Enter Your Department	
	Enter your Title	
	What is your Role	Individual Contributor or People Manager or Head of the Department

Main Body of Questionnaire

Sr No	H1 - Leadership / Managerial	New Question
1	Vision & Mission of Leader	I have clarity about my role from my leader and it excites me to give my best
2	Leadership Style	Leadership Style of my manager affects me drastically
3	Democratic Leadership	My leader makes decision based on my and my team members inputs
4	Autocratic Leadership	My Leader make decision without taking inputs from any of team member
5	Laissez-Faire Leadership	My Leader doesn't take me review and gives me complete ownership of my results
6	Strategic Leadership	My Leader has strategy in place to deal with uncertainties
7	Transformational Leadership	My Leader puts me out of my comfort zone and always motivates me to do more
8	Transactional Leadership	My Leaders give me Clears Roles and Responsibilities along with Timeline and KPIs.
9	Coach-Style Leadership	My leader knows my strengths and Weakness and he guides me accordingly
10	Bureaucratic Leadership	My Leader doesn't not appreciate new and innovative ways of working

11	Coaching by Manager	My Manager provides me with regular coaching/feedback
12	Camaraderie with Colleagues	I Enjoy my camaraderie with my Colleagues
13	Relationship with Manager	My Manager is supportive & I like interacting with him
14	Performance Pressure	Pressure with respective to performance affects me drastically
15	Low Pressure	There is low pressure with respect to performance
16	Healthy Pressure	There is Healthy pressure impacting my performance positively
17	High Pressure	There is Continuous Pressure impacting me drastically
18	Empowerment	There is empowerment with respect to my role
	H2 - Institutional	
19	Brand Image	I feel proud to be associated with my organisation
20	Responsibility	I feel happy when I have entrusted with Responsibility
21	Technology	Technology impacts my performance positively
22	Infrastructure	Infrastructure supports me a lot in my current role
23	Production Systems	It is my experience that Production systems plays a important role in increasing Productivity
24	Structure	Reporting / Org Structure affects my performance drastically
25	Indian / MNC	I prefer to work with MNCs
26	Organisational Stability	Organisational Stability Impacts me performance drastically
27	Market Position	I feel proud about my organisations market position
	H3 - Job Related	
28	Job Fit	I like my job if my skills my matching with offered role
29	Clear Goals and Expectations	Clear Goals & Expectations helps me in achieving my Targets
30	Training provided	I feel Training provided helps me grow in the organisation
31	Tools and Equipment / Resources	Tools and Equipment's help me improve my productivity
32	Work Life Balance	I take break from work, which rejunuvates me and helps me to improve my focus on work
33	Usage of Cutting-Edge Technology	Technology help me improve my productivity
34	Risk associated with Job	I feel worried if I perceive risk in the job
35	Location of work	Location of Work impacts my performance drastically
36	Reputation/Status of the Job	I like to work for reputed / Status focused jobs

#		
37	Diversity in Job	I like to have diversity in my work
	H4 - Organisational Culture	
38	Culture	Organisational Culture affects me drastically
39	Clan Culture	My Organisation friendly, Innovative, committed and provides me mentoring
40	Adhocracy Culture	My Organisation is Dynamic, Innovative, Transformational and Learning from mistakes
41	Market Culture	My Organisation is Agile and Flexible to meet customer & market demand
42	Hierarchy Culture	My Organisation is Structured, Stability oriented and Cost oriented
43	Communication	Communication affects my performance drastically
44	Communication to Inform	I feel low when I am just communicated to inform
45	Communication to Involve	I feel motivated when I am included/involved in the communication
46	social learning	I Learn from my colleagues and also enthusiastically share my learnings with them
47	Ethics	I am proud to work with organisation of high ethics and repute
48	Innovation	I believe Innovation is key towards organisational growth
49	Discipline	My Discipline helps to improve organisations productivity
50	Standardization	My Organisation has required level of standardization
51	Reputation in eyes of Customer	I feel proud to work when customer are satisfied with our product
	H5 - Opportunity	
52	Development Opportunities	I feel passionate to perform when I see development opportunities in my organisation
53	Career Path	I feel motivate when my managers discuss career path with me
54	Growth Options	I feel motivated when in grow in the organisation
55	Job Security	I feel worried if job security is a concern
56	Diversity	Diversity in my team keeps me excited about my role
	H6 - Motivation	
57	Motivation	My Manager motivates me at my job/work
58	Recognition	I feel good when my efforts are recognised
59	Job Enrichment	I feel motivated when additional responsibilities are entrusted upon me.
60	Job Satisfaction	I give my best when I am satisfied with my Job
61	Passion towards car	I Love Automobiles (Cars / Bikes / Auto)
62	Ability	My ability impacts my performance drastically

63	Performance Appraisal Process	I feel satisfied when I performance appraisal process is fair and transparent
	Performance Question	Performance Assessment Questions
64	Targets	I am able to complete my targets
65	Satisfaction / Motivation	My Organisations management is happy with my work
66	Timeline	I am able to complete my targets within the timeline
67	Satisfaction / Motivation	My manager is Happy with my work
68	Recognition from Colleagues	I am recognised by my team mates for quality of my work
69	Recognition from Management	I am getting recognition I deserve
70	Helping others	My Colleagues approach me for Challenges they face at work
71	Growth	I got the growth that I deserve in the organisation
72	Motivation	I feel good to attend work

"A study of Non-Monetary factors impacting employee's performance in selected automobile manufacturing industry"

THESIS
SUBMITTED
TO
SAVITRIBAI PHULE PUNE UNIVERSITY

FOR THE AWARD OF DEGREE OF

DOCTOR OF PHILOSOPHY

FACULTY OF MANAGEMENT

SUBMITTED
BY
Mr. Kunal Shriram Kumawat

UNDER THE GUIDANCE OF

DR. KULDIP S. CHARAK

RESEARCH CENTRE

D Y PATIL SCHOOL OF MANAGEMENT CHAROLI,

LOHEGAON,

Pune – 05

January 2022

CHAPTER 5

Findings

Below are the findings under the 6 Factors which we focused for study

1. Leadership / Managerial Factors

Among the total number of respondents, 52.9% of respondents were always agreed for I have clarity about my role from my leader and it excites me to give my best

Among the total number of respondents, 40.1% of respondents were always agreed for Leadership Style of my manager affects me drastically

Among the total number of respondents, 31.3% of respondents were always agreed for My leader makes decision based on my and my team members inputs

Among the total number of respondents, 52.2% of respondents were often agreed for My Leader make decision without taking inputs from any of team member

Among the total number of respondents, 48.3% of respondents were always agreed for My Leader doesn't take me review and gives me complete ownership of my results

Among the total number of respondents, 42.1% of respondents were always agreed for My Leader has strategy in place to deal with uncertainties

Among the total number of respondents, 44.2% of respondents were always agreed for My Leader puts me out of my comfort zone and motivates me to do more

Among the total number of respondents, 43.8% of respondents were always agreed for My Leaders give me Clears Roles and Responsibilities along with Timeline and KPIs.

Among the total number of respondents, 46.4% of respondents were often agreed for My leader knows my strengths and Weakness and he guides me accordingly

Among the total number of respondents, 43.8% of respondents were often agreed for My Leader doesn't appreciate new and innovative ways of working

Among the total number of respondents, 45% of respondents were often agreed for My Manager provides me with regular coaching/feedback

Among the total number of respondents, 47% of respondents were often agreed for I Enjoy my camaraderie with my Colleagues

Among the total number of respondents, 48.1% of respondents were always agreed for My Manager is supportive & I like interacting with him

Among the total number of respondents, 45.4% of respondents were often agreed for Pressure with respective to performance affects me drastically

Among the total number of respondents, 45.4% of respondents were often agreed There is low pressure with respect to performance

Among the total number of respondents, 47.6% of respondents were often agreed There is Healthy pressure impacting my performance positively

Among the total number of respondents, 41.3% of respondents were often agreed There is Continuous Pressure impacting me drastically

Among the total number of respondents, 45% of respondents were always agreed for There is empowerment with respect to my role

2. **Institutional Factors**

Among the total number of respondents, 66.6% of respondents were always agreed for I feel proud to be associated with my organisation

Among the total number of respondents, 63.5% of respondents were always agreed for I feel happy when I am entrusted with Responsibility

Among the total number of respondents, 64.4 % of respondents were always agreed for Technology impacts my performance positively

Among the total number of respondents, 41.8% of respondents were always agreed for Infrastructure supports me a lot in my current role

Among the total number of respondents, 64.9% of respondents were always agreed for It is my experience that Production systems plays a important role in increasing Productivity

Among the total number of respondents, 36.8% of respondents were often agreed for Reporting / Org Structure affects my performance drastically

Among the total number of respondents, 55.8% of respondents were always agreed for I prefer to work with MNCs

Among the total number of respondents, 42.8% of respondents were always agreed for Organisational Stability Impacts me performance drastically

Among the total number of respondents, 56% of respondents were always agreed for I feel proud about my organisations market position.

3. **Job Related Factors**

Among the total number of respondents,66.6 % of respondents were always agreed for I like my job if my skills my matching with offered role

Among the total number of respondents,70.4% of respondents were always agreed for Clear Goals & Expectations helps me in achieving my Targets

Among the total number of respondents,45.9% of respondents were always agreed for I feel Training provided helps me grow in the organisation

Among the total number of respondents,63.2% of respondents were always agreed for Tools and Equipment's help me improve my productivity

Among the total number of respondents,39.9% of respondents were often agreed for I take break from work , which rejuvenates me and helps me to improve my focus on work

Among the total number of respondents,65.9% of respondents were always agreed for Technology help me improve my productivity

Among the total number of respondents,40.4% of respondents were sometimes agreed for I feel worried if I perceive risk in the job

Among the total number of respondents,38.7% of respondents were always agreed for Location of Work impacts my performance drastically

Among the total number of respondents,58.4% of respondents were always agreed for I like to work for reputed / Status focused jobs

Among the total number of respondents,51.4% of respondents were always agreed for I like to have diversity in my work.

4. **Organisational Cultural Factors**

Among the total number of respondents,48.1% of respondents were always agreed for Organisational Culture affects me drastically

Among the total number of respondents,43.8% of respondents were always agreed for My Organisation friendly, Innovative, committed and provides me mentoring

Among the total number of respondents,48.1% of respondents were always agreed for My Organisation is Dynamic, Innovative, Transformational and Learning from mistakes

Among the total number of respondents, 53.1% of respondents were always agreed for My Organisation is Agile and Flexible to meet customer & market demand

Among the total number of respondents, 55% of respondents were always agreed for My Organisation is Structured, Stability oriented and Cost oriented

Among the total number of respondents, 43.8% of respondents were always agreed for Communication affects my performance drastically

Among the total number of respondents, 45.7% of respondents were often agreed for I feel low when I am just communicated to inform

Among the total number of respondents, 65.3% of respondents were always agreed for I feel motivated when I am included/involved in the communication

Among the total number of respondents, 56.3% of respondents were always agreed for I Learn from my colleagues and also enthusiastically share my learnings with them

Among the total number of respondents, 74.8% of respondents were always agreed for I am proud to work with organisation of high ethics and repute

Among the total number of respondents, 83.4% of respondents were always agreed for I believe Innovation is key towards organisational growth

Among the total number of respondents, 65.6% of respondents were always agreed for My Discipline helps to improve organisations productivity

Among the total number of respondents, 43% of respondents were always agreed for My Organisation has required level of standardization

Among the total number of respondents, 88.7% of respondents were always agreed for I feel proud to work when customer are satisfied with our product.

5. Opportunity Factors

Among the total number of respondents, 80.8% of respondents were always agreed for I feel passionate to perform when I see development opportunities in my organisation

Among the total number of respondents, 58.4% of respondents were always agreed for I feel motivate when my managers discuss career path with me

Among the total number of respondents, 67.3% of respondents were always agreed for I feel motivated when in grow in the organisation

Among the total number of respondents, 35.6% of respondents were often agreed for I feel worried if job security is a concern

Among the total number of respondents, 51.4% of respondents were always agreed for Diversity in my team keeps me excited about my role.

6. Motivational Factors

Among the total number of respondents, 40.9% of respondents were always agreed for My Manager motivates me at my job/work

Among the total number of respondents, 70.4% of respondents were always agreed for I feel good when my efforts are recognized

Among the total number of respondents, 64.9% of respondents were always agreed for I feel motivated when additional responsibilities are entrusted upon me.

Among the total number of respondents, 79.8% of respondents were always agreed for I give my best when I am satisfied with my Job

Among the total number of respondents, 72.1% of respondents were always agreed for I Love Automobiles (Cars / Bikes / Auto)

Among the total number of respondents, 51.9% of respondents were always agreed for My ability impacts my performance drastically

Among the total number of respondents, 45.9% of respondents were always agreed for I feel satisfied when I performance appraisal process is fair and transparent

7. Performance factors

Among the total number of respondents, 49.5% of respondents were often agreed for I am able to complete my targets

Among the total number of respondents, 48.1% of respondents were often agreed for My Organizations management is happy with my work

Among the total number of respondents, 49.8% of respondents were often agreed for I am able to complete my targets within the timeline

Among the total number of respondents, 48.6% of respondents were always agreed for My manager is Happy with my work

Among the total number of respondents, 56.5% of respondents were always agreed for I am recognized by my team mates for quality of my work

Among the total number of respondents, 50.7% of respondents were often agreed for I am getting recognition I deserve

Among the total number of respondents, 48.8% of respondents were always agreed for My Colleagues approach me for Challenges they face at work

Among the total number of respondents, 50.7% of respondents were often agreed for I got the growth that I deserve in the organisation

Among the total number of respondents, 65.6% of respondents were always agreed for I feel good to attend work.

All the Factors are positively impacting employee's performance.

Table 57: Summary of Regression Model for all the factors.

Factors	R-Square	Anova	Regression	Correlation Coefficient (R) and +slope
1. Leadership/Managerial factors	R square = 0.348, 34.8% Variations Explained	F = 221.379 & p value = 0.00 < 0.05	Y = 16.630 + 0.305*X	+ correlation coefficient (R = 0.590) & + slope (0.305)
2. Institutional factors	R square = 0.344, 34.4% variation explained	F = 217.483 & p value = 0.00 < 0.05	Y = 14.050 + 0.636*X	+ correlation coefficient (R = 0.587) & + slope (0.636)
3. Job Related factors	R square = 0.264, 26.4.0% variation Explained	F = 148.139 & p value = 0.00 < 0.05	Y = 16.965 + 0.512*X	+ correlation coefficient (R = 0.513) & + slope (0.512)
4. Organizational Cultural factors.	R square = 0.444, 44.4% of variation explained	F = 330.176 & p value = 0.00 < 0.05	Y = 7.996 + 0.502*X	+correlation coefficient (R = 0.666) & + slope (0.502)
5. Opportunity factors	R square = 0.223, 22.3% Variation Explained	F = 118.642 & p value = 0.00 < 0.05	Y = 20.575 + 0.839*X	+ correlation coefficient (R = 0.472) & + slope (0.839)
6. Motivational factors	R square = 0.424, 42.4% Explained	F = 304.236 & p value = 0.00 < 0.05	Y = 11.141 + 0.883*X	positive correlation coefficient (R = 0.651) & positive slope (0.883)

With reference to above table researcher has observed following findings.

1. Motivation Factors are having highest impact on employee's performance considering the slope of variable Motivational factors (X) is 0.883 implies that the Performance of Employee would be increased by 0.883 per unit increase in variable Motivational factors (X).

2. Opportunity Factors are having second highest impact on employee's performance considering the slope of variable Opportunity factors (X) is 0.839 implies that the Performance of Employee would be increased by 0.839 per unit increase in variable Opportunity factors (X).

3. Institutional factors are having Third highest impact on employee's performance considering the slope of variable Institutional factors (X) is 0.636 implies that the Performance of Employee would be increased by 0.636 per unit increase in variable Institutional factors (X

4. Job Related Factors are having fourth highest impact on employee's performance considering slope of variable Job-Related factors (X) is 0.512 implies that the Performance of Employee would be increased by 0.512 per unit increase in variable Job-Related factors (X).

5. Organisational Cultural Factors are having fifth highest impact on employee's performance considering slope of variable Organisational Cultural factors (X) is 0.502 implies that the Performance of Employee would be increased by 0.502 per unit increase in variable Organisational Cultural factors (X).

6. Leadership/Managerial Factors are having fifth highest impact on employee's performance considering slope of variable Leadership / Managerial Factor (X) is 0.305 implies that the Performance of Employee would be increased by 0.305 per unit increase in variable Leadership / Managerial Factor (X).

Based on the above study researcher is proposing below model to ensure highest performance of employees in Auto industry.

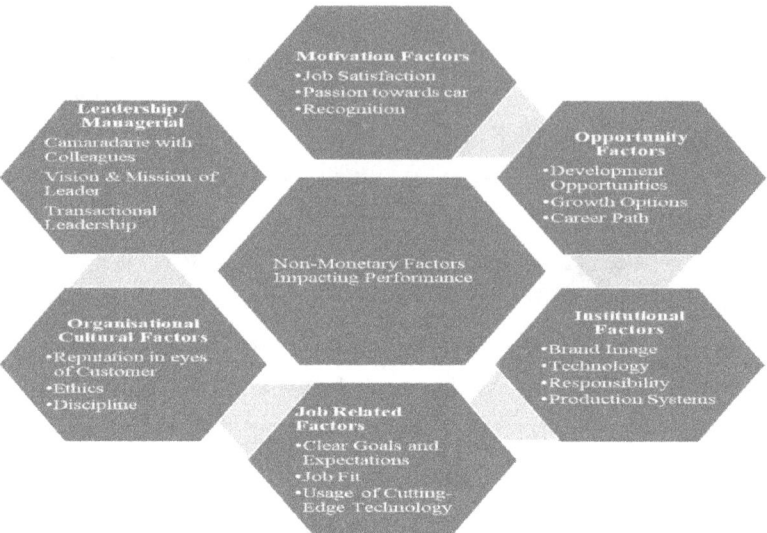

Figure 3: Conceptual Model

Elaboration on Conceptual Model Based on the analysis and findings of study

1. Motivation factor has highest impact on the performance of employee, in which motivation Job satisfaction, Passion towards car and Recognition plays a crucial role in improving the performance of employee.

2. Opportunity Factor has second highest impact on the performance of employee, in which Development opportunities, Growth Options and Clarity of Career path excites employee to deliver high performance

3. Institutional Factors has third highest impact on the performance of employee, in which subfactors like Brand Image, Technology used, Responsibility and Production system used play significant role in supporting employee performance.

4. Job Related Factors has fourth highest impact on the performance of employee, Clear goal setting, Correct Job Fit and Usage of cutting age technology highly positively impacts employee performance.

5. Organisational culture factors has fifth highest impact on performance of employee, sub-factors like Reputation in eyes of Customer, Organisational Ethics and Discipline are important.

6. Leadership / Managerial factor has lowest impact in all the factors, but Camaraderie with Colleagues, Vision & Mission of Leader and Transactional Leadership Subfactors impact most on the employee performance.

Top 10 Factors impacting employee's performance in Auto Industry in Rank Order.

Table 58: – Top 10 Factors Impacting Employee's Performance

Sr No	Factor	Sub-Factor
1	Motivational Factors	Job Satisfaction
2	Organizational Cultural Factors	Reputation in eyes of Customer
3	Motivational Factors	Recognition
4	Organizational Cultural Factors	Ethics
5	Opportunity Factors	Development Opportunities
6	Organizational Cultural Factors	Discipline
7	Job Related Factors	Clear Goals and Expectations
8	Motivational Factors	Passion towards car
9	Organizational Cultural Factors	Communication to Involve
10	Job Related Factors	Job Fit

Communication

Communication plays an important role in success and failure of organization at the same time it also plays a very crucial role in the impacting employee performance. In general, & broadly there are 2 types of communication styles, Communication to Involve and Communication to Inform. It has been found that Communication 83.4% respondents agree that communication impacts performance drastically and in communication, if Style of communication used is "Communication to Involve" then employee will feel motivated and included and will highly impact performance. 95.2% employees prefer "Communication to Involve" Style of motivation.

Organisational Culture

91.6% respondents agreed that the auto OEM's has a "Hierarchy Culture" – which is more towards, Structured, Stability Oriented and Cost Oriented. A mixed or "hierarchy" culture and "Market Culture" would be a good combination to have high performing employees in the organization. 98.1% respondent feel proud when they see customer satisfying with their product.

Leadership

87.02% respondents agree that "Vision & Mission of Leader" impact employee's performance. If the leader provides clear and exciting Vision and Mission which is compelling in nature employees will be excited to give good performance. Vision Literacy, Loftier Vision and Missions should be percolated within the employees.

81.73% respondents believe that if their managers knowns their strengths and weakness and guides / coaches them accordingly the employee can achieve better performance

Passion for Cars / Autos

96.2% respondents agree that if they have passion for cars/auto segment their performance will be better.

Production Support Systems

92.3% respondents agreed that technology used in production of Auto impacts their performance followed by Production systems to which 90.09% respondents agree followed by Infrastructure to which 80.5% respondents agree.

Job Related Factors

Location and Work and Risk associated with the Job are the least impaction factors to employee's performance.

Opportunity Factors

97.1% respondent agreed that the performance passionately when they see development opportunities in the organization, this should be complemented by also provided growth – promotion, Special projects, short term projects to make employee feel that they are growing.

Proud Feeling in Respondents

98.1% respondents feel proud to work when customer is satisfied with their products.
97.6% respondents feel proud to work with organization of high ethics and repute.
92.3% respondents feel proud to be associated with my organization.
85.1% respondents feel proud about my organizations market position.

Based on the above findings we can observe that Customer Satisfaction, Ethics/Reputation & Market positions makes respondent feel proud about their association with their employer in turn impacting their performance.

CHAPTER 6

Conclusion

The study examined the effect of monetary and non-monetary reward factors on employee performance. The organizational challenge is to determine the optimal balance between monetary and non-monetary factors that will improve employee performance supporting in achieving the organization's objectives. Both monetary and Non-Monetary play a crucial role in supporting employee performance.

The study's first purpose was to catalogue the non-monetary factors employed by the automobile industry. According to the study, non-monetary factors considerations such as motivation, recognition, communication, leadership, vision & mission are frequently used the automobile industry. In the automobile industry, non-monetary benefits broadly are categories int 6 categories Motivational, Cultural, Opportunity, Job Related, Institutional and Leadership/Managerial.

A questionnaire containing questions was developed and distributed to the Auto OEM company employees based on the non-monetary aspects in place. The questionnaire included 72 questions on five-point Likert scale about non-monetary factors, in order to explore the research objectives.

Objective 1 - Identify of Non- Monetary of Factors which impact performance in Automobile manufacturing industries.

The study's first purpose was to catalogue the non-monetary factors employed by the automobile industry. According to the study, non-monetary factors considerations such as motivation, recognition, communication, leadership, vision & mission are frequently used the automobile industry. In the automobile industry, non-monetary benefits broadly are categories int 6 categories Motivational, Cultural, Opportunity, Job Related, Institutional and Leadership/Managerial. After exhaustive Literature Review overall we identified 45 factors which were later combined in 6 umbrella factors to carry out the study.

F1-Leadership / Managerial	F2 - Institutional	F3 - Job Related
Vision & Mission of Leader	Brand Image	Job Fit
Leadership Style	Reponsiblity	Clear Goals and Expectations
Coaching by Lead	Technology	Tools and Equipment / Resources
Camaradarie with Colleagues	Infrastructure	Work Life Balance
Relationship with Manager	Production Systems	Usage of Technology
Performance Pressure	Structure	Risk associated with Job
Empowerment	Indian / MNC	Location of work
	Organisational Stability	Reputation/Status of the Job
	Market Position	Diversity in Job

F4 - Organisational Culture	F5-Opportunity	H-6 Motivation
Culture	Development Opportunities	Motivation
Communication	Career Path	Recognition
social learning	Growth Options	Job Enrichment
Ethics	Job Security	Job Satisfaction
Innovation	Diversity	Passion towards car
Discipline		Ability
Standardisation		Performance Appraisal Process
Reputation in eyes of Customer		

Figure 4: Factors and subfactors Identified for study impacting employee's performance.

Further for the studies we also considered various dements of Sub-Factors like Communication types, Leadership Styles, Pressure/Stress etc. The identification of these monetary factors impacting performance have given all together a new perspective to factors impacting performance.

Objective 2 - To establish relationship between Non-Monetary factors and performance of employee.

The second purpose of this study was to ascertain the relative importance of monetary and nonmonetary rewards in the case study. As a result, the study establishes a favorable correlation between monetary factors and employee performance. Job Satisfaction and Recognition are the most influential variables. so, the business should develop policies that effectively handle these two factors, which will result in increased motivation and retention rates in the long run. Additionally, automobile industry includes non-monetary incentives, which will result in increased employee motivation in turn resulting into employee performance. Thus, the author can assert that non-monetary benefits have an effect on the organization's employees' performance.

Table 59: Regression Summary

Factors	R-Square	Anova	Regression	Correlation Coefficient (R) and +slope
1. Leadership/Managerial factors	R square = 0.348, 34.8% Variations Explained	F = 221.379 & p value = 0.00 < 0.05	Y = 16.630 + 0.305*X	+ correlation coefficient (R = 0.590) & + slope (0.305)
2. Institutional factors	R square = 0.344, 34.4% variation explained	F = 217.483 & p value = 0.00 < 0.05	Y = 14.050 + 0.636*X	+ correlation coefficient (R = 0.587) & + slope (0.636)
3. Job Related factors	R square = 0.264, 26.4.0% variation Explained	F = 148.139 & p value = 0.00 < 0.05	Y = 16.965 + 0.512*X	+ correlation coefficient (R = 0.513) & + slope (0.512)
4. Organizational Cultural factors.	R square = 0.444, 44.4% of variation explained	F = 330.176 & p value = 0.00 < 0.05	Y = 7.996 + 0.502*X	+correlation coefficient (R = 0.666) & + slope (0.502)
5. Opportunity factors	R square = 0.223, 22.3% Variation Explained	F = 118.642 & p value = 0.00 < 0.05	Y = 20.575 + 0. 839*X	+ correlation coefficient (R = 0.472) & + slope (0. 839)
6. Motivational factors	R square = 0.424, 42.4% Explained	F = 304.236 & p value = 0.00 < 0.05	Y = 11.141 + 0.883*X	positive correlation coefficient (R = 0.651) & positive slope (0.883)

With the help of statistical tools like Annova and Regression we have established relationship between different factors like Motivational, Cultural, Opportunity, Job Related, Institutional and Leadership/Managerial whose summary is mentioned in above table.

Further it can be concluded that there is positive correlation / impact of all the six factors identified on the impact of employee's performance. This was also tested with **Hypothesis 1** of the study.

Its evident from the study that the employers have put calibrated & balanced efforts to ensure these factors in a right mix to have optimum levels of performance from employees.

Objective 3 - To establish or rank non-monetary factors based on their positive impact on employee's performance.
Table No. -

The third purpose of this study was to establish or rank non-monetary factors based on their positive impact on employee's performance. According to respondents, all the 6 factors positively impact employees' performance. Employees are more likely to stay with a company if they are Satisfied, Recognized, Values and Coached. Employees wish to enhance their professional qualifications through exposure to cutting-edge technology and exposure to latest Auto Production systems.

Table 60: Regression Summary

Factors	R-Square	Anova	Regression	Correlation Coefficient (R) and +slope
1. Leadership/Managerial factors	R square = 0.348, 34.8% Variations Explained	F = 221.379 & p value = 0.00 < 0.05	Y = 16.630 + 0.305*X	+ correlation coefficient (R = 0.590) & + slope (0.305)
2. Institutional factors	R square = 0.344, 34.4% variation explained	F = 217.483 & p value = 0.00 < 0.05	Y = 14.050 + 0.636*X	+ correlation coefficient (R = 0.587) & + slope (0.636)
3. Job Related factors	R square = 0.264, 26.4.0% variation Explained	F = 148.139 & p value = 0.00 < 0.05	Y = 16.965 + 0.512*X	+ correlation coefficient (R = 0.513) & + slope (0.512)
4. Organizational Cultural factors.	R square = 0.444, 44.4% of variation explained	F = 330.176 & p value = 0.00 < 0.05	Y = 7.996 + 0.502*X	+correlation coefficient (R = 0.666) & + slope (0.502)
5. Opportunity factors	R square = 0.223, 22.3% Variation Explained	F = 118.642 & p value = 0.00 < 0.05	Y = 20.575 + 0.839*X	+ correlation coefficient (R = 0.472) & + slope (0.839)
6. Motivational factors	R square = 0.424, 42.4% Explained	F = 304.236 & p value = 0.00 < 0.05	Y = 11.141 + 0.883*X	positive correlation coefficient (R = 0.651) & positive slope (0.883)

Study concluded that the all the non-monetary factors are positively impacting employee's performance. Further based on the data following is the rank of factors impacting employee's performance.

Rank 1 - Motivational Factors
Rank 2 - Opportunity Factors
Rank 3 - Institutional Factors
Rank 4 - Job Related Factors
Rank 5 - Organisational Culture Factors
Rank 6 – Leadership/Managerial

Based on the above ranking employers can calibrate the Employee life cycle management process, focus of factors and make sure that we have optimum level of performance.

Objective 4 - Based on the finding of study, Creation of Model/structure to enhance performance of employees.

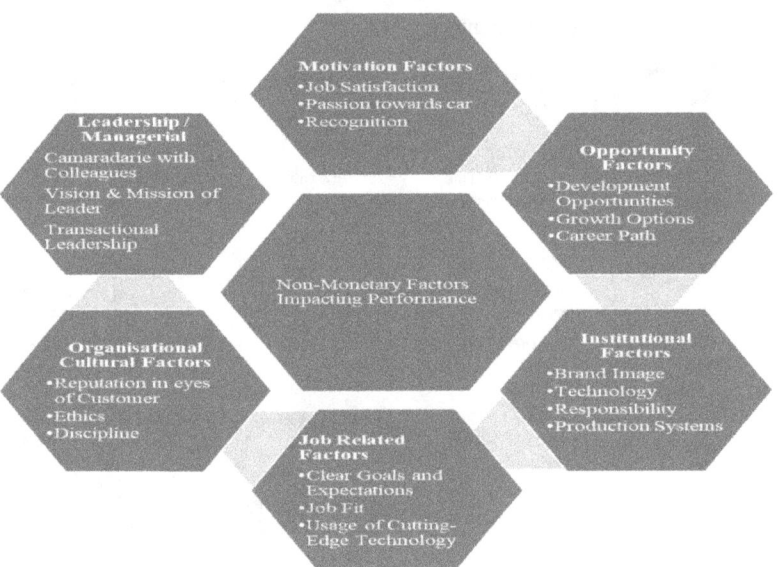

Figure 5: Creation of Model/structure to enhance performance of employees.

Based on the study the author is proposing to have well balanced and synergized combinations of the 6 factors and their Subfactors which will impact employee's performance. Figuring out the right mix is itself a challenge as we are dealing with human beings and not machines, person the person the factors may vary as well.

Finally, it can be demonstrated that "there is in the automobile business, non-monetary factors have a strong and considerable beneficial link with employee performance. The ability and motivation, declarative knowledge, procedural knowledge, motivation to work, attainment of specified goals, staff competence, and established standards all contributed to these performances.

Employment security, decent working circumstances, participation in goal planning and achievement, staff recognition, job expansion, incentives that address social needs, improved working conditions, and fringe benefits were revealed as non-monetary motivations.

Employees have requirements that should be met by their employer to minimize demotivation or distraction from work. As a result, the automobile industry must place a premium on non-monetary motivators in order to maintain, attract, and improve employee performance, satisfaction, and commitment.

Other future research may wish to investigate additional elements affecting employee performance that were not examined or focused on in this study, including employee loyalty, employee emotions, work time flexibility, business culture and values, and employee retention. Another conceivable expansion of this study is to include complete coverage of both companies' other geographical areas. Given that this study did not include enough managers, it would be interesting for future research to include a representative sample of managers and conduct interviews to augment the data collection procedure. If possible, inputs for future publications could come from other sources, such as the outcomes of the companies' performance rating procedures; this would assist assure a more accurate depiction of the data.

Other independent variables, such as the work environment, could be further dissected and analysed in greater detail by focusing on their various facets. For instance, the work environment encompasses office lighting, workstation spacing, office design, and noise levels. Future research may examine the effect of various factors on employee performance by comparing the "before" and "after" effects of these factors. For example, employee performance might be measured before to and following training in order to compare and assign a value to the training received. Additional studies could also look at other demographic aspects and regional trends. Finally, future research may

Chapter 7

Further Scope of Research

Future studies should examine the influence of non-monetary rewards on employee performance in industries other than the automobile sector. Again, additional research should be conducted to determine the effect of non-monetary rewards on employee job satisfaction, security, work environment, job match, and participative management.
Study is focusing on OEM which further can be expanded to Auto Suppliers as well. Blue Collars are not part of the study as they are governed by law of the land and the benefits are as per the Settlement signed between union and company management. Further Going ahead blue collars can also be included in the scope of study.

A study on Monetary factors can be carried out and merged with findings of current study to create a Holistic and robust model understand impact of both the factors on the employee's performance. Geographical Scale be increased and study and be further expanded to the two-wheeler, three-wheeler and truck and Tractor manufacturing plant across the geography of India, also it Can be expanded to manufacturing & IT industries as well to understand the impact of Non-Monetary factors on performance.

Depending on the financial need factor of employees, both monetary and non-monetary play different role in impacting employee performance. A study can be carried out to understand linkage in Financial need factor of employee and his performance.

The conceptual model proposed herein can be implemented in few Auto Industries and its results can be validated by observing actual impact on performance of employee, the study on implementation of model based on the observation can help to calibrate the model and make is more scalable, robust and precise.

As a part of this journey researcher proposes to provide excerpts of this study to auto industry body for their consumptions.

CPSIA information can be obtained
at www.ICGtesting.com
Printed in the USA
BVHW051350110423
662126BV00017B/779